China

CURRENT HISTORY BOOKS

Founded in 1914, *Current History* is the oldest U.S. publication devoted exclusively to world affairs. Drawing on the best that this distinguished journal has to offer, *Current History* Books will present timely, comprehensive, and accessible overviews of regions and topics related to international affairs and policy.

South Asia
Edited by Sumit Ganguly

China: Contemporary Political, Economic, and International Affairs
Edited by David B. H. Denoon

China

Contemporary Political, Economic, and International Affairs

Edited by

David B. H. Denoon

NEW YORK UNIVERSITY PRESS

New York and London

NEW YORK UNIVERSITY PRESS
New York and London
www.nyupress.org

Library of Congress Cataloging-in-Publication Data

China : contemporary political, economic, and international
affairs / edited by David B. H. Denoon.
p. cm.—(Current history books)
ISBN-13: 978-0-8147-1999-2 (cloth : alk. paper)
ISBN-10: 0-8147-1999-6 (cloth : alk. paper)
ISBN-13: 978-0-8147-2000-4 (pbk. : alk. paper)
ISBN-10: 0-8147-2000-5 (pbk. : alk. paper)
1. China—Politics and government—1976–2002.
2. China—Politics and government—2002–
I. Denoon, David.
DS779.26.C47346   2007
951.05'9—dc22   2006036708

New York University Press books are printed on acid-free paper,
and their binding materials are chosen for strength and durability.

Manufactured in the United States of America

c 10 9 8 7 6 5 4 3 2 1
p 10 9 8 7 6 5 4 3 2 1

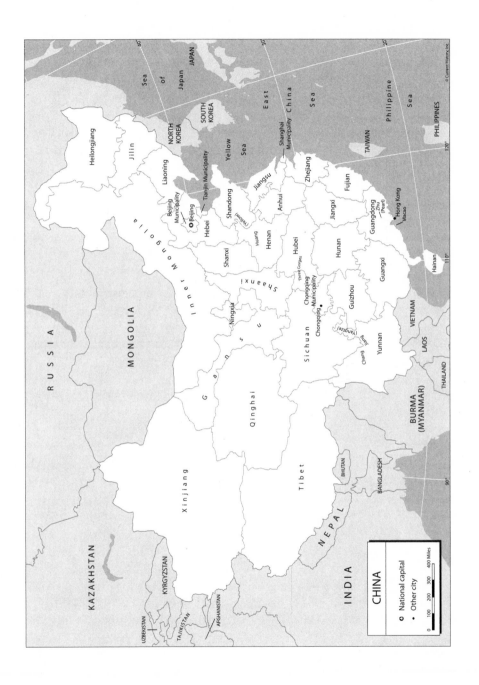

Contents

Introduction: Is China's Transformation Sustainable?   1
David B. H. Denoon

Part I: Foreign Policy and National Security

1. The People's Army: Serving Whose Interests?   17
June Teufel Dreyer   *September 1994*

2. Uncertainty, Insecurity, and China's Military Power   27
Paul H. B. Godwin   *September 1997*

3. Does China Have a Grand Strategy?   39
Michael D. Swaine   *September 2000*

4. Sino-American Relations since September 11: Can the New Stability Last?   51
David Shambaugh   *September 2002*

5. Asia in the Balance: America and China's "Peaceful Rise"   64
Robert Sutter   *September 2004*

Part II: Economic Policy and Social Issues

6. The Long March from Mao: China's De-Communization   77
Liu Binyan   *September 1993*

7. China's North-South Split and the Forces of Disintegration   85
Edward Friedman   *September 1993*

8. The Dangers of Economic Complacency   96
Barry Naughton   *September 1996*

9. Rumblings from the Uyghur   106
Dru C. Gladney   *September 1997*

10. Beijing's Ambivalent Reformers   114
Bruce J. Dickson   *September 2004*

11. China's New Exchange Rate Regime   127
Barry Eichengreen   *September 2005*

Part III: Domestic Politics and Governance

12. Is Democracy Possible?   137
Merle Goldman   *September 1995*

13. The Leader in the Shadows: A View of Deng Xiaoping   147
Lucian W. Pye   *September 1996*

14. Village Elections: Democracy from the Bottom Up?   162
Tyrene White   *September 1998*

15. An All-Consuming Nationalism   172
Michael Dutton   *September 1999*

16. Understanding Falun Gong   182
Richard Madsen   *September 2000*

17. China's New Leadership: The Challenges to the Politics of Muddling Through   192
Tony Saich   *September 2002*

18. China's Environmental Challenge   204
Elizabeth Economy   *September 2005*

Chronology of Recent Events   217

About the Contributors   243

Introduction: Is China's Transformation Sustainable?

DAVID B. H. DENOON

China is the only large country in the world today where political leaders have systematically understated their economy's growth rate. They do this because the scale and dynamism of China's economy have already caused apprehension among neighbors and trading partners.

In 2005, the understated numbers became too glaring to ignore; Beijing's Central Statistical Office revised its gross domestic product (GDP) estimates for 2004, adding $280 billion to previous figures.[1] This "omission" was an amount roughly equal to the entire current GDP of India. The new figures ranked China as the world's fourth largest economy, with a net product larger than France and the United Kingdom.[2] In addition, most economists presume the yuan, the Chinese currency, is significantly undervalued. So, if the yuan were allowed to appreciate to levels determined by market forces, this would probably add another 15–30% to national income estimates.

Moreover, China's dynamism is by no means limited to the economy alone. Enrollments in secondary and higher education are rapidly expanding and new means of communication (cellular phones, cable and satellite TV, and e-mail) are vastly increasing the information available to the Chinese public. In two decades, the Chinese government has also transformed its foreign relations.

China has joined the World Trade Organization, launched the Shanghai Cooperation Organization with Russia and the Central Asian states, started a free trade area with Southeast Asia, and has been a principal mover behind East Asian regionalism and the East Asian summit process. All of these steps have meant that officials in Beijing are now consulted on virtually every key development within the region, whereas 20 to 55 years ago

China was inwardly focused and still suffering from the excesses of the Cultural Revolution.

The main area where China has seen much slower change is in its internal political development. The Communist Party of China (CCP) still dominates all aspects of political life: the Politburo is still self-selecting, party congresses have carefully scripted agendas, province governors are chosen by Beijing, censorship is widespread, and treatment of dissidents is harsh. Though there are some elections at the township and village levels, competition is limited and few are so bold as to directly challenge the CCP.

The intent of this volume is to give readers a chronicle of China's recent transformation and, by selecting articles published over the past 15 years, to highlight how some of the leading scholars of China saw key issues as they developed.

Structure of the Volume

This collection is divided into three sections: (1) Foreign Policy and National Security, (2) Economic Policy and Social Issues, and (3) Domestic Politics and Governance. Many recent books on China have concentrated on either its economic or its domestic political and social changes. These topics are clearly essential and we will deal with them in the second and third sections of the volume.

We have decided to start with foreign policy and national security because they are the areas most completely dominated by the Chinese leadership and represent the actions by which Beijing wants the outside world to judge its intent. The claims that China's rise will be peaceful and that trade, investment, and technology flows will be used for internal economic development are central to Beijing's strategy for modernizing the economy while continuing to allow the CCP to hold the reins of power tightly. Friction with its neighbors or, even worse, a war would seriously hamper China's rapid pace of development.

Thus, Chinese foreign policy since the early 1990s has been subordinated to broader modernization goals. Chinese diplomacy has also been remarkably skillful as China's image has been transformed from troublesome neighbor to that of a boundless, open market. Fortuitously for Beijing, this strategy could be implemented in a period when its principal Asian rival, Japan, was stagnating economically and the Bush administration had chosen to concentrate on counterterrorism and the Middle East.

So, China moved to center stage in East Asia with a low-keyed approach and little challenge from potential competitors.

Why *Current History*?

There are several reasons to present an edited volume on China of *Current History* articles:

1. *Current History* is written to be scholarly and accurate, but in a style that is accessible to a broad audience. Therefore, these selections should highlight essential developments in China for researchers who want to check key turning points in the past two decades, while, at the same time, being clearly presented to the general public and to undergraduates and graduate students.

2. *Current History* publishes an annual volume on China in which many of the leading specialists in the field summarize trends and present their interpretations of recent developments. These articles provide a superb snapshot or cross-section of developments in a given period. Also, since the articles in each section of this volume have been arranged chronologically, they can be read to provide an overview of the main issues during China's rapid transformation.

3. The editors of *Current History* make considerable effort to select authors who try to present developments in an objective manner and explain competing assessments of major trends. This means that both researchers and nonspecialists can read this volume to find both mainstream and alternative analyses of events.

4. Finally, each issue of *Current History* includes a chronology that summarizes recent major political, economic, and social developments. We have taken these chronologies for China, Hong Kong, and Taiwan for the 1993–2005 period and edited them for readers here. This provides a resource for researchers who want to check the timing or sequence of events on a topic of interest to them.

Foreign Policy and National Security

The transformation of Chinese foreign policy in the past three decades has been truly remarkable. As Mao Zedong and Zhou Enlai passed from the scene in the mid-1970s, the Cultural Revolution was simmering down, but outsiders had no idea what would follow. Mao's chosen successor, Hua Guofeng, was a weak, compromise candidate and was soon pushed aside by Deng Xiaoping. Although Deng had been previously labeled a "capitalist roader," he was a member of the first generation of Communist leadership and few observers anticipated the dramatic changes that China was about to undergo. Mao had approved the rapprochement with the United States in 1972, but it was seen by many as a purely pragmatic way to deal with the Soviet threat and not necessarily a sign of a broad, sweeping opening to the West.

Once Deng Xiaoping consolidated his power in 1978, however, the changes came in quick succession. Deng phased out communes in China's rural areas and used market incentives to encourage agricultural production; established Special Economic Zones (SEZs, essentially protected free trade areas) along China's eastern coast; and visited the United States in early 1979 (which no Chinese leader had done in 30 years of communist rule).

Moreover, despite two decades of Chinese support for the leadership in Hanoi, Deng ordered the invasion of Vietnam—after he returned from Washington in January 1979—in retaliation for Vietnam's occupation of Cambodia. The incursion into Vietnam signaled to all concerned that China's foreign policy was going to be more focused on Chinese interests than communist solidarity.

The lowest point in Deng's rule took place in June 1989, when he ordered Chinese troops to clear Beijing's Tiananmen Square of protestors. The resulting bloodshed and use of armed troops against civilians led to sanctions against China by Japan and most Western states, and there was a period in the early 1990s when it appeared that China might move back in a more autarkic, isolated direction. Nevertheless, Deng was committed to China's modernization and opening to the outside world, and he reinforced this during his trip to Guangdong province in 1992 when, despite some internal criticism, he reiterated that the growth of the private sector must continue.

On balance, the pragmatic steps initiated by Deng Xiaoping in economic and foreign policy have been continued by his successors, presidents Jiang Zemin and Hu Jintao. By the mid-1990s, under Jiang Zemin and Prime Minister Zhu Rongji, the pace of change accelerated. The SEZs proved so successful that most of the country was opened for foreign investment and this provided a flood of foreign capital. Equally important, the foreign direct investment (FDI) brought with it the latest technology as foreign firms took root in the manufacturing sectors. So, China not only received a vast injection of foreign savings but also know-how and first-rate technology as well.

As we will see in the economic section below, by 2004 China was receiving new commitments of up to $60 billion of FDI per year, which revolutionized its manufacturing capabilities and helped build up the world's largest pool of foreign exchange reserves.[3] This surge of capital inflows helped maintain the country's growth rate and made it feasible for leaders in Beijing to buy much of the foreign military equipment and technology they wanted. Economic performance enhanced foreign policy and national security options.

Two of the chapters in this volume deal directly with the modernization of the People's Liberation Army (PLA).[4] June Teufel Dreyer's 1994 piece, "The People's Army: Serving Whose Interests?" highlights the dilemmas that China's political leadership faced in downsizing the military and increasing its professionalization. Dreyer notes that, in the early 1990s, Russia was in such dire economic straits that Moscow was willing to sell some of its highest performance aircraft to China and license the technology for manufacturing many of the systems as well.

This anomaly of a former opponent becoming a key arms supplier, combined with rapid increases in the PLA budget, meant that the favored parts of the PLA were upgrading quickly. However, the lower-tech infantry and less favored specialties were reducing troops and looking for any source of income they could find. This led many parts of the PLA to go directly into business and blurred the line between military and civilian enterprises. In addition, the resulting differences in income and living standards between divisions of the PLA produced resentment and further pressures for corruption that are a continuing problem.

Paul H. B. Godwin's chapter, "Uncertainty, Insecurity and China's Military Power," explores what priority the Chinese military receives from the political leadership. Of the "Four Modernizations" that the Politburo stressed in the 1990s (agriculture, industry, science and technology, and the military), the PLA ranked last. Yet, Godwin notes that the poor performance of the Chinese forces in Vietnam in 1979 and the recognition, after the Gulf War of 1991, that a high-tech military is essential have given priority to those parts of the PLA that can best use modern surveillance equipment and weaponry. This has meant the nuclear forces, submarine fleet, air force, and assorted forms of high-tech licensed manufacturing of foreign-designed components have received first call on funding.

Michael D. Swaine's contribution is to step back and ask: "Does China
Have a Grand Strategy?"[5] He concludes that Beijing's leaders have clear priorities for the military, ranked as follows: preservation of domestic order,
defense against threats to sovereignty and territory, and attainment and
maintenance of geopolitical influence as a major, perhaps primary state in
the Asia-Pacific region and beyond.

Swaine saw the CCP pursuing a pragmatic, nonideological foreign policy, using force only selectively and seeking an enhanced role in international forums where the gains in influence outweigh the costs of
involvement. Swaine then speculated that, depending upon economic, political, and military trends, China might begin to play a higher profile role
after 2010, potentially placing more emphasis on increasing its power, developing alliances, and attempting to "redress past wrongs."

Then we assess the two big changes in U.S.-China relations after 2000:
the U.S. preoccupation with counterterrorism and the Middle East and obvious signs that China's influence is growing rapidly.

In "Sino-American Relations since September 11," David Shambaugh
analyzes how the interaction between Beijing and Washington has changed
after Al Qaeda attacked the World Trade Center and the Pentagon. Shambaugh identifies a series of steps that China took after 9/11 that supported
the U.S. counterterrorism effort: voting for United Nations Security Council and General Assembly resolutions condemning terrorism, supporting
U.S. attacks on the Taliban in Afghanistan, encouraging President Musharraf of Pakistan to support the war against the Taliban, sealing the Chinese
boundary with Afghanistan to prevent Al Qaeda operatives from migrating
into China's western region of Xinjiang, and inspecting bank accounts in
Hong Kong and China to see if they were connected to terrorist groups. All
of these moves were, not surprisingly, appreciated by Washington and
helped shift the rhetoric in the Bush administration about China from talk
of "strategic competition" to various sorts of engagement.

Robert Sutter's discussion about China's claim that it seeks a "peaceful
rise" ties together several of the earlier themes in this volume. China's soaring economic growth combined with declining American attention to Asia
has changed the strategic picture on the Pacific Rim. Although Japan shows
some signs of economic recovery, China has had fortuitous circumstances
to pursue its goal of greater influence on its periphery. Beijing has operated
in a subtle fashion as well. Its offer of a free trade area with the Southeast
Asian states, without requiring immediate reciprocity, was seen as a sign of
good will; and the 2002 accord on managing territorial disputes over the

Spratly Islands was seen as an improvement over former incidents using force.

Sutter also demonstrates that China is carefully laying the basis for expanding its regional influence, while at the same time limiting Washington's options. By taking a lawyerly approach to differences in World Trade Organization forums and criticizing U.S. bilateral alliances in East Asia (as holdovers from the Cold War), Beijing is deftly encouraging Asian states to choose policies that are more independent of U.S. leadership.

Thus, the thrust of the Foreign Policy and National Security section of the volume is to show that critical changes are under way in Asia, with China's dynamic economy getting the public attention but important strategic changes occurring with less press attention.

Economic Policy and Social Issues

There is an extensive literature on the causes of China's surge in economic growth in the 1990s and the impact of this booming economy on its neighbors.[6] Our purpose here is to select chapters that highlight the dilemmas that China's leadership faces as income differentials by region and class grow and as other nations increasingly see China's exports as a threat to their economies.

The most fundamental question the Chinese Politburo must deal with is: Will the public accept the bargain it has proposed? The CCP asked Chinese citizens to agree to their tight hold on all political life in exchange for rapid economic growth and a dramatic rise in living standards.

In "The Long March from Mao: China's De-Communization," Liu Binyan (now deceased) argued that the CCP was originally seen by the Chinese public as liberators from the corrupt rule of Chiang Kai-shek's Kuomintang. The Great Leap Forward and the Cultural Revolution squandered that legitimacy, and the CCP has been hoping to reestablish its credibility by managing a multidecade experiment in rapid economic growth.

Will this Faustian bargain work? Liu was doubtful because he was optimistic that the Chinese public would demand its personal liberties soon and not wait for the multidecade transformation of the economy. The number of protests against the Chinese government has grown rapidly. The government's own statistics indicate that there were 87,000 "public order disturbances" in 2005 alone.[7] However, the fact that the government openly reports these numbers and that only one protest, at Tiananmen

Square in 1989, directly challenged overall CCP rule, means that a country-wide revolt is not yet at hand.

Edward Friedman's discussion of China's "North-South Split" raises a critical aspect of Beijing's development strategy. In 1993, when the piece was written, the sharpest income differentials were between the south, Guangdong, and Fujian provinces where the private sector was booming, and the rest of the country. Today, most of the east coast and the major cities are surging ahead, while the agricultural areas and populations are lagging. So, though the geographical locus of the income split has become more complex, it remains a key issue for Chinese society because at least 80% of the population still lives in the rural areas.

President Hu Jintao and Prime Minister Wen Jiabao have taken a number of steps to reduce the urban-rural income gap: ending the grain tax, abolishing the household registration system, which limited the chances for farmers to obtain permanent jobs in cities, and imposing various credit and other controls on the export sector while trying to stimulate domestic consumer demand. Nevertheless, when the east coast and major cities have such enormous advantages in location, infrastructure, and education levels, the resentments that Friedman highlights will doubtless be a semiper-manent part of the Chinese scene.

The essays by Barry Naughton and Bruce J. Dickson were written eight years apart (1996 and 2004 respectively) but they get at another ongoing issue that inevitably arises from the development strategy the CCP has chosen. The party's leaders want a world-class manufacturing sector and are willing to let private investors have considerable leeway in selecting the location and equipment for their facilities.

What the party is not willing to do, however, is let foreigners control the main banks or key state enterprises. This means that there is a conflict be-tween the goal of efficiency and the political imperative of preserving the power of the state. Hence, both Naughton and Dickson allow us to see that, though Marxism is no longer an accepted guiding principle, Leninist views of state control clash with capitalist methods of achieving efficiency.

In "Rumblings from the Uyghur," Dru C. Gladney introduces a further complication facing Beijing's planners. Although roughly 90% of Chinese citizens are of Han ancestry, the non-Han ethnic groups resent their mar-ginal status. Moreover, many of the Uyghur and Hui are Muslim and have further grievances against rule by a secular Han state. Uyghur separatists set off bombs in Urumqi and Beijing in 1997, leading to harsh countermea-sures and 20 executions in retaliation.

The Gladney essay was written before 9/11 but it was prescient in emphasizing not only the Uyghur dissatisfaction with rule from Beijing but also the growing desire among Xinjiang's Muslims for ties with Central Asia and the rest of the Muslim world. Since the mid-1990s, China's diplomacy has been quite skillful at maintaining links with Pakistan, the countries of Central Asia, and states in the Persian Gulf region. As a country with a sharply growing demand for imported oil, the dulcet diplomacy in the Muslim world is understandable. The question is whether China can continue to maintain close external ties in the Muslim world while imposing tight controls on its more than 20 million Muslims at home.

In addition to regional and ethnic income differentials and the balance between public and private firms, China must also decide what role its export sector should play. Since the early 1990s, exports have been the leading edge of the economy. First, with the Special Economic Zones, and then with broadened approvals for foreign investment, China has used exports to generate income, employment, and modern manufacturing skills as the leading sector of its burgeoning economy.

Like most of the other successful Pacific Rim countries before it, China has stimulated exports by having an undervalued exchange rate. So, besides having abundant cheap labor, China has made its exports attractive by underpricing its currency. This has helped make Chinese goods very price-competitive and allowed the country to take market share from other suppliers.

The question becomes: How much longer can Beijing keep the yuan undervalued? The Chinese government has already revalued the yuan upward by 2.1% in July 2005 and widened the price band in which the currency can fluctuate. However, because China continues to run massive trade surpluses, the International Monetary Fund (IMF) and individual countries have protested. Moreover, several U.S. senators have proposed legislation that would add import surcharges to Chinese goods unless the yuan is revalued upward.

There are also solid macroeconomic reasons for thinking it is in China's interest to gradually move the exchange rate to its real market value. The Chinese economy is currently growing at over 11% per year, inflation is picking up, and the central banking authorities have been raising reserve requirements for banks along with higher benchmark lending rates for loans.[8] The undervalued currency is an economic stimulus, so there is a conflict between the banking system restraints and the pro-growth incentives from the low exchange rate.

In "China's New Exchange Rate Regime," Barry Eichengreen explores the factors that Chinese authorities are considering in deciding whether to raise the exchange rate significantly. There are two key issues: 1) What would be the ideal level for the new rate? and 2) Should China move to a true "fluctuating rate system" or stay with a "fixed rate?"

Although a revaluation upward would slow the economy and make it easier for Chinese consumers to pay for imported goods (thus lowering the trade surplus), it would make it harder for marginal firms to compete, so the exporting community inside China favors keeping the rate low. If the government chose a fluctuating rate, market forces would determine the level, but the Chinese would then have to give up currency controls and this would allow foreigners to hold unlimited amounts of Chinese currency. Once foreigners held large amounts of currency, they could press for ownership shares of prime Chinese assets that are currently held locally.

Hence, the decision about an exchange rate system rewards different groups inside and outside China and has a very high political content. It could be that the Chinese will choose an intermediate step of raising the currency's value but keeping it at a fixed level so that they can maintain controls.

Domestic Politics and Governance

To give readers two decades of perspective on politics inside China, we have chosen three essays from the 1990s on aspects of democratization and political control. Although the press and Internet in China provide more information than before, it is striking to note how similar the issues are today in comparison with those raised a decade ago. In addition, we have selected two chapters on movements (nationalism and Falun Gong) that appear to be filling a void left by the loss of respect for communism. These are followed by a discussion of the current, fourth generation of political leadership, and a concluding essay on the environment and the quality of life in China.[9]

The chapters by Merle Goldman, Lucian W. Pye, and Tyrene White each illustrate the difficulty of making generalizations about the pace at which democratization is proceeding in China. Merle Goldman, in 1995, was impressed with the nascent signs of civil society: a lively popular culture, greater use of the courts to challenge the CCP and state, and the rise of over 2,000 newly launched newspapers. Goldman indicated, however, that the Chinese middle class lacked the independence and cohesiveness found in South Korea and Taiwan (before those countries made their democratic transitions). She also notes that regional autonomy may be more acceptable as a means to loosen Beijing's grip than individual rights and open expression of political opinions.

Lucian W. Pye's chapter, "The Leader in the Shadows: A View of Deng Xiaoping," on the other hand, emphasizes how the traditional levers of power in China can still be manipulated in the current era. Pye stresses that Deng stayed in the background and used the mystique of authority to enhance his power. He mentions that Deng rarely appeared in public or on TV. It was a veritable sensation, in January 1992, when Deng used a TV interview during his "southern trip" to press for continued economic reform. Pye also says Deng understood political timing and that the "paramount leader" became "the man on the spot when the Chinese were ready to turn their backs on the Maoist road to modernity."

White's discussion of village elections focuses attention on how hard it is to judge the pace and extent of democratization in China. In June 1998 the National People's Congress passed the Organic Law of Villagers Committees, which permitted Villagers Councils (to represent each household), Villagers Representative Assemblies (to establish delegates nominated by the villagers), and Villagers Committees (of actual selected leaders). If this law had led to open political competition between candidates with different approaches to governing, it might well have been the beginning of real grassroots democracy. However, that clearly has not happened; in the last eight years, most of the village candidates have been approved in advance by the local CCP and the amount of open contestation is usually limited.[10] White ends by cautioning that this experiment in local democracy depends on the extent to which Beijing will let open contests develop, so the first eight years have obviously had mixed results. For those who saw the Villagers Committees as the first step toward township and province elections, that progression has not developed either.

Michael Dutton and Richard Madsen concentrate on political developments in China that are outside the CCP. In Dutton's analysis, the student protests of the 1999 U.S. bombing of the Chinese embassy in Belgrade were a reflection of "An All-Consuming Nationalism." He asserts that the subsequent riots and violence (at the U.S. embassy in Beijing) were not instigated by the Chinese leadership, but, instead, are an indication the CCP has let nationalism become a substitute for the former faith in communism.

Madsen makes a similar point about Falun Gong, the cult that combines elements of Buddhism, ritual exercise, and worship of its leader, Li Honzhi. What startled the CCP was Falun Gong's organizational ability and skill at assembling a ring of protesters around the leadership compound in Beijing. Although Falun Gong members were predominantly middle-aged women, they were seen as a threat to the CCP because of their adeptness at communicating throughout China. A country with a vibrant civil society would have seen Falun Gong more as a curiosity than as a challenge.

In Tony Saich's analysis of China's fourth-generation leadership, he notes that Deng Xiaoping was clever at initiating reforms on those features of the Maoist state that had drawn the most criticism. So, ending communes in the rural areas and setting up the Special Economic Zones were likely to generate quick support. Saich argues that designing and implementing a new social welfare system and dealing with chronic federal budget deficits are much tougher issues to handle. Political leaders in other countries have struggled with the same problems, but China has two significant advantages in its high savings rate and enormous foreign exchange reserves. The high savings rate indicates that the public is expecting only limited services from the state and the foreign exchange can always be used to import products if various constituencies are to be rewarded. Since the current members of the CCP Politburo are all trained as engineers, we will see whether they address these fundamental questions in a technical, non-ideological fashion.

Elizabeth Economy reviews "China's Environmental Challenge," noting that, by 2002, six of the world's ten most polluted cities were in China. The problems of deforestation, flooding, desertification, and water scarcity all require immediate attention. She argues that China's economic success has come at a very high price and further environmental degradation could bring the country to its knees. Will redressing these environmental problems require a mobilized middle class that has a clear concern for the future? Or is this a situation in which China's Politburo engineers can lead?

As we reflect on domestic politics and governance in China, it is striking to see how consistent the CCP has been in implementing its strategy of opening the economy while keeping power tightly held within its elite.

Is the Current Chinese Development Strategy Sustainable?

China's transformation is a national social experiment in the world's largest state. The CCP is attempting to guide 1.3 billion people through a wrenching set of changes. About 100 million have now reached middle-class living standards, and prospects are good that several hundred million Chinese will follow them in the next 15 years. Yet, that still leaves two-thirds of the society living a marginal existence and, almost certainly, becoming increasingly resentful of being left behind.

Is this model of societal change as viable for the next generation as it has been for the past 25 years? Any answer to that question must be qualified.

At one extreme, if urban-rural income differentials grow, if protests spread unabated, and the middle class wants its political freedom, the CCP cannot keep its tight hold on power.

At the other extreme, if national income more than doubles every decade, the middle class continues to focus on material gains, and the rural population thinks its chance is coming soon, the CCP may prolong its stay at the apex of power.

We will not make a forecast here, but this volume should help readers to make their own judgment. Is China a pressure cooker with a limited number of escape valves? Or is it an exceptional cornucopia with endless opportunities and more sense of national pride than at any time since the 1500s?

The three sections of this book represent the three pillars on which the CCP is erecting its monument.

The current *foreign policy* can stay intact as long as the CCP is in charge and not threatened by a fundamental external military or economic challenge.

Economic policy has become the engine for the country's transformation. Current rates of foreign direct investment are not likely to be sustained and GDP growth rates will almost certainly decline, but most countries would be happy with a growth rate that is half of what China has been able to maintain. With unlimited cheap labor for at least another 20 years, high savings rates, good transportation facilities, and pragmatic managers, how many countries have a more favorable environment for growth?

The *domestic political* base is the shakiest of the pillars. The short run appears stable, but the sheer size and complexity of Chinese society require an exceptional balancing act to hold it together. It is hubris to assume that a small elite can do this indefinitely, but then the CCP may not have an un-limited time horizon. Clearly, however, the CCP is not going to reveal its hand before it is ready to share or drop the reins of power.

NOTES

1. In 2006, an entire revised time series of GDP estimates, going back to 1994, was released as well.

2. Only the United States, Japan, and Germany have larger economies.

3. By mid-2006, China had official foreign exchange reserves of approximately $850 billion.

4. The name PLA applies to all three services—though the PLA Navy and PLA Air Force are separate bureaucracies.

5. This chapter draws on Swaine's jointly authored book with Ashley Tellis, *China's Grand Strategy: Past, Present, and Future* (Santa Monica, Cal.: Rand, 2000).

6. See, for example, W. Overholt, *The Rise of China—How Economic Reform Is Creating a New Superpower* (New York: W.W. Norton, 1993) and Chung Min Lee, "China's Rise, Asia's Dilemma," *The National Interest*, no. 81 (Fall 2005), pp. 88–94.

7. J. Kahn, "Pace and Scope of Protest in China Accelerated in 2005," *New York Times*, January 20, 2006, p. A-10.

8. D. Lague, "China Moves to Curb Lending for the Second Time in Five Weeks," *New York Times*, July 22, 2006, p. C-3.

9. The first generation of leaders who survived in power were Mao Zedong and Zhou Enlai, the second was unitary leadership under Deng Xiaoping, the third were Jiang Zemin and Zhu Rongji, while the fourth are the present leaders, Hu Jintao and Wen Jiabao.

10. A. Nathan, "Present at the Stagnation," *Foreign Affairs*, vol. 85, no. 4 (July–August 2006), pp. 177–182.

PART I

Foreign Policy and National Security

1. The People's Army: Serving Whose Interests?

September 1994

JUNE TEUFEL DREYER

A curious dichotomy has emerged between how the outside world views the Chinese military and how the People's Liberation Army is seen at home. Other countries have become concerned with the possibility of aggression by an increasingly militarily capable China as well as the effects of Beijing's arms sales on the global balance of power. At the same time, the leadership in China is becoming more concerned about the armed forces' loyalty, and worries that the military's growing business empire may affect its combat capabilities. Although evidence can be marshaled for both sides' contentions, the interaction between the military's foreign and domestic roles makes it unlikely that the Chinese military will embark on a course of territorial aggrandizement, or that the military will prove to be the sole determinant in the struggle for the succession to Deng Xiaoping.

The Arms Business

The People's Liberation Army (PLA) has continued to reach out to foreign militaries, receiving visiting groups from more than 40 countries last year and sending its own abroad. By far the most newsworthy of these contacts has been the relationship with Russia. Defense Minister Pavel Grachev was first among many high-ranking military officials to journey to Beijing, signing a five-year cooperation agreement with his Chinese counterpart. A few months before, ships from Russia's Pacific Fleet had visited Qingdao for the first time in 37 years. President Boris Yeltsin placed the value of military sales to China in 1992, before the agreement was signed, at $1.8 billion; this included at least 26 Su-27 fighter planes and 100 S-300 surface-to-air missiles. Talks were continuing on the purchase of the SS-25, Russia's most modern, mobile intercontinental ballistic missile; Kilo class diesel-electric submarines; aircraft carriers; and late-model T-80 tanks. More than a thousand Russian scientists visited China in the space of two years to help with the Chinese military effort, and an estimated 300 to 400 Chinese defense specialists were sent to Russia for training. Weapons designs were reportedly being faxed to China, amid Western fears that Russia's system to keep track of its weapons specialists had broken down.

A slow thaw has also begun in military relations between the United States and China, which were frozen after the June 1989 military crackdown in Tiananmen Square. Military Commission vice chairman Liu Huaqing has noted that he was strongly in favor of this, prompting Russian sources to surmise that China intends to play the United States off against Russia for technology—as it had done successfully with the Soviet Union in the past.

China has also acquired military technology from Israel, sometimes against Washington's wishes. The People's Republic was reportedly using Patriot missile technology sold to it by Israel to upgrade Soviet-designed surface-to-air defense weapons and to develop ballistic missile reentry vehicles that can evade American defensive systems. The aim was assumed to be capture of a larger share of the growing demand for weapons by third world states. Pentagon analysts opined that China would be selling cruise missiles and other military systems as well.

That China is selling weapons is of less concern than that certain countries are buying them. Beijing has denied United States allegations that it was selling M-9 and M-11 missile parts to Pakistan, despite an earlier promise not to; the wording of the Chinese statement, however, seemed less than forthright. China also reportedly stepped up cooperation with Iran on missile technology, and last year it signed an agreement to help the Iranians build a nuclear power plant. Hong Kong authorities discovered that American-made military aircraft parts were being modified in China and then shipped to Iran via the crown colony on commercial flights. In addition to garnering foreign exchange, China's motives were believed to include the desire for continued access to Iranian oil and Teheran's agreement, tacit or otherwise, to eschew support for growing fundamentalist sentiment among China's Muslims.

An incident especially embarrassing for the United States occurred last August. Washington charged that a Chinese cargo ship, the *Yinhe,* was carrying chemicals used to make mustard gas and nerve gas to the Middle East. Given Iraq's use of chemical warfare against Iran and its own Kurdish minority, the claim assumed major proportions. China countercharged that the United States was harassing its ship, and denied that the *Yinhe* was transporting the chemicals. After several weeks of high-level negotiations, during which the ship continued on its journey, the two sides agreed an inspection would be carried out in Saudi Arabia. No chemicals were discovered. American intelligence sources maintained that the banned chemicals were still on board when the captain had managed to off-load his controversial cargo before reaching the Persian Gulf. Almost simultaneously the State Department announced a two-year ban on technology sales to 10 Chinese aerospace companies because of their dealings with Pakistan. These events slowed, at least temporarily, the thaw in Sino-American military relations.

North Korea, an international pariah because of its apparent violation of the nuclear Non-Proliferation Treaty, has also been the recipient of Chinese military technology. The United States Defense Intelligence Agency concluded that China had collaborated with North Korea in the development of a new long-range missile. Other sources confirmed that two of China's major arms importer-exporters, China North Industries and Poly Technologies, were working with North Korean weapons scientists. The quid pro quo was thought to be Pyongyang's agreement to allow China to export missiles and other arms to the Middle East via North Korean ports. This may also explain China's reluctance to support United Nations sanctions against North Korea for Pyongyang's unwillingness to allow inspection of its nuclear facilities.

China is also the military mainstay of yet another international outcast, the ruling State Law and Order Restoration Council in Myanmar (Burma). Arms deliveries to the junta have topped $1 billion, and include tanks, armored personnel carriers, and multiple rocket-launcher systems, presumably for use in counterinsurgency operations. A joint venture factory was constructed in Myanmar for the manufacture of machine guns and ammunition. China also assisted in the building of three highways from the border of Yunnan province into Myanmar; Burmese dissidents worry that Beijing could use these as invasion routes in a takeover of their country. The Chinese military has supplied Myanmar's air force with A5-m ground attack planes suitable for counterinsurgency activities, and F-7 fighters. But its neighbor's navy most interests the PLA: the regime in Myanmar can provide China with an outlet to the Bay of Bengal and the Andaman Sea. Hainan-class fast attack craft and support personnel began arriving in Myanmar in 1991, and several existing naval bases in the country are being improved, including those in Mergui and the Cocos Islands. New Chinese-made radar has been installed in the Cocos base, which will allow China's intelligence personnel to better monitor the area.

In Thailand, two separate caches of Chinese-made weapons were discovered only a few weeks apart. One was described as the largest such find in Thai history, containing enough firepower to defend a small country. Both were believed to be destined for the Khmer Rouge across the border in Cambodia. In keeping with UN efforts to end the bloodshed there, China has pledged not to arm the Khmer Rouge. The two caches do not necessarily constitute evidence that this promise has been violated, since it is possible they were private business transactions between corrupt PLA members and their Thai counterparts. Still, the international repercussions are potentially embarrassing for Beijing.

Red Flag Rising?

These activities have caused concern in many countries. China's presence in the Cocos Islands is particularly troublesome to India, which has a naval base of its own in nearby Port Blair and considers the Indian Ocean part of its preserve. India's invitation to Indonesia to take part in joint naval exercises in the Indian Ocean this year may be an attempt to create cooperation to counter what is perceived as a growing common threat; Indonesia has long been wary of Chinese expansionism at its expense. The increasing capabilities of China's navy have also aroused apprehension among the many countries that contest the ownership of the Spratly Islands in the South China Sea with China.

Japan, which has several unresolved claims with China in the South China Sea, is uneasy about the Chinese military presence in Mergui, near the entrance to the Strait of Malacca, which connects the South China Sea with the Indian Ocean. This channel is not only strategically important in itself but is also a crucial transit point for the oil Japan imports from the Middle East. Earlier this year Japanese Foreign Minister Tsutomu Hata and United States Defense Secretary William Perry agreed to monitor China's military buildup closely. At a bilateral security meeting in Beijing a few weeks later, Tokyo formally solicited greater "transparency" on military matters. The Japanese suggested that China make military information public—perhaps, as is common international practice, through the publication of a defense white paper. Meanwhile, in Taiwan attention was focused on a document issued by the Military Commission of the Chinese Communist party's Central Committee on the subject of the possible invasion of Taiwan.

These concerns may be exaggerated, or at least premature. China has indeed been developing and purchasing new weapons, but it will be many years before they can be perfected and integrated into combat plans. And increased capabilities do not necessarily indicate an intention to use them. Confronted with its neighbors' anxieties, Chinese officials have been careful to stress that the military buildup is for defensive purposes only. Still, there is evidence to support the argument that at least the upper echelons of the armed forces favor a more assertive international role for China. Elderly generals have complained that party General Secretary Jiang Zemin has been far too accommodating toward the United States, and a group of them supposedly advised him in writing at least twice to take a harder line. The precipitating causes were the *Yinhe* incident and the rejection of Beijing's bid to host the Olympics in the year 2000, in favor of Sydney, Australia.

Changing of the Guardians

With 90-year-old paramount leader Deng Xiaoping in visibly failing health, the fate of his chosen successor, General Secretary Jiang Zemin, is unclear. Jiang will need the support of the armed forces to maintain his position, yet he has no military experience and had no ties with the military on his anointment in June 1989. During the past few years he has visited various PLA units about once a month to inspect the troops and, presumably, to forge links with the officers. The elevation of six men to the rank of general last June—the first such promotions since the military reinstituted ranks in 1988—was seen as another of Jiang's efforts to curry favor with the military.

Early this year the outlines of the third major transfer of senior officers since the Tiananmen incident became discernible. The rationale behind military transfers is not usually publicly stated. Since little is known about the careers of the individuals involved, analysts must hypothesize on the basis of sparse information. Sometimes the reasons may involve no more than the desire to rejuvenate the officer corps by moving younger people into command positions or giving promising officers experience in more than one area by rotating them around the country. In the case of the first major reshuffle after Tiananmen, in spring 1990, an additional concern appears to have been maintaining the officers' willingness to enforce the hard line advocated by Deng Xiaoping and China's president, General Yang Shangkun; the promotion of martial law spokesperson Zhang Gong to commissar of the Beijing Military Region is a case in point. Other promotions were thought to have been designed to enhance the power of the Yang faction, which included Yang Shangkun's younger half-brother Yang Baibing.

The second set of reassignments, in late 1992, seemed to indicate a softening of the hard line and a desire to reduce the power of the Yang faction so as to enhance Jiang Zemin's chances of political survival. Zhang Gong was transferred to the less prestigious Chengdu Military Region, Yang Shangkun retired, and Yang Baibing was removed from all military positions, though given membership in the Politburo. The third set early this year continued the trends established by the second; Zhang Gong was reassigned to a still less powerful position as commissar of the Academy of Military Sciences in Beijing, and more than a hundred high-ranking officers, many of whom reportedly had ties with the Yang family, retired or were reassigned. A number of Jiang protégés are believed to have received promotions. Whether this will be sufficient to ensure Jiang's leadership remains to be seen.

The Budget Question

The steady growth in the PLA's budgets since 1989 have also increased international anxiety about Beijing's military intentions. The expansion has been substantial, and seems all the more so in light of the austerity budgets Deng had granted the military since his accession to power (the one exception being 1979, to cover the costs of the military expedition into Vietnam that year).

Chinese sources have tried to allay concerns by pointing out that there has been substantial inflation during this period—sometimes exceeding 20 percent in major cities—and saying that increases have done little more than compensate the military for losses in buying power. However, it is difficult to adjust defense budget figures to account for inflation, since official inflation rates tend to be several points lower than estimates by foreign analysts. Moreover, they do not necessarily affect the military and other sectors of the economy equally. In many years the increases in the defense budget have outstripped the increases in other sectors, such as education and agriculture—that one would expect to have higher priority when the threat of external attack is minimal. And although officials point out that military expenditures are a modest 8.6 percent of the state budget and 1 percent of China's gross domestic product, foreign analysts note that China does not follow standard accounting procedures; actual defense expenditures are estimated to be two to three times the published numbers.

Some discount government contentions that the military budget is low by international standards as little more than an anodyne for international concerns over an emerging Chinese juggernaut. However, the authors of a book entitled *Can China Win the Next War?*, as yet unavailable in translation and clearly meant for internal circulation only, are distressed at the slow progress of military modernization and lament both antiquated equipment and poor troop quality.[1] The book leaves the clear impression that China may not be able to perform well in any future confrontation. Although the authors tend to concentrate on the need for new military hardware, they also cite other areas that they believe require improvement. For example, PLA salaries have failed to keep pace with many civilian jobs, thus causing some young men to avoid military service and others, such as air force pilots, to leave early for better pay in commercial ventures. The apparently large increase in this year's defense budget is believed to be mainly to finance the first pay raise for the armed forces in many years: salaries of recruits and junior officers were increased by about one-third, and those of senior officers by 50 percent or more. In addition to easing the difficulties of recruiting, it was hoped that better wages would reduce the alarming increase of corruption in the military.

An Officer and a Businessman?

The military budgets of the early 1980s did not indicate a low regard for the armed forces on Deng's part; rather, the paramount leader, who considered military service an important part of his own career, was convinced that a

---

1. A partial translation can be found in *Orbis* (Summer 1994).

strong military could not be grafted onto a weak economy; economic modernization was thus his first priority. The PLA was enjoined to do its utmost in the effort to modernize, including turning some of its production lines over to civilian production and marketing both consumer goods and weapons. Between 25 and 30 percent of the military's expenses are now met through its industries and businesses.

The PLA's venture into the commercial sector is less surprising in the Chinese context than it would have been for foreign armies: from the earliest days of the Red Army, soldiers had been asked to reduce the military's burden on society by raising their own food, building their own barracks, and producing their own uniforms. This new démarche, however, was on an unprecedented scale, and quickly came to be associated with profit rather than mere subsistence.

The military responded with alacrity; according to official statistics, the more than 1,000 large- and medium-size defense enterprises have increased civilian output by 20 percent each year since being ordered to convert from defense production in 1978. Washing machines, refrigerators, socks, and the like are said to account for nearly 70 percent of defense sector production. But new problems have emerged too. Almost immediately there were reports of corruption. Some units engaged in stealing luxury cars from Hong Kong and transporting them to the mainland, where they were sold for large gains. Other units sold the fuel the government had allocated them to civilians.

Naval vessels have even stopped foreign ships in international waters, forced them into military ports, and off-loaded their cargoes for resale. After 16 Russian vessels were attacked in the East China Sea early last year, Moscow began deploying warships in the area, which ended the problem for its ships. For vessels from other countries—particularly those flying flags of convenience like Panama's or Liberia's, which could not expect protection from those nations' navies—problems continued. After a representative of the International Maritime Organization visited Beijing, China announced new regulations for registering its own vessels and for boarding and inspecting ships. But given the many ways in which units can evade these, it would be naive to assume the piracy problem has been resolved.

Military units also earn extra money by selling their license plates, which allow the purchasers to avoid vehicle inspections, road tolls, and other impediments to their businesses. The practice became so widespread in some areas that authorities issued new plates, in a different style, to military units, and set up dragnets to catch vehicles bearing old-style plates. Officials admitted, however, that this was only a temporary fix, since the newly issued license plates could be sold in turn. The PLA's exemption from inspection had tragic consequences in the Shenzhen Special Economic Zone in southern China last August, when a military-owned factory exploded, killing 70 people and injuring several hundred others.

While some of the income from military enterprises may have been used to help the armed forces modernize their weapons, improve training techniques, and better the troops' living standards, most of the profits seem to have been spent on luxury goods for a relatively small number of officers. The trickle-down effect appears to have been minimal, judging from Military Commission directives urging military officials to bear the hardships of service proudly. Other directives have been aimed at ensuring adequate food supplies to the troops, and reassuring military suppliers that they will be paid market prices for their grain while guaranteeing military units that grain will be supplied them at fixed prices.

Unsurprisingly, straitened circumstances have caused morale problems among those members of the military who are unwilling to participate in corrupt schemes or who are simply not in a position to avail themselves of the new opportunities. The discrepancy between their salaries and those of less scrupulous officers certainly runs counter to the Communist party's carefully cultivated image of an egalitarian military establishment in which officers and men share "weal and woe." An anguished major was quoted in a leading Chinese magazine as saying: "If the units managed to deal with [their troops] fairly and honestly, the enlistees would naturally apply themselves to their work and study to excel. But such is not the case in certain units today. You want to transfer to the volunteers, join the party, enroll in school or become a cadre? You have no connections, nobody ready to give you a little help? Then forget it. A junior enlistee from a small place. What connections can you possibly have? None. Then you have to cultivate your ties. Look up fellow villagers, acquaintances, friends, relatives. How? Send a gift when a gift is called for, send money when money is called for."

In some localities the PLAs' special privileges have caused friction, since the military competes with civilian enterprises from a favored position. In other areas officials and officers appear to have collaborated, creating fear in Beijing over the possible rise of "independent kingdoms" that can evade the central government's control. Even when they do not, military enterprises appear to distort the operation of markets rather than facilitate China's evolution toward a free market economy.

Repeated admonitions to the military to eschew private uses for profits from enterprises—referred to as "keeping small treasuries" or "practicing external circulation"—have had no noticeable effect. A recent Chinese Academy of Science report suggested the PLA's removal from business. Its industries, the report said, should be purchased for a fair price, enabling soldiers to return to their real vocation: training for the defense of their country. Members of the military should be paid fair salaries, to be provided through taxes rather than military commerce.

The 1994 pay raise is one government attempt at this, as are directives ordering the military to extricate itself from business dealings. Yet, in seeming contravention of these, in March the PLA command in Guangdong announced that it would set up a "military tourism zone" on one of its bases, where domestic and foreign visitors could sky dive, practice marksmanship at indoor and outdoor shooting ranges, and participate in heavy-weapons maneuvers.

Worries Within and Without

While the outside world worries about the expansionist motives of a modernizing PLA, the Chinese leadership frets about deficiencies in its military technology and the quality of the troops being recruited. Leaders are concerned as well about the military's loyalty to the regime, and wonder whether the commitment of individual military men to self-enrichment might not outweigh their institutional commitment to defend the country. They warn that "the Great Steel Wall," as the PLA is often called, "may self-destruct."[2] Both fears appear to be exaggerated. But the military's domestic political role is substantial, and it would be difficult for any government to change this easily or quickly. Given the tenuous ties Deng's chosen successor, Jiang Zemin, has with the military, and his need for its backing if he is to maintain his position after Deng's death, it will be particularly difficult for him to carry out this change. Meanwhile, to the extent the PLA continues to play a major part in market enterprise, the enhancement of its military capabilities will be inhibited.

2. See Li Chu, "Chi Haopian Personally Handles Smuggling Cases in the Military," *Cheng Ming,* September 1, 1993.

2. Uncertainty, Insecurity, and China's Military Power

September 1997

PAUL H. B. GODWIN

When Deng Xiaoping came to power in 1978, he inherited a defense establishment that was little more than a lumbering giant. In the 20 years following the Sino-Soviet split of 1959–1960 and Moscow's termination of military assistance, China's military power had eroded into obsolescence. The country's defense industrial base was incapable of producing anything more than copies of Soviet designs from the 1950s, and the defense research and development (R&D) infrastructure was equally backward. Even the nuclear weapons program, developed at great cost and to the neglect of conventional weaponry, had produced only crude strategic systems, including a single nuclear-powered ballistic missile submarine that had yet to launch a missile. Moreover, during this time the Chinese armed forces had become intensely involved in Mao Zedong's domestic political campaigns, especially the Cultural Revolution, and were no longer an effective combat force, a reality demonstrated by their poor performance in the 1979 incursion into Vietnam.

Deng Xiaoping's long-term objective for the military reforms he introduced in 1979 was to build a self-sustaining defense establishment so that China could not be intimidated by any military power, and Beijing's foreign policies would not be constrained by military weakness. Rebuilding military strength, however, was not given first priority in Deng's strategy for modernizing China. In the "four modernizations" that defined his program for transforming China into a nation capable of assuming a leading role in world politics, renovating national defense came fourth, after the modernization of agriculture, industry, and science and technology.

Apprehension in Asia and the United States that China's military power was becoming potentially dangerous to the region did not emerge until the cold war's end. Four major developments in Beijing's defense policies intersected to create the image of potential peril. First, in 1985 Beijing transformed its national military strategy: China's armed forces were directed no longer to prepare for a major, possibly nuclear, war with the Soviet Union but for local, limited wars on China's borders. Second, annual double-digit percentage increases in Beijing's defense budgets began in 1989 (and continue), sustained by the dramatic growth in China's economy, which suggested a potential change in priorities. Third, the armament and military technology linkage established with the Soviet Union in 1990, and upheld by Russia after the Soviet Union's disintegration, was viewed as potentially revitalizing China's defense industrial base in addition to providing advanced weaponry. Finally, in the early 1990s, improvements in China's conventional forces were joined by the development of a new series of short-range, tactical battlefield ballistic missiles and land- and submarine-based strategic missiles.

These four elements converged as China's military security, in Beijing's own assessment, became more assured than at any time in the previous 150 years. Even as the threat to China's security diminished, Beijing demonstrated an assertive, if not aggressive, nationalism in its approach to territorial claims in the South and East China Seas. An assertive, nationalistic China, facing no major military threat but with growing military muscle bolstered by a rapidly expanding economy and increasing military expenditures, raised serious questions about Beijing's long-term international intentions. Beijing's belligerent use of military exercises to intimidate Taiwan in the summer of 1995 and the spring of 1996, leading to United States deployment of two aircraft carrier battle groups near Taiwan, served only to exacerbate these concerns.

China's Military Strength in Context

Military power is relative, not absolute; any evaluation of a state's military strength must be comparative and placed in context. Despite widespread apprehension in Asia and the United States that Beijing's military modernization programs could overturn East Asia's balance of power early in the twenty-first century, China's military leadership has no such confidence. To the contrary, it looks forward to the twenty-first century with uncertainty and a sense of insecurity, knowing that the Chinese People's Liberation Army (PLA), as all four services and branches are collectively named, will enter the next century with armaments and equipment just beginning to incorporate technologies from the 1970s and 1980s. It is not that Beijing perceives an immediate military threat to China, but that in an uncertain future with military technology evolving quickly, the PLA's relative obsolescence is becoming increasingly difficult to overcome.

Even apart from America's overwhelming military strength, Beijing looks out on an Asia undergoing major military renovation that in many areas exceeds the PLA's current capabilities and will continue to outmatch China's programs for at least a decade. As Beijing examines Asia's defense modernization programs, its concerns can be fully understood. Notwithstanding Tokyo's long-standing security relationship with the United States, including the protection provided by American nuclear forces and ongoing discussions about joining the United States theater missile defense program, Japan's euphemistically named Self-Defense Forces (SDF) are technologically the most sophisticated in the region and supported by Asia's most advanced defense industrial base. Nor are these forces small. Japan's maritime Self-Defense Forces constitute the region's largest modern navy, with 63 major surface combatants and 17 submarines; many of these are armed with the most advanced military technology in the world. With the capability to operate up to 1,000 nautical miles from the home islands, Japan's navy is supported by a land-based air arm deploying cutting-edge antisubmarine and antiship weapons on 110 aircraft and 99 armed helicopters. Japan's air Self-Defense Forces are equally powerful, deploying 90 American F-4Es, 189 domestically produced copies of the United States F-15 (considered the world's finest interceptor), and 50 indigenous F-1 ground attack fighters, all supported by airborne warning and control system (AWACS) aircraft. Furthermore, Tokyo's current plans call for continued modernization of its air, ground, and naval forces with a defense budget, $46.8 billion, that is the third largest in the world.

Tokyo clearly intends to sustain Asia's most powerful navy and air force, even though the Soviet Union no longer exists to threaten Japan and its security ties with the United States are politically strong. Further heightening Beijing's insecurity is the fact that the PLA and Japan's SDF began their modernization programs at about the same time (Tokyo's

National Defense Program Outline that guided the SDF to its current status was announced in 1976, and Deng Xiaoping's military reforms were initiated in 1979). In the two decades since China and Japan began modernizing their armed forces and defense industries, Tokyo has clearly made the most progress, and its edge will continue into the foreseeable future.

In addition to Japan, throughout East Asia most defense establishments have been rapidly modernizing their armed forces with advanced combat aircraft, ships, and submarines. Thailand is about to deploy the region's first aircraft carrier—the Spanish-built *Chakkrinareubet*. Displacing only about 11,500 tons, and intended for search-and-rescue and humanitarian operations, this carrier nevertheless can embark a small number of helicopters and aircraft, and thus represents East Asia's first sea-based airpower.

In Southeast Asia, naval forces are being acquired that, in combination with modernizing air forces deploying a variety of United States F-16 and F/A-18 combat aircraft and Russian MiG-29s, will be better able to defend territorial and maritime interests. Taiwan in particular continues programs to extensively upgrade its air and naval forces, including air defense capabilities highlighted by the deployment of Patriot surface-to-air missiles. Taiwan is also acquiring French and American combat aircraft, ships, and air defense systems that will be on line within the decade.

From Beijing's perspective, the renovation of China's armed forces is part of a pattern of Asian military modernization that began in the late 1970s and continues, with few exceptions, today. Furthermore, United States defense alliances and forward-deployed military forces provide an added complication to any net assessment Beijing would make of its regional capabilities. This is true not only of formal United States treaty relationships but also of America's less formal commitments. Beijing could not ignore the fact that the first of two United States aircraft carrier battle groups to arrive off Taiwan during the March 1996 crisis was based in Japan. Similarly, it is American technology and research that threaten to erode the credibility of China's small nuclear deterrent force and tactical battlefield missiles through the promise of theater missile defense systems and national missile defenses, both plausible in the next century. Once again, Japan's defense industrial and R&D capabilities are highlighted by United States pressure on Tokyo to join the theater missile defense research program and agree to future deployment.

Rethinking National Military Strategy

When the Soviet Union was China's principal threat and Beijing's military strategy was based on defending continental China, most of the PLA's technological weaknesses could be overcome by a strategy of protraction, attrition, and the threat of nuclear retaliation—the so-called people's war under modern conditions. Continental defense, including the ability to conduct offensive operations short distances beyond China's borders, benefited from the sheer size of the 4 million-man PLA and the ultimate strategy of falling back into China's vast interior and simply exhausting an adversary through protracted war.

As the cold war ended, China began preparing for local, limited war on its periphery, including the defense of maritime borders and territorial claims in the East and South China Seas; this new orientation accentuated the obsolescence of the PLA's arms and equipment far more than had the requirements for continental defense. Beijing's new national military strategy required the PLA to prepare for early, offensive operations designed to defeat an adversary quickly and decisively, and potentially at some distance from the mainland. In modern warfare, these operations depend on the synergistic effect of ground, air, and naval forces operating together for common military objectives. China's armed forces had no experience with these complex operations, and therefore lacked the joint service command, staff, and logistic support to prepare them for the demands of the new military strategy.

Moreover, existing and emerging warfare technologies make defense against a sudden attack or a preemptive military operation far more difficult than in the past. Standoff weaponry has become significantly more accurate and lethal, offers precision targeting at far greater ranges, and can be used at night and in other low-visibility conditions. Limited war involving high-technology weapons and equipment raises the importance of the initial engagement far beyond what it was a decade ago. Equally important for military operations, the development of surveillance technology is making the battlefield increasingly transparent. The significance of contemporary military technologies was underlined by the devastatingly swift defeat of Iraqi forces by the United States–led coalition in 1991. While the PLA knows it is extremely unlikely it will face such capabilities in the near future, it recognizes that China's military environment is becoming more demanding with the spread of advanced weapons and equipment throughout

East Asia. In a direct response to the Gulf War's demonstration of high-technology warfare, China's military leadership modified its definition of future military contingencies from "limited, local war" to "limited war under high-tech conditions."

The PLA's Emerging Capabilities

The PLA is undoubtedly seeking to overcome the deficiencies highlighted by the demands of China's revised national military strategy.[1] It is also the case that access to Russian military technology and weapons, and Israeli technological and design support, have hastened the day when China's defense industries and the PLA will be more competent and capable. The difficulty is determining when that day will arrive, and to what extent China's capabilities will exceed those of its neighbors—nearly all of whom are committed to continued modernization of their defense forces. The question for Asia, however, is not whether the PLA will be better able to defend China in the improbable event of an attack on its mainland; apprehension within the region is instead based on China's potential force projection capabilities, especially as they apply to the future of Taiwan's and Beijing's territorial claims in the East and South China Seas. Thus, it is not the sheer size of China's armed forces and the vast amounts of largely obsolescent equipment it deploys, but the direction and intent of current modernization programs that are the source of anxiety.

Beijing has not sought to hide its recent focus on air and naval power. The PLA also has not tried to obscure its concentration on building "crack troops" capable of responding effectively to the kinds of military contingencies outlined in China's new national military strategy. For the past decade, but especially during the past five years, the PLA has focused on training and equipping selected ground units for quick-reaction and amphibious warfare roles. These are the "fist" (*quantou*) and "rapid response" (*kuaisu*) units, such as the 15th Group Army (Airborne) and the PLA navy's brigade-strength marine corps. Similarly, the PLA is attempting to establish command-and-control and logistic support systems that can effectively coordinate and sustain operations involving ground, air, and naval units. Training and exercises are explicitly concentrated on joint service

1. See the June 1996 issue of *The China Quarterly*, which is devoted to a thorough analytic survey of China's military affairs. Much of my assessment draws on this issue.

operations. This training includes amphibious warfare exercises and naval maneuvers involving underway replenishment, as task forces train for surface combat and antisubmarine warfare.

Beijing's current weapons, equipment, and technology acquisition programs support the needs of its national military strategy. Air and naval forces answer the demand to defend far-flung maritime sovereignty claims, including Taiwan and those in the South China Sea. Strategic weapons are being replaced because of their age and the need to make new systems more survivable and accurate in the next century. Analyzing these acquisitions within the operational doctrine of today's PLA and Asia's military environment provides a measure of capability. There are, nonetheless, specific constraints that must be kept in mind as part of such an assessment.

Before Moscow began military technology transfers in 1990, the Western powers had placed stringent limits on what they would sell China. Following the Tiananmen tragedy of 1989, the West—with the exception of Israel—essentially embargoed all arms and military technology transfers to China. Because of these constraints, China's experience with advanced military technology is limited to, at most, the past five years, when the PLA began receiving Russian arms. Until China's defense industries place advanced weapons and equipment into series production, they cannot be considered an effective defense industrial base for China's armed forces. Equally important, the small number of weapons purchased and the time it takes to train the first crews and maintenance personnel mean that it will be many years before the PLA can be considered modern.

Acquiring and Projecting Power

China has pursued programs designed to update obsolescent equipment with foreign technologies and develop new indigenous designs. The failure of these programs to meet the PLA's needs can be seen in acquisitions from Russia. The 1994 purchase of four Kilo-class diesel-electric-powered attack submarines from Russia indicates that China's own submarine programs were unsatisfactory. The submarine force is large, but 50 percent of the 50 or so deployed are based on outdated Soviet Romeo-types from the 1950s. China's newer designs are the 12 Romeo-derived Ming-class, and a single Song-class of more modern design currently undergoing operational evaluation. These ships are supplemented by 5 Han-class nuclear-powered submarines based on older technologies, and therefore undoubtedly very noisy and easily targeted by modern antisubmarine warfare systems. Similarly, the purchase in 1997 of 2 Russian Sovremenny-class destroyers is a strong indication that the new Luhu-class destroyer and Jiangwei-class frigate developed by China using primarily Western technologies are less than successful. Only 2 Luhus and 4 Jiangweis have been built in the past five years.

Long-standing efforts to improve the PLA air force and navy fleet air arm include the F-8, now operational but at best representing early 1960s technologies, and the FB-7, originally developed for the navy but not yet in series production. The future of China's airpower is tied to the F-10 that is being developed with Israeli assistance, and to the agreement for licensed production of Russia's Su-27 following the purchase of 72 completed aircraft. Over time these new aircraft will replace, but in much smaller numbers, China's obsolescent airpower composed primarily of about 4,400 fighter and ground attack aircraft derived from Soviet MiG-17, MiG-19, and MiG-21 designs. There is as yet no sign that the bomber force of some 420 aircraft derived from 1950s Soviet Il-28 and Tu-16 designs is to be replaced.

Forty-eight of the 72 Su-27s purchased from Russia have been delivered. Licensed production of these aircraft from complete kits supplied by Russia could begin in a year or so, but full Chinese-content Su-27s cannot be built for many years. It is unclear when the Israeli-assisted F-10 will enter production; even after years of development there is as yet no flying prototype. Two of the Kilo-class diesel-electric submarines have been delivered, and their first crews are completing Russian training programs. The two Sovremenny destroyers may be delivered by the end of this century and could be operational around 2004. Thus, from the PLA's point of view, true modernization of its weapons and the process of integrating them into operational and tactical doctrine have only just begun.

Military power projection requires the ability to sustain expeditionary forces in combat some distance from their home base. For the pla, as with any other military, time and distance are critical variables in offensive operations. Should the PLA be called on to defend China's sovereignty claims in the South China Sea, military operations would require sustaining forces in combat as far as 600 miles (960 kilometers) from Hainan Island. If China sought to invade Taiwan, it would require an amphibious and/or air assault some 100 miles (160 km) from the mainland—essentially the distance covered by the allied invasion of France in 1944. At least for the next decade, China's armed forces will be incapable of successfully performing either operation against determined resistance.

With the exception of its ancient bomber fleet, combat operations in the South China Sea are beyond the effective range of China's airpower, which is entirely land-based and has no aerial refueling capability. Furthermore, Beijing's naval forces lack effective defenses against cruise missiles and air attack. Deployed naval air defenses consist of surface-to-air missiles (SAM) with a range of seven miles (11 km), providing an adversary the opportunity to launch antiship missiles beyond the range of the defending SAMs. Chinese warships have no defense against cruise missiles, since they do not mount radar-controlled close-in weapons systems designed for this purpose. Moreover, even with recent improvements, Chinese warships do not deploy antisubmarine warfare (ASW) systems capable of defeating modern, quiet submarines.

Should Beijing attempt combat air patrols over the South China Sea without aerial refueling, even its most modern fighter-bombers would have at most five minutes of loiter time. Without AWACS aircraft to detect and assign targets, the combat air patrols would be ineffective. Any of China's obsolescent long-range bombers deployed would be dangerously exposed to SAM defenses and modern interceptors firing medium-range air-to-air missiles. China can maintain a naval presence in the South China Sea, but it cannot conduct sustained combat operations like those rehearsed for three weeks this April in the region by Australia, Singapore, Malaysia, Brunei, and Britain (the British Commonwealth's Five-Power Defense Arrangement group). This exercise, dubbed "Flying Fish," involved the deployment of 160 aircraft and 36 ships, including a British aircraft carrier and nuclear-powered submarine.

An assault on Taiwan would be perhaps even more difficult for the PLA because of improvements in the island's defenses. Taipei is acquiring 60 French Mirage 2000 fighter-bombers, 150 United States F-16s, and 4 American E-2 AWACS aircraft, making it extremely difficult for the PLA to gain air superiority over the Taiwan Strait. Taipei's acquisition of 6 French La Fayette-class frigates, the construction of 6 improved United States Perry-class frigates, and the lease of 6 modernized United States Knox frigates (which augment 22 updated older American destroyers) provide Taiwan's navy with far more advanced ships than those currently deployed by the pla. In particular, the Perry's SAM defenses have a range of at least 60 miles (97 km), and defense against cruise missiles is provided by close-in weapons systems. These ships also employ very effective ASW systems and surface-to-surface missiles. On a ship-to-ship basis, Taiwan's navy can outshoot China's. An amphibious assault across the 100 miles (160 km) of the

Taiwan Strait would require air superiority and sea control. Even with a large submarine force, it is doubtful the PLA could achieve such predominance except at great cost and over a considerable period of time.

Time is an extremely important consideration for Beijing. By deploying two carrier battle groups off Taiwan in response to China's aggressive military exercises, the United States clarified its commitment and added a clear complication to any PLA planning. Put simply, the PLA cannot plan military operations designed to subdue Taiwan without including the contingency of United States involvement. To the extent that Taiwan can prevent the PLA from rapidly achieving air superiority and sea control, American military support in the defense of Taiwan becomes more probable.

The Nuclear Dimension

Beijing's strategy for nuclear deterrence is straightforward: China shall have the capability to respond to any nuclear attack with a second strike lethal enough to seriously harm the attacker. Beijing believes that this strategy can deter the kinds of nuclear threats made by the United States during the Korean War and the Taiwan Strait crises of the 1950s, and faced from the Soviet Union in the 1960s, 1970s, and 1980s.

China's small, aging, liquid-fueled intercontinental ballistic missile (ICBM) force of some 17 missiles was initially deployed in the mid-1970s and early 1980s. Deployment of its intermediate-range ballistic missile (IRBM) force of perhaps 70 weapons began in the late 1960s. To provide a survivable, quicker-reacting nuclear deterrent in an era when the United States and Russia continue to deploy thousands of strategic weapons and when missile defense is on the horizon, this force had to be modernized. Survivability is being sought through tactical mobility, with both the new solid-fueled 7,500-mile (12,000-km)-range DF-41 ICBM and the 5,000-mile (8,000-km)-range DF-31 designed to be road- and rail-mobile. The DF-41 is not anticipated to be operational before 2010, but the DF-31 will perhaps begin deployment in a year or two.

Solid fuels improve booster reliability and provide quicker response time, thereby reducing the missiles' vulnerability to a counterforce first strike. Solid propellants, however, have less boost power than liquid fuels, which means that the change to solid fuels required smaller warheads with greater yield-to-weight ratios. Smaller warheads have also been developed to prepare for the time when China masters multiple reentry vehicle technologies and missile defenses require penetration aids.

China's single nuclear-powered submarine (SSBN) entered service in 1983. This ship is not known to have test-launched a missile in a decade and may not be operational, if it ever was. Nonetheless, a new submarine-launched missile—the JL-2—has been derived from the DF-31, and it is assumed that a follow-on SSBN is under construction to take the weapon.

There are indications that some of Beijing's military strategists believe China's strategic forces are too small to be considered a credible deterrent. They would have China change from minimum deterrence, where a relatively small number of warheads capable of inflicting considerable damage in a second strike are considered sufficient, to a more robust strategy that calls for the deployment of a larger number of strategic forces. In an era when missile defenses are likely to be put in place, there will be continuing pressure on China to deploy more systems, with warheads equipped with multiple reentry vehicles, including penetration aids. Development of these technologies is almost certainly under way, but some years of testing will be required before they can be employed. This will provide sufficient lead time to determine that a major shift in nuclear strategy has occurred and that the number and capability of China's strategic systems are increasing.

A Mirror-Image Future

Beijing's military planners face an increasingly difficult dilemma. Rapid advances in military technologies have created requirements that China's defense R&D infrastructure and industrial base cannot meet. Beijing's national military strategy and the proliferation of high-technology arms and equipment nonetheless accentuate the role of advanced technologies in operations conducted by China's conventional forces, especially offensive operations, and in maintaining a viable nuclear deterrent. Yet, despite China's undoubted ambition to become a full-fledged great military power and its quest for Russian assistance in achieving this objective, there is no evidence that Beijing has embarked on a crash course to correct all its well-known deficiencies. Rather, Beijing's limited purchase of advanced weapons and equipment, and its continued preference for technology over end-use items, demonstrate that China's defense modernization strategy remains long-term and incremental. Modernization of China's defense industrial base and R&D, as this term is understood in the United States,

Europe, Russia, and Japan, remains at least two decades into the future—decades during which the rest of Asia will not be standing still, least of all Japan.

Need East Asia worry? Of course. Although China's capabilities are currently limited, Beijing's ambition to achieve the status of a major military power has never been hidden. Two or three decades from now, assuming China's economy can continue to support the long-term strategy of building a largely self-reliant defense establishment, Asia could have in its midst a new primary military power. How Beijing will choose to use this power is the critical uncertainty. Hence, the central question for East Asia's security analysts is how long the United States will continue to deploy the military forces that are such a crucial element in the region's military balance. Despite Washington's constant reiteration that significant United States forces will remain, much of the buildup in East Asia reflects uncertainty about the American commitment and the misgiving that in a decade or two the region will contain two giants, China and Japan, each potentially seeking dominance. Thus, in an ironic twist, the uncertainty and consequent insecurity marking the PLA's perception of the twenty-first century is mirror-imaged by the rest of the region.

3. Does China Have a Grand Strategy?

September 2000

MICHAEL D. SWAINE

C oncern has arisen in the West and among many Asian nations over the implications of China's steadily growing economic and military prowess. Much of this concern focuses on measuring and interpreting upward changes in the "objective" determinates of national power, such as the capabilities of China's military and the size and rate of growth of China's GDP. Although extremely important, these estimates convey little meaning unless they are placed in a larger context that describes how China's leaders employ the attributes of national power and to what ends. In short, any accurate assessment of the ultimate significance of China's growing power for the international community requires an understanding of China's grand strategy.

Some analysts of China's approach to security argue that the Chinese state has never deliberately pursued a grand strategy. Others argue that the premodern Chinese state was primarily concerned with ensuring its cultural and ideological preeminence through proper ritual and right conduct, and that the modern Chinese nation-state similarly emphasizes status and prestige over state power. Yet although China's grand strategy has never been explicitly articulated in a comprehensive manner by its rulers, China, like any other state, has pursued a grand strategy in the past and is pursuing a grand strategy today.

China's Grand Strategy Defined

China's grand strategy is keyed to achieving three interrelated objectives: first and foremost, the preservation of domestic order and well-being in the face of social strife; second, defense against persistent external threats to national sovereignty and territory; and third, the attainment and maintenance of geopolitical influence as a major and perhaps primary state in the Asia-Pacific region and possibly beyond.

For most of Chinese history, efforts to attain these objectives have produced a security strategy oriented toward maintaining internal stability and prosperity along with achieving Chinese preeminence, if not control, along a far-flung geographic periphery. To carry out this strategy, China has relied on a strong authoritarian government that has employed a monolithic, hierarchical value system, frequent and at times intense coercive force, a wide range of highly pragmatic diplomatic stratagems involving balance and maneuver, and the many advantages resulting from the preservation of a dominant cultural and economic system throughout most of Central and East Asia.

During the premodern era, strong unified Chinese states sought to control their strategic periphery and assert Chinese preeminence by eliciting deference from nearby peoples, preferably through the establishment of unambiguous suzerainty relations that were backed, if possible, by superior military force. When faced with various internal and external obstacles to such methods (including domestic resistance to a prolonged, intensive use of force), strong Chinese states used a variety of noncoercive external security strategies, including appeasement, alliances, culturally based sinocentric patterns of interaction, and personal understandings among rulers, as well as a heavy reliance on static defenses.

Weak or declining Chinese states depended primarily on noncoercive tactics to stave off foreign attacks or maintain stability along the periphery while avoiding the offensive use of force. When such strategies proved unsuccessful, weak regimes would sometimes resort to desperate military means, at times in response to the demands of dominant conservative domestic leadership factions. Such resistance invariably met with little success, and a regime severely weakened or completely collapsed would result in major reductions in Chinese control over the periphery and, in some instances, the loss of Chinese territory to foreigners. Strong unified Chinese regimes would eventually reemerge and seek to recoup these losses. The interaction among changing foreign and domestic capabilities and domestic elite attitudes and behavior thus created a pattern of expansion, consolidation, and contraction of Chinese control over the periphery that coincided with the rise, maintenance, and fall of Chinese regimes.

China's basic security objectives have remained unchanged during the modern era (roughly 1850 to the present). However, significant changes have occurred in China's threat perceptions, its definition of the periphery, requisites for periphery control, state capacities, and internal as well as external requirements of domestic order and well-being. Together these present implications for the specific type of security strategies pursued by the Chinese state. In particular, the modern era has witnessed the emergence of a hybrid weak-strong state security strategy that combines elements of traditional strong-state efforts to control the strategic periphery through military and political means with elements of a weak-state approach employing a primarily territorial defense-oriented force structure and a relatively high level of involvement in diplomatic balance and maneuver.

In recent decades, following the absorption of many former periphery areas into the Chinese state and the emergence of increasingly strong industrial powers along China's periphery, China's weak-strong state security approach has produced a calculative grand strategy that is neither assertive nor cooperative. This strategy has three guiding elements. First, it is based on a highly pragmatic, nonideological policy approach tied to market-led economic growth and the maintenance of amicable international political relations with all states—especially the major powers. Second, the strategy depends on a general restraint in the use of force, whether toward the periphery or against more distant powers, combined with efforts to modernize and streamline the Chinese military, albeit at a relatively modest pace. Third, it calls for an expanded involvement in regional and global interstate politics and various international, multilateral forums, with an emphasis on attaining asymmetric gains whenever possible.

The roots of this grand strategy can be traced to China's position as a relatively weak power. It requires high levels of undistracted economic and technological growth and hence significant geopolitical quiescence to ensure domestic order and well-being and to effectively protect its security interests along the periphery and beyond. The need for undistracted growth has been basic to the reform policies under way since the late 1970s.

The guiding elements of China's calculative grand strategy are clearly reflected in the policies China is pursuing in four separate areas: policies toward the United States; policies toward military modernization; policies toward territorial claims and the recourse to force; and policies toward international regimes.

Still Weak, but Rising

Given China's accurate appreciation of its status as a weak yet rising power, the thrust of Beijing's security-related policies toward the United States as the world's preeminent power can be characterized as a two-sided effort focusing on co-optation and prevention. The effort at co-optation focuses essentially on developing and maintaining cordial relations with the United States to encourage it to consistently underwrite the continuing growth in Chinese power; prevention seeks to hinder any American efforts that could frustrate the expansion in Chinese capability, status, and influence. This two-pronged strategy is grounded in the Chinese leadership's recognition that the United States subsists "in economic terms as an important trading partner and major investor" in China, while simultaneously remaining, "in nationalistic terms, [a] major rival in a competition for 'comprehensive national strength.'"[1]

The efforts at co-optation and prevention are manifested in direct and indirect forms. At the direct level, they are oriented at convincing the United States to accept the rise of China as a stabilizing event internationally and regionally. Convincing the United States that the inevitability—indeed, the desirability—of a more powerful China is essential to prevent any attempts at containment either by the United States and its allies or by other Asian powers. It is also essential to forestall a heightened defensive American counterresponse to a rising China, especially one that, if it leads to greater military acquisitions, increased forward deployments, and accelerated military research and development, would not only increase the gap in power capabilities between the United States and China still further, but also provide Beijing's regional competitors with the political cover under which they could challenge Chinese interests more effectively.

A Thoroughly Modern Military

As part of its current calculative strategy, China has sought to develop a range of military capabilities to sustain an expanded level of political and operational objectives. These objectives include securing the defense of Chinese sovereignty and national territory against threats or attacks from

1. Xiaoxiong Yi, "China's U.S. Policy Conundrum in the 1990s," *Asian Survey,* August 1994, p. 681.

all opponents, including highly sophisticated military forces; acquiring the ability to counter or neutralize a range of potential short-, medium-, and long-term security threats along China's entire periphery (especially in maritime areas); learning to use military power as a more potent and versatile instrument of armed diplomacy and statecraft in support of varied regional and global policies; and eventually developing the power projection and extended territorial defense capabilities commensurate with the true great-power status expected in the twenty-first century. These objectives may be summarized as an effort to reduce China's existing vulnerabilities while increasing the utility of its military forces for purposes of securing diplomatic and political leverage.[2]

The attempt to reduce vulnerability has materialized at two levels. The first consists of a slow but determined effort at nuclear modernization designed to reduce the vulnerability of China's small and relatively primitive strategic nuclear force to preemptive strikes by the industrialized powers' larger and more sophisticated forces. This program has been directed primarily toward improving "the survivability of [its] strategic forces, develop[ing] less vulnerable basing modes, and mak[ing] general improvements in the accuracy, range, guidance, and control" of its missile forces.[3] It is not aimed primarily at expanding significantly the overall size of China's nuclear arsenal.[4] China is also attempting to modernize its conventional weaponry; its labors in this area are much more concerted and its achievement more significant. Because China's contiguous land borders are relatively secure—thanks both to Chinese diplomacy and a current unwillingness on the part of China's potential neighboring adversaries to press their claims—the most visible dimensions of China's conventional modernization efforts have involved air and naval forces. Contingencies involving Taiwan in particular have provided a sharp focus for China's conventional modernization efforts in recent years. These include developing both interdiction (including morale-breaking) capabilities aimed at

2. A good summary of the multidimensional facets of China's military modernization can be found in the "Special Issue: China's Military in Transition," *The China Quarterly,* June 1996.

3. John Caldwell and Alexander T. Lennon, "China's Nuclear Modernization Program," *Strategic Review,* Fall 1995, p. 30.

4. However, the deployment by the United States of even a limited national missile defense system (NMD) (that is, one designed to intercept 20 to 25 long-range ballistic missiles) would likely compel the Chinese to increase significantly both the size and sophistication of their nuclear force beyond existing planned levels. A limited NMD system, when combined with a devastating first strike by the United States, would almost certainly eliminate even a modernized yet small Chinese arsenal.

Taiwan as well as denial capabilities targeting Taiwan's potential defenders, primarily the United States.

In their effort to achieve the objectives of developing a force capability that resolves near-term challenges while simultaneously supporting longer-term aspirations, Chinese security managers have recognized that the state's military modernization efforts must be built on a foundation of indigenous scientific, technological, and economic capabilities. Hence, the level of resources devoted to military modernization has increased at a pace that is intended neither to undermine the attainment of essential civilian development priorities nor to unduly alarm both the peripheral states and the major powers and thus erode the generally benign threat China faces today. This is, in essence, the clearest manifestation of the calculative strategy.

Territoriality and the Use of Force

China's approach to territorial claims remains a subset of its general strategic approach toward the peripheral states under the calculative strategy. Under this strategy China has pursued a generalized good-neighbor policy that has focused on strengthening its existing ties in Northeast and Southeast Asia, mending ties wherever possible in South and West Asia, and exploring new relationships in Central Asia.

Beijing has adopted a two-pronged approach in dealing with territorial issues. If the territorial dispute in question is marginal to China's larger interests, the government has sought to resolve it amicably to pursue its larger goals. The border disputes with Russia, for example, are evidence of this approach; China's overarching interest in improving political relations with Moscow and securing access to Russian military technology has resulted in quick, hopefully permanent, solutions to these disputes.

If the dispute in question is significant but cannot be resolved rapidly to China's advantage by peaceful means, Beijing has advocated an indefinite postponement. This tactic has been adopted in territorial disputes with India, Japan, and the Association of Southeast Asian Nations (ASEAN) states; China has steadfastly avoided conceding any claims with respect to the dispute while simultaneously trying to prevent disturbing the environment that China needs to complete its internal transformation successfully. Beijing has applied the same logic to the dispute over

Taiwan, whose presently ambiguous status the government would like to freeze. China would prefer not to employ force to resolve the issue, but may be compelled to do so because the principle of avoiding significant territorial loss—especially of an area possessing enormous nationalistic significance as a Chinese province—would demand a military reaction, no matter how costly, if the Taiwanese sought to change the status quo unilaterally. The reluctance to employ force to resolve outstanding territorial disputes remains a good example of the calculative strategy at work.

Cooperation vs. Defection

Beijing's calculative strategy has led it to adopt an "instrumental" attitude toward international regimes. This implies that China possesses neither commitment nor antipathy to existing international norms and organizations but approaches these in terms of a pragmatic calculation centered on the benefits and drawbacks of participation and nonparticipation. Consequently, it has pursued a wide range of strategies regarding existing and evolving international regimes that can range from full participation in search of asymmetric gains, and contingent cooperation in pursuit of reciprocal benefits, to overt or covert defection.

This wide range of behaviors is by no means unique to China: it is typical of most states. Consistently simple and straightforward behaviors—either in the direction of cooperation or defection—are usually manifested only by those few states that disproportionately benefit from the regime or are disproportionately penalized by it. The established great powers usually fall into the first category, the "revisionist" states into the second. Those states that occupy the middle ground—either favored or disadvantaged by prevailing regimes—would adopt behaviors similar to China's. Since Beijing encounters a variety of international regimes in the areas of economic development, trade, technology transfer, arms control, and the environment, this calculus is often reflected in different ways.

China either participates or has sought to participate in all regimes that promise asymmetric gains where accretion of new power or maintenance of existing power is concerned. It has also tried to participate in all international organizations and regimes where consequential policies adverse to China's interests might be engineered if Beijing were absent. At the same time, China has sought to undercut—through participation—those regimes that threaten the political interests of its communist government. And China has attempted to overtly or covertly undercut or leave those regimes that threaten its political and strategic interests, and generally to adhere to those regimes that advance such interests. China has remained a member of those international regimes that notionally provide joint gains, if the initial private costs of participation can either be extorted, shifted, or written off. China has also participated in regimes where the costs of unilateral defection were very high (for example, China continues to adhere to the Comprehensive Test Ban Treaty).

The Calculative Strategy: Benefits and Risks

China's calculative grand strategy has resulted in significant security gains for the Chinese state during the past decade. Most important, it has greatly strengthened domestic order and well-being by producing sustained high rates of economic growth and major increases in the living standards of many Chinese. It has greatly increased China's international leverage, especially along its periphery, and raised its overall regional and global status and prestige. The strategy has resulted in an expansion in China's foreign economic presence and an increase in its political involvement and influence in Asia and beyond. It has also generated a huge foreign currency reserve as well as provided the Chinese state with the financial ability to purchase advanced weaponry and critical technologies from foreign states, thus partially compensating for the continued shortcomings in its military capabilities (for example, Chinese purchases of advanced weapons from Russia are to a significant extent a testimony to the failure of China's defense industry to domestically produce many such critical systems). In perhaps the greatest achievement of all, the calculative strategy has contributed—despite the many unresolved disputes between China and its neighbors—to the maintenance of a relatively benign external environment that allows Beijing to continue to focus on internal economic growth.

The calculative strategy has thus paid off handsomely for China, putting it on a path that, if sustained, could see China become the largest economy in the world sometime in the first half of the twenty-first century. More significant, it has allowed this growth through an export-led economic program that increasingly employs imported technology and inputs. China has been able to rely on the markets and, increasingly, the resources of its partners to create the kind of growth that might eventually pose a major concern to its economic partners—without greatly unnerving those partners in the interim. This does not imply that China's economic partners are unconcerned about the implications of China's growth in power. It does indicate that such concerns have not resulted in efforts to constrain China's growth because the desire for absolute gains on the part of all (including China) has outweighed the corrosive concerns created by relative gains.

This represents the true success of the calculative strategy: because the strategy has been explicitly premised on a refusal to provoke fear and uncertainty through Chinese actions, Beijing has succeeded, whether intentionally or unintentionally, not only in desensitizing its trading partners to the problems of relative gains but has also, by rhetoric and actions aimed at exploiting all sides' desire for absolute gains, created the bases for the kind of continued collaboration that inevitably results in further increases in Chinese power and capabilities. Carried to its natural conclusion, the Chinese transition to true great-power status could occur in large part because of its partners' desire for trade and commercial intercourse, so long as Beijing is careful not to let any security competition short-circuit the process.

China's calculative grand strategy is not risk-free. Confrontation or conflict with the United States or its Asian allies could occur as a result of "normal" disputes between states—especially those arising from perceived threats to China's domestic order and China's territorial integrity—and not from explicit or implicit struggles over control of the international system. The current tensions between the United States and China over Taiwan provide the foremost example of this type of "normal" dispute.

A Future Grand Strategy

If current economic, military, and domestic political trends hold, by 2015–2020 at the earliest—and more likely by 2020–2025—China might begin an extended transition phase to a new grand strategy. This phase could last for one or two decades, and its span will largely be determined by how quickly and fully Beijing can consolidate its power capacities relative to other great powers in the international system, including the United States.

If China acquires a relatively high level of national capabilities during this period—such that a power transition at the core of the global system becomes possible—what would Beijing's new grand strategy look like? Clearly, it is unlikely to persist with the calculative strategy because this plan, which was born primarily of weakness and dependence, will have transformed the circumstances that generated it and will have outlived its necessity and usefulness. The calculative strategy would slowly transmute into another that better comports with China's new power and capabilities. Three basic alternative strategies are possible: a chaotic China, a cooperative China, or an assertive China.

China's political, economic, and social order will probably not disintegrate into chaos in the near term or during the transition beyond the calculative strategy. It is also unlikely that a more cooperative China will emerge during this period if Beijing's relative power grows to the point where a systemic power transition becomes plausible. Instead, growing Chinese power will most likely result, over the long term, in a more assertive China. And China could reasonably be expected to pursue most, if not all, of the core elements of those assertive grand strategies pursued by major powers in the past. These include efforts to augment its military capabilities in a manner commensurate with its increased power; develop a sphere of influence by acquiring new allies and underwriting the protection of others; acquire new or reclaim old territory for China's resources or for symbolic reasons by penalizing, if necessary, any opponents or bystanders who resist such claims; prepare to redress past wrongs it believes to have suffered; attempt to rewrite the prevailing international "rules of the game" to better reflect its own interests; and, in the most extreme policy choice, even perhaps ready itself to thwart preventive war or to launch predatory attacks on its foes.

How to Handle a Rising China

Even if the rise of Chinese power and its associated assertiveness should occur, preemptive containment and preemptive appeasement strategies would be counterproductive for the foreseeable future. As long as some chance exists that the predicted outcome of assertiveness may fail to materialize, or may be less severe than anticipated because of economic failure or the emergence of a more cooperative, democratic China, American strategy should neither create the preconditions for its occurrence nor retreat with the expectation that its occurrence is inevitable. And if it appears that the worst ravages of future security competition between the United

States and China can be avoided, American grand strategists are bound both by the dictates of prudence and moral sensibility to explore every possibility that reduces international turmoil. Hence, a policy that assumes the need to realistically engage China over the course of the calculative strategy is the optimal approach.

To maximize the desired effects of such engagement, United States policy must orient the concept of engagement to include three different but related strands of policy: to pursue, whenever feasible, the possibilities of cooperation aimed at attaining deeper levels of encounter, stronger degrees of mutual trust and confidence, more clearly defined notions of reciprocity or equity, and greater levels of integration into the international system, and to use the resulting expanded level of cooperation and integration to encourage movement by China toward a democratic form of government; to discourage or, if ultimately necessary, prevent China's acquisition of capabilities that could unambiguously threaten the most fundamental core national security interests of the United States in Asia and beyond; and to remain prepared, if necessary, to cope with—by means of diplomacy, economic relations, and military instruments—the consequences of a more assertive and militant China with greater capabilities in a variety of political, strategic, and economic issue-areas.

United States policy must maintain a clear understanding of the ends to which engagement is pursued by developing a short list of objectives, preferably centered on China's external security behavior in key issue areas of interest to the United States, such as the American presence and alliance structure in Asia, the open economic order, and the proliferation of weapons of mass destruction. American policy should also clearly appraise the multiple instruments available to support the three central strands of engagement just described and assess the trade-offs inherent in the use of these instruments. Overall, the development of a more effective engagement policy requires a more thorough understanding of how the operational elements of China's calculative strategy might evolve over time as China's capabilities change.

Even as this sharper assessment of engagement is developed, it is important to clarify America's own grand strategy and the objectives to which it aspires. The engagement of China should not be a policy prescription designed to assist the growth of Chinese power so that it may eventually eclipse the United States, even if peacefully. Rather, engagement must be focused on encouraging a more cooperative China, whether strong or weak, while also preserving American primacy in geopolitical terms. Together, the predicates of engagement should also focus on assisting Beijing to recognize that challenging existing American leadership would be both arduous and costly and, hence, not in China's long-term interest.

America's effort to engage China will be facilitated if China becomes a democratic state, more fully integrated into the international order and thus less inclined to employ military force. If Beijing eschews the use of force and works peacefully to adjust to and shape the future international system, the most destabilizing consequences of growing Chinese power will be minimized and, if the advocates of the democratic peace thesis are correct, a United States–led international order of democratic states that includes China might even be able to avoid the ravages of security competition. Unfortunately, the historical record suggests that achieving this goal will be difficult because the structural constraints imposed by competitive international politics will interact with the chaotic domestic processes in both the United States and China to produce antagonism between these two countries at the core of the global system.

4. Sino-American Relations since September 11: Can the New Stability Last?

September 2002

DAVID SHAMBAUGH

Ayear after the devastating terrorist attacks on the United States, Sino-American relations are their most stable since they began their decade-long deterioration and constant fluctuation following the events of June 1989. The prospects for continued stability are positive as long as neither nation infringes on the core security interests of the other. Some would dispute this assessment, including many analysts in China, since they see limited benefits from post–September 11 Sino-American cooperation and continuing underlying tensions and frictions in the relationship.[1] Of course, problems do exist and, given the fluctuant history of Sino-American relations, it would be a mistake to proclaim that the new-found stability is permanent or can endure indefinitely. Yet, the roller coaster of relations during the 1990s—when security tensions were frequent and disputes over human rights and trade were constant—is absent today.

China's support of the American war on Al Qaeda and global terrorism has certainly contributed to this new stability, but improvement in bilateral ties was noticeable before September 11 and is the result of more than simply cooperation in counterterrorism. Joint actions since September 11 have certainly contributed to improved ties, but this cooperation capitalized on momentum begun early in the Bush administration, particularly in the immediate aftermath of the April 2001 incident in which an American EP-3 surveillance plane was forced to make an emergency landing on Chinese territory.

---

1. See, for example, Aaron L. Friedberg, "11 September and the Future of Sino-American Relations," *Survival* (Spring 2002), pp. 33–50, and David M. Lampton, "Small Mercies: China and America after 9/11," *The National Interest* (Winter 2001/2002), pp. 106–113.

China's Reaction to September 11

When the hijacked airplanes ploughed into the World Trade Center, Pentagon, and a Pennsylvania field on September 11, Chinese President Jiang Zemin watched the tragedy unfold live on CNN. Jiang immediately ordered his government to issue solemn condolences to the American people and to fully cooperate with the United States government's efforts to track down the perpetrators.[2] For his part, the Chinese president activated the dormant hotline to the White House to personally convey condolences to President George W. Bush (Jiang was reportedly the second foreign leader, following Russian President Vladimir Putin, to get through). Thereafter the Chinese government took a number of steps to offer tangible assistance to the United States:

- helping draft and pass two key resolutions in the UN Security Council and General Assembly;
- supporting, in principle, the coalition attacks on the Taliban regime in Afghanistan (Beijing's vote on Resolution 1368 marked the first time that China had voted in favor of—rather than its usual practice of abstaining from—authorizing the international use of force);
- diplomatically working quietly behind the scenes with its close partner Pakistan to persuade General Pervez Musharraf's government to support the war against the Taliban regime;
- sharing intelligence with the United States on Al Qaeda and the Taliban;
- initiating a series of exchanges with the United States on counterterrorism, leading to a practical working relationship in this field;
- sealing China's short border with Afghanistan to prevent Al Qaeda or Taliban fighters from migrating into the Xinjiang Autonomous Region;
- inspecting bank accounts in Hong Kong and China for links to terrorist groups;
- offering aid for Afghan refugee resettlement in Pakistan and some reconstruction aid in Afghanistan.

China took these steps to unambiguously support the United States in the aftermath of September 11, but it has not done as much as other neighboring nations or other countries in the world. For example, China did not offer military overflight or basing rights—as did every nation surrounding

2. Author interview with senior Chinese Foreign Ministry official, October 9, 2001, Beijing.

Afghanistan (except Iran). China claims it has problems doing so because of longstanding sensitivities regarding sovereignty. Other nations, however, overcame such sensitivities and rose to the occasion. Nor did China commit any military units to the multinational force in Afghanistan. China's reluctance to become militarily engaged in the Afghan conflict tarnishes its otherwise positive record in the war against terrorism. Even more troubling and mystifying is China's failure to grasp the opportunity to contribute to the postconflict reconstruction of Afghanistan. China has pledged $150 million in reconstruction aid, but it has chosen not to become involved in training the new Afghan army or police forces, nor has it sent engineers, construction workers, or equipment to help rebuild the country. China's decision to send civilian police to East Timor proved to be an effective contribution to the maintenance of security and nation building there. China could—and should—contribute to these initiatives as a concrete expression of its international responsibilities as a major world power and member of the UN Security Council.

A Return to Engagement

China's cooperation with the United States in fighting terrorism certainly helped improve bilateral relations, but it only added momentum to the strengthening of ties that had been evident over the three months prior to September 11. The EP-3 incident in April and May 2001 certainly increased tensions and strained relations between the two countries, but once it was resolved both sides moved quickly to put it behind them and begin a dedicated process of engagement with each other. Immediately following the release of the EP-3 crew, the United States administration began to signal a shift in tone and policy toward China. Despite the bitter taste left by the Chinese government's handling of the incident, President George W. Bush, in a Rose Garden speech announcing the release of the detained crew, put Beijing and his bureaucracy on notice that he sought an improvement in relations. By using such terms as "constructive and productive relationship" and avoiding the standard refrain of "strategic competitor," the president signaled his willingness to improve ties. Keenly aware of the fissures in the administration's thinking about China, and the president's previously neutral stance toward the contending factions, the Chinese government saw a silver lining in the speech and was quick to grasp the opportunity to improve ties.

The responsibility for implementing the new and more positive policy fell to the State Department, which initiated a series of reciprocal official visits during the early summer, culminating in Secretary of State Colin Powell's own trip to Beijing in late July 2001. The tone of these visits was positive; both governments were looking forward to the first meeting of the two presidents at the Asia-Pacific Economic Cooperation conference in Shanghai in October. Thus, improvement in the United States–China relationship was evident before September 11.

While the Bush administration and Bush himself came to office arguing that China was a "strategic competitor," and while many members of his administration saw China as a potential adversary, a coalition of key officials (including the president, secretary of state, and national security adviser Condoleezza Rice) sought to establish a more stable, cooperative, and enduring relationship with Beijing. The rationale behind the shift in tone and policy was not dissimilar from the strategic logic that had guided the China policies of the six previous administrations: a China that is positively engaged with the world, and not withdrawn into a nationalistic cocoon, is conducive to the stability and security of the Asia-Pacific region and to American national security interests.

This realistic approach was soon to pay dividends after September 11. Sino-American cooperation against terrorism paved the way for Bush's visit with Jiang in Shanghai. The two presidents met again in February 2002, when Bush paid a two-day official visit to Beijing. Two American presidential trips to China in the space of four months are unprecedented, and the two leaders have also spoken by telephone a number of times during the past year. Although their chemistry is reported to be businesslike but not warm, such high-level contact is an important element in the overall relationship. It provides a personal sense of the other leader (an important criterion in Bush's worldview) and a channel of direct and uncensored communication on sensitive issues; it also energizes the two governments' bureaucracies to generate areas of joint cooperation.

In May 2002, Chinese Vice President Hu Jintao, who has been groomed to succeed Jiang Zemin in one or more positions at and after the sixteenth congress of the Chinese Communist Party that is scheduled for this autumn, also paid an official visit to the United States at the invitation of Vice President Dick Cheney (Hu had been to the West only once before with a November 2001 visit to Western Europe). Hu toured New York and New Jersey, Washington, D.C., the San Francisco Bay region, and Hawaii. In all his meetings, Hu impressed his interlocutors with a firm and detailed grasp of the issues, even if he did not stray from his carefully scripted "talking points." In Washington, Hu met with more than half the United States cabinet in two days of meetings. His discussions, while often pro forma, covered the gamut of issues on the bilateral agenda: human rights, Tibet, Taiwan, regional security in Asia, the Middle East, counterterrorism, nonproliferation, and United States–China military relations.

The past year has not only witnessed this set of high-level meetings but also the full reinstitutionalization of bilateral exchanges. Virtually every United States cabinet official (with the notable and glaring exception of Secretary of Defense Donald Rumsfeld) has now met his or her Chinese counterpart for discussions—some several times. Exchanges between the State Department and the Chinese Foreign Ministry have been particularly intensive. Secretary of State Powell and Deputy Secretary of State Richard Armitage have held several rounds of similar discussions with Foreign Minister Tang Jiaxuan, Executive Vice Foreign Minister Li Zhaoxing, and Assistant Foreign Minister Zhou Wenzhong. Vice Foreign Minister for Asia Wang Yi has exchanged views with his State Department counterpart, James Kelly, and Director for Arms Control and Disarmament Liu Jieyi has met with Assistant Secretary Avis Bohlen and Undersecretary John Bolton to discuss missile defense, nonproliferation, and arms control issues. Director of Policy Planning Richard Haass and Foreign Ministry Director of the Policy Research Office Cui Tiankai held the first of several exchanges on global security issues. Other delegations have also been exchanged in the areas of counterterrorism, human rights, public health, trade, transnational crime, and narcotics.

The lack of military-to-military exchanges is a notable exception to the reinstitutionalization of bilateral relations. Secretary of Defense Rumsfeld suspended all bilateral exchanges with the People's Liberation Army (PLA) following the EP-3 incident. Any such exchanges were to be approved on a case-by-case basis and by the secretary personally. Rumsfeld and other senior officials in the Defense Department are deeply suspicious of the value of these exchanges to the United States. They have the perception that past exchanges have benefited the PLA much more than the United States military, and have primarily been an avenue for Chinese military espionage. Because of the lack of Chinese transparency and reciprocity, the United States, they believe, receives little tangible benefit from military exchanges. Despite this predisposition at the Pentagon, Bush has proposed on two occasions to Jiang Zemin that the two militaries should resume exchanges. The State Department is also pushing for a resumption.

Reluctantly, Rumsfeld met with Hu Jintao (who also holds the portfolio of vice chairman of the Central Military Commission) and discussed the possibility of renewing military exchanges. Assistant Secretary of Defense for International Security Affairs Peter Rodman was dispatched to Beijing in June 2002 for exploratory discussions with the PLA leadership. Exchanges still have not resumed, however. If they do, they are likely to remain limited, given the reigning perception in Washington that the United States has little to gain from them as long as the PLA refuses to open its bases and military establishment on a truly reciprocal basis. This view is not only prevalent at the Pentagon, but also in Congress. In July 2002 the bipartisan congressional U.S.–China Security Review Commission issued its first annual report, which was extremely suspicious and critical of the Chinese military.[3]

The "Armitage–Wolfowitz Vision"

While bilateral exchanges in the military realm lag, the Bush administration has otherwise adopted the same strategy of "engagement" as had the previous six administrations. In this respect Bush's China policy is centrist and has continuity with his predecessors.[4] But this process of engagement represents just one strand of the Bush administration's China policy. It is dialectically paired with another set of actions aimed at countries and actors around China's periphery.

While some officials in the Bush administration do not even favor the engagement element of the administration's China policy, a consensus seems to have emerged early in the administration that China had to be engaged and not ignored, confronted, or contained. Secretary of State Powell, national security adviser Rice, and the president himself were key in forging this consensus. China was, in their estimation, a "major power" (like Russia) with which the United States had important equities and national security interests that mandated as much engagement and cooperation as possible. Yet, as part of this recognition, the administration also strongly believes that the approach to China must include other regional

3. Report to Congress of the U.S.–China Security Review Commission, *The National Security Implications of the Economic Relationship Between the United States and China* (Washington, D.C., July 2002).

4. This perspective is elaborated in David Shambaugh, "From the White House, All Zigzags Lead to China," *Washington Post*, February 17, 2002.

elements and that the United States should place much greater priority on these regional actors than it places on China. A central Republican Party critique of the Clinton administration's China policy was that it erred by placing inordinate emphasis on dealing with Beijing, to the neglect of real allies and partners elsewhere in Asia. Although this critique is disingenuous, during Clinton's second term a high priority was placed on building ties with China. This perspective is not new to the current Bush administration—it was presaged by the second Reagan administration and was conceptualized in that earlier era by the key officials responsible for East Asia policy—particularly the late Gaston Sigur, James Lilley, Richard "Dixie" Walker, Paul Wolfowitz, Richard Armitage, and James Kelly.

Today Wolfowitz and Armitage—now the deputy secretaries of defense and state, respectively—have played the dominant roles in conceptualizing the administration's broad Asia strategy. In their view, America's China policy should be embedded in a broader Asia policy, rather than vice versa. This basic conceptualization is not tantamount to a policy of containing China, although it certainly does have the effect of strengthening America's strategic and military ties all around China's periphery (which, to many in China, is precisely a form of neocontainment). While no existing public document describes it, what can be described as the "Armitage–Wolfowitz vision" for China and Asia policy involves at least the following core elements:

- Emphasize Japan. America's entire relationship with the Asia-Pacific region is anchored to the United States–Japan alliance—an alliance that, in Armitage's view, needs substantial strengthening and redefining so that it bears a closer resemblance to the United States–Britain alliance (an unrealistic desire if, for no other reason, Japan does not seek such a relationship);
- Stress and strengthen America's other four regional alliances (South Korea, Thailand, the Philippines, Australia) and its security partnerships (especially Singapore);
- Work to build security ties with Malaysia, Indonesia, Brunei, and possibly Vietnam;
- Vastly enhance overall relations with India—political, commercial, and military;
- Build security partnerships with Central Asian states (this was true September 11 and has become actual policy since then);

- Rebuild relations with Pakistan and help keep Pakistan from becoming a failed state that encourages and exports terrorism;
- Strengthen political and military ties with Taiwan;
- Maintain a robust forward military presence throughout Asia.

In the Armitage–Wolfowitz vision, China must be dealt with as amicably as possible, but within this broader strategic context. This vision is apparently shared by national security adviser Rice, Secretary of State Powell, and Trade Representative Robert Zoellick—while Secretary of Defense Rumsfeld and Vice President Cheney (and key members of their staffs) have much more hawkish views of China. Yet with this "vision" these policymakers have forged a consensus and coalition on Asia and China policy in the Bush administration.[5]

On Taiwan the Bush administration has also undertaken many new initiatives aimed at giving the government and people on the island greater confidence and dignity. In 2001 it approved the largest arms sales package for the Taiwanese military since the previous Bush administration agreed to sell 150 F-16 fighters in 1992. While it did not include the hotly debated Aegis-equipped naval cruisers, it did involve a number of weapons previously denied to Taipei (including submarines). The Defense Department has also moved to upgrade other forms of military assistance to Taiwan's armed forces in a variety of areas (an initiative begun during the second Clinton administration but intensified by the Rumsfeld Pentagon). The administration also broke with past policy by authorizing Taiwan's leaders (president and vice president) to make occasional "transit" visits to major American cities. It also permitted an unprecedented visit by Taiwan's minister of defense, who attended a conference in Florida where he met with Deputy Secretary of Defense Wolfowitz and Assistant Secretary of State Kelly. In another unprecedented move, former Taiwanese vice president and leader of the Kuomintang (Nationalist Party), Lien Chan, was invited to a conference and dinner at the White House. With the exception of former President Lee Teng-hui's controversial trip to the United States in 1995, these moves by the Bush administration are unprecedented in the 23 years since the United States derecognized the government on Taiwan. President Bush contributed the most notable policy departure of all by announcing in a nationally televised interview that his administration

---

5. For a similar assessment, see John Garver, "Sino-American Relations in 2001," *International Journal* (Spring 2002), pp. 283–310.

"would do whatever it takes to help Taiwan defend itself." This was a marked departure from the 30-year policy of "strategic ambiguity" (although both Taipei and Beijing have long assumed American intervention under scenarios short of Taiwan's outright declaration of independence). Although the Bush administration professes adherence to the "one China" policy and has explicitly said that it will not support a Taiwanese declaration of independence, these recent moves nonetheless have had the net effect of strengthening United States ties with Taiwan across the board. They also have support in Congress and from much of the American public.

Beijing is deeply concerned about and vigorously protests these initiatives, but they have not led to a major rift in the Sino-American relationship. For its part, Beijing is also recalibrating its relationship with Taiwan. The mainland's policy toward the island appears to have four main thrusts: economic integration, political co-optation, military intimidation, and international strangulation. All four elements work in tandem and are collectively intended to make Taiwan increasingly more dependent on the mainland, while sowing seeds of division in the island's domestic politics and closing Taiwan's international options. While official cross-strait dialogue remains suspended and hung up on disagreement over the "one China" issue, interchange of all kinds is rapidly deepening and accelerating. According to People's Republic sources cited in the January 25, 2002 *China Daily*, in 2001 cross-strait trade reached $32 billion, Taiwan invested $6.9 billion in 4,100 projects, and 2.9 million Taiwanese visited the mainland. It is estimated that Taiwan has invested a total of nearly $150 billion on the mainland. Approximately 300,000 Taiwanese now reside in Shanghai. While the magnets of commerce and culture are drawing the two sides continually closer, in terms of popular identity and politics a large gap remains across the strait. The interaction of these two sets of variables will, over time, be far more decisive than military factors in determining the future of the China–Taiwan relationship.

Potential Problems on the Horizon

Although the Sino-American relationship has experienced newfound stability over the past year, difficulties and potential problems remain. These fall in the areas of relations with Taiwan, nonproliferation, missile defenses, and the American military presence in Asia.

On Taiwan, the Bush administration has been able to achieve what many previous administrations failed to accomplish: strong and stable relations with Beijing and Taipei simultaneously. It has been able to do so by largely pursuing relations with each on independent tracks, rather than worrying about what a move toward one will do to the other. The administration, by proceeding to stabilize relations with the People's Republic first, has given itself the latitude to subsequently strengthen its ties to Taiwan. But ultimately there is a linkage between the two policy tracks. In particular, the Bush administration risks a confrontation and serious deterioration in relations with China if it continues to upgrade military relations with Taiwan, sell more advanced weapons to it, and permit senior Taiwanese officials to visit the United States. At present, Taipei is pushing hard for a possible visit by President Chen Shui-bian to Washington, and some members of Congress are interested in inviting him to address a joint session. That would be a profound affront to China and would likely trigger a major political crisis in Sino-American relations.

The United States is similarly risking a deterioration if it proceeds to further link the Taiwanese and American militaries in "joint" ways with integrated communications systems, command and control, and intelligence, along with joint force planning, logistics, training, or exercises. Any or all of these acts would, in the eyes of Beijing, reconstitute de facto the military alliance with Taiwan that the United States terminated in 1979 as a condition for the normalization of diplomatic relations with the People's Republic. It is one thing to sell weapons to Taiwan—which Beijing does not like but tolerates—but it is quite another to integrate the two militaries in these ways. It may make military sense to do so in the event that the United States must come to Taiwan's defense, but this is, in fact, a *political* issue: it directly contravenes the commitments of the Carter administration when the United States normalized relations with China in 1979. Even if the Pentagon does not undertake these initiatives on its own, Congress may force it to do so. Section 1202 of the National Defense Authorization Act for Fiscal Year 2003 (H.R. 4546), currently before Congress, mandates that the Department of Defense implement many of these measures within 180 days of passage into law. If the legislation is passed and implemented, it will likely ignite a major crisis in United States–China relations and may precipitate the very military confrontation the measures are intended to address. It is highly unlikely that the Bush administration is going to spend valuable political capital in Congress by working to remove the language and requirements from the draft bill—to the contrary, it seems inclined to support and adopt such measures. The administration should be prepared for adverse consequences.[6]

The arms buildup on both sides of the Taiwan Strait is also dangerous and destabilizing. An action-reaction arms-race dynamic has developed in the last few years, with Beijing buying specific weapons from Russia to counter those sold by the United States to Taiwan, while the United States selects weapons for sale to the island specifically designed to counter those sold by Russia to China. This escalatory dynamic is costly and risky.

The second concern, China's proliferation of ballistic missiles and missile components to other countries—particularly Iran, Iraq, Libya, and Pakistan—has been a longstanding problem. Despite years of negotiations, a bilateral agreement in November 2000, and countless Chinese denials and pledges, China's ballistic missile proliferation apparently continues. During the past year, the United States State Department slapped sanctions on 12 Chinese companies involved in such proliferation. China is a signatory to the nuclear Non-Proliferation Treaty and claims to oppose the proliferation of weapons of mass destruction, yet its continued leakage of such dangerous technologies or whole missiles (in the case of Pakistan) is a significant source of friction in United States–China relations and contributes to instability in already unstable parts of the world. It also links China directly to such "rogue states." In a speech to the Asia Society in Hong Kong this February, the American ambassador to China, Clark Randt, termed China's proliferation a "make or break issue" in the relationship. Although this may be an overstatement, if Beijing does not cease such activities and fully implement the November 2000 bilateral accord on ballistic missile proliferation, it risks deterioration in its relations with Washington.

The missile defense issue has also been an irritant for several years now, with China repeatedly expressing its opposition to the United States withdrawal from the Anti-Ballistic Missile Treaty in 2002 and development and deployment of such defenses. For China the issue centers on the number of ballistic missile interceptors deployed in Alaska as part of a national missile defense system. If a "minimal architecture" of 100 or fewer interceptors was deployed, Chinese military and civilian strategists suggest that it would not endanger their present "second-strike" nuclear retaliatory capability—and, hence, China could probably live with it and not undertake major increases in its own intercontinental force. But if a more robust architecture

6. Also see the discussion in Michael D. Swaine, "Bush Has a Tiger by the Tail with His China Policy," *Los Angeles Times,* June 17, 2002.

were deployed, China would be forced to build up its intercontinental ballistic missile and submarine-launched missile forces so as to ensure its deterrent. In its *Annual Report on the Military Power of the People's Republic of China* that was released July 12, 2002, the United States Department of Defense predicted that China's force of approximately 20 intercontinental ballistic missiles will likely grow to "around 30 by 2005 and may reach 60 by 2010." Irrespective of potential United States missile defense deployments, China is modernizing its entire missile force by moving from liquid to solid fuels, from fixed to mobile launchers, and from single to multiple warheads.

China is opposed not only to national missile defense, but also to the possibility of theater missile defenses in Northeast Asia—especially if they are deployed on or around Taiwan. If theater missile defense deployments were intrinsically linked to American systems, they would bring Taiwan under the United States defense umbrella and would reconstitute the severed military alliance. Yet, ironically, China's continuing buildup of short-range ballistic missiles opposite Taiwan—currently approximately 350 and growing by 50 per year—may likely precipitate extending theater missile defenses to the island (beyond the Patriot batteries already deployed). By continuing this buildup, China may find itself with the very outcome it seeks to prevent. A wiser path for China would be to seize the political initiative by proposing a unilateral freeze or reduction of its short-range ballistic missile deployments in exchange for an agreement by the Bush administration not to transfer theater missile defense *and* restrain its sales of conventional weapons to Taiwan. Such a move by Beijing would be diplomatically astute and an important confidence-building measure with Taipei; it would also place the Bush administration in a tricky position. A Chinese initiative along these lines, if matched by the United States, would arrest the current arms-race dynamic, decrease the militarization of Taiwan, and improve the atmosphere for the resumption of direct dialogue between the governments in Taipei and Beijing.

The final potential problem on the horizon of Sino-American relations concerns the growing United States military presence around China's periphery. Deployments in Pakistan and Central Asia as part of the war in Afghanistan, along with the rapidly improving United States–India military relationship; five bilateral alliances and improved security partnerships between the United States and several Southeast Asian states; and the already existing 100,000 forward deployed forces in Northeast Asia give China pause for concern. Many Chinese strategists perceive American encirclement and believe that China's national security environment has significantly deteriorated since September 11. If this perception grows and hardens among Chinese officialdom, and if China perceives these deployments as oriented against China, this military presence could become a problem in the Sino-American relationship. It is a positive sign that Chinese officials have told their American counterparts over the past year, for the first time, that China does not seek to evict the United States from East Asia and respects American interests in the region. This is not quite the same as saying that China agrees (with the United States and other countries) that the American presence is, in itself, a stabilizing force in the region, but it is reassuring.

The Outlook

Although Taiwan, missile proliferation, missile defense, and the American military presence in Asia and Central Asia have the potential to upset Sino-American relations over the next year, the current stability is reason for cautious optimism since other irritants to the relationship, such as human rights and trade, should be manageable. Neither country needs or seeks a deterioration of relations or a return to the roller coaster of the 1990s. Indeed, both are otherwise preoccupied. The United States is committed to the war against terrorism and improving the domestic economy. China faces a major leadership transition with the party congress this fall, and it also is in the early stages of a prolonged and wrenching process of implementing the terms of its accession to the World Trade Organization.

The United States and China share a host of interests and concerns that bind the two nations. With nearly $120 billion in two-way trade and substantial direct investment, each is of enormous economic importance to the other (China is now America's fourth-largest trading partner, while the United States is the third-largest for China). Only an absence of tension and confrontation will allow the two nations to fully tap their positive potential relationship. It is not preordained that the United States and China become adversaries. If wisely managed by both sides—and if the key sensitivities of each are respected rather than provoked—the new stability in Sino-American relations may endure.

5. Asia in the Balance:
America and China's "Peaceful Rise"

September 2004

ROBERT SUTTER

Backed by a dynamic economy and strengthened military power, China has developed an increasingly moderate and flexible approach to its Asian neighbors over the past decade. The result has been a remarkable expansion of influence in the region. Senior Chinese leaders have kept busy schedules, meeting with Asian counterparts from small as well as large countries. China has launched a wide array of economic, political, security, and cultural initiatives designed to foster closer bilateral and multilateral arrangements. Beijing has even shown flexibility on some territorial issues that in the past prompted rigid and assertive postures.

The impact of these efforts has been more or less favorable for China's influence throughout the region, with the exception of Taiwan and, possibly, Japan. The greatest gains have come in South Korea and several countries in Southeast Asia. The rapid growth of the Chinese economy has attracted or compelled businesspeople in these areas to seek closer relations with China, while China's attentive diplomacy and willingness to accommodate the concerns of South Korea and some Southeast Asian nations have won high marks from officials in those countries. In South Korea a "China fever" has prevailed for the past few years, with elite and popular opinion showing China to be more highly regarded than any other power. Beijing's increasing willingness to work closely with regional groupings centered on the Association of Southeast Asian Nations (ASEAN) has combined with China's economic dynamism and flexibility over territorial issues to help win broad support among Southeast Asian neighbors.

This record of generally positive accomplishment in Asia has been accompanied by little debate among Chinese and foreign observers about the objectives behind the new approach. There is general agreement that, still preoccupied with difficult economic and political issues at home, China's leaders seek a stable environment in Asia that will allow them to focus on domestic concerns. Fearful that Asian neighbors may react anxiously and perhaps try to resist China's growing power and influence, Beijing has pursued an active diplomacy designed to offset regional worries about a Chinese "threat." Meanwhile, economic modernization is essential to China's internal stability and greater international power, and the economies of Asia are a focal point of Chinese interest. Chinese efforts to isolate and pressure Taiwan also have encouraged improved relations with other Asian countries with the goal of making them less likely to interact with Taiwan in ways not approved by Beijing.

The significance of these changes is not lost on the United States. Some American specialists, recalling China's past strident objections to US leadership in the region, conclude that China wants to expand its influence at the expense of America's, and to weaken the US position in Asia. Others take the opposite tack, noting Beijing's diplomatic moderation toward the United States and its efforts to seek cooperative relationships and partnership with Americans in dealing with Asian affairs. The latest Chinese policy framework for the region—emphasizing China's "peaceful rise" in Asia—seems to support the latter view, although leaders in Beijing continue to debate and discuss that framework.

Implementing the "Peaceful Rise"

China's new approach to Asia has seen repeated summits and other high-level political, economic, and military discussions with Asian leaders. There also has been an unprecedented wave of Chinese activism in multilateral organizations. China has entered into free trade arrangements and security initiatives with ASEAN, and it has strengthened ties with Russia and Central Asia. Meanwhile, China's trade with Asia has expanded dramatically, attracting widespread positive attention and not a little concern from neighbors anxious to take advantage of opportunities in China's growth but fearful of the competition coming from China's rapid advances. China has become the main export destination for South Korea, Japan, and Taiwan.

Chinese leaders and officials have generally avoided the defensive assertiveness that characterized Chinese policy in Asia in the past, trying
wherever possible to accommodate the interests of the smaller Asian states.
In 2002, Beijing reached an accord to manage disputes with other Asian
claimants of islands in the South China Sea. It also began to ameliorate its
criticisms of the United States. In the 1990s, China had accompanied its
generally positive approach to Asian neighbors with rhetoric and actions
designed to weaken the American position in the region. It attacked US alliances and "cold war thinking" and encouraged Asian states to pursue
policies independent of US leadership, which Chinese officials tended to
view as "hegemonic." Such criticism of the United States was markedly reduced by mid-2001, before the September 11 attacks on America, as Chinese
leaders calculated their interests were better served by cooperation than
confrontation with the US superpower.

A similar pragmatism has also affected Chinese-Russian relations. During the 1990s, Beijing relied on Russia for political support against the
United States, and Russia was China's main source of modern weapons imports. Sino-Russian military cooperation has continued smoothly, and
trade relations have developed from a relatively low base. However, President Vladimir Putin by early 2001 saw Russian interests better served by
constructive relations with the United States, and he deemphasized anti-
US themes in interactions with China. In addition, Putin showed less commitment to the Chinese relationship as Russia maneuvered to obtain
advantageous arrangements for the sale of Siberian oil to bidders from
China and Japan. Chinese officials came to recognize that the Sino-Russian
"strategic partnership" was subject to adjustments by Russian leaders pursuing narrow national interests. China's leaders reacted pragmatically to
these changed circumstances, expecting less help from Russia when dealing
with their own differences with the United States.

China has, however, joined with Russia and four Central Asian
states—Kazakhstan, Tajikistan, Uzbekistan, and Kyrgyzstan—to deal
with terrorist issues, border security, and economic cooperation in the
regional grouping called the Shanghai Cooperation Organization. The
SCO excludes and appears at odds with US and Western influence in
Central Asia, but the organization has had to adjust to an abrupt up-
swing of US military power and deployments in the area as a result of
the invasion of Afghanistan in 2001. As the chief financial and political
supporter of the SCO, China has continued incrementally to expand

its influence in Central Asia, recognizing that most governments in the region still give higher priority to their relations with Russia or the West.

In another illustration of China's new approach to Asia, Beijing has pursued a slow process of reconciliation with India while sustaining active support for India's strategic opponent, Pakistan. The attractiveness and the competitiveness of the Chinese economy have drawn Indian business interest, and trade has grown from relatively low levels. China's constructive approach to New Delhi has positively influenced elite opinion and Indian officials, but they remain wary of Chinese objectives, especially given Beijing's continued support for Pakistan. Some Indian leaders are concerned about expanding Chinese influence in Burma and elsewhere in South Asia, which appears at odds with Indian security interests.

China's booming economy has also changed relations with Australia, the other continental power in the region. Chinese industry is increasingly important to Australian raw material exporters, while Australian manufacturers see a growing need to deal with competition from the People's Republic. Adroit Chinese diplomacy has reinforced Australian tendencies not to upset an overall beneficial relationship with China as the Australian government continues to side closely with its American allies.

Behind the New Moderation

What are the implications of China's moderate policies and growing regional influence for US leadership in Asia? Although Chinese party, government, and military specialists can provide a systematic outline of the purpose and scope of the moderate approach to domestic development and foreign policy captured under the heading of "peaceful rise," they acknowledge that there remain issues of debate and uncertainty because the process of establishing a firm policy remains incomplete. Consultations this author held in mid-2004 with 50 Chinese officials and specialists in Beijing and Shanghai, and with officials and nongovernment specialists in Taiwan, South Korea, Japan, Singapore, Australia, and India, helped to clarify the importance of Chinese leaders' strategic thinking for US interests in the region.

In contrast to Western commentary depicting the new Chinese strategy as evidence of greater confidence among the leaders in dealing with

Major Asian Exporters to China
(as a percentage of their total exports)

	1990	2003
Japan	2.1	13.6
South Korea	0.0	20.5
Hong Kong	24.8	42.7
Singapore	1.5	7.0
Indonesia	3.2	7.4
Malaysia	2.1	10.8
Philippines	0.8	12.0
Thailand	1.2	7.1
India	0.1	6.4

Source: International Monetary Fund.

domestic and foreign affairs, most Chinese officials interviewed stressed Chinese diffidence and preoccupations. Apart from numerous domestic concerns and worries, the main international uncertainty they addressed involved the United States. Specifically, they recognize that rising powers of the past, such as imperial Germany before World War I and imperial Japan before World War II, became powerful in ways that challenged the prevailing international order. In the event, other powers aligned against and destroyed them.

Chinese officials see the United States as the dominant power in Asian and world affairs, and the main potential international danger that can confront and complicate China's development and rising power. The US preoccupation with the Iraq quagmire has not fundamentally altered the Chinese view of American power. Under these circumstances, Chinese officials and specialists say they are determined that the United States not see China's rise as a challenge to America. To reduce the likelihood of this outcome, they have worked to solidify trends evident since mid-2001, with Chinese commentary reducing past attacks on a wide range of US domestic and foreign policies and practices. Chinese officials say Beijing is prepared, for example, to restrain condemnation of US "hegemony." In general, Chinese officials have tried to narrow criticism of US policies and behavior to areas that relate to Taiwan. Meanwhile, Chinese officials assert that they accept US leadership in Asian and world affairs.

China's recent moderate approach is strategic and long-term, officials and experts emphasize. But they add that it also depends on circumstances, notably a constructive US response to Chinese moderation.

US-China differences over Taiwan represent an immediate challenge in this regard. As US national security adviser Condoleezza Rice discovered during meetings in China this July, Chinese officials and specialists want the Bush administration to do more to curb the Taiwan government's signals and actions pointing toward a more formal independent status for the island. They want America to cut back military support for Taiwan, and they are disappointed that the United States continues such support as it seeks to deter China from using force against Taiwan.

Chinese officials and specialists also admit that Japan poses a special problem for China's peaceful and moderate approach to Asia, and that US support for Japan feeds into this problem. Thus, China has shown less moderation toward Japan than toward the United States, India, or other countries that Chinese officials and commentary attacked in the past. Officials and specialists say the fundamental problem is Chinese domestic politics, as well as Japanese domestic politics, which make it very difficult for the two countries to moderate differences over history, territorial issues, and other disputes. Not surprisingly, Japanese officials have a mixed view of China's rising power and influence in Asia. They generally welcome economic cooperation with China, but some Japanese officials and specialists make clear that Japan is unlikely to fully embrace China's avowed peaceful intentions until Chinese military doctrine, deployments, and force improvements clearly reflect a peaceful intent. Partly as a result, Japanese officials continue to rely closely on the US security alliance.

Chinese officials and specialists also acknowledge that it may be difficult for the United States to fully embrace and reciprocate China's moderate approach. US officials have been surprised by Beijing's recent moderation, by its avowed acceptance of US leadership in Asian and world affairs, and by the narrowing of significant differences in the Sino-American relationship to focus on the Taiwan issue. Although China no longer is the prime target of US foreign policy debate as it was prior to September 11, 2001, the United States still has wide-ranging differences with Chinese policies and practices over values, economic issues, security concerns, and sovereignty questions that are unlikely to be silenced by the shift in China's stance toward greater moderation. Moreover, American security planners, like their Japanese counterparts, are unlikely to fully embrace Beijing's avowed peaceful intent until China reduces its strong military modernization efforts targeted at Taiwan and at US forces that might intervene in a Taiwan contingency.

China's "Gulliver Strategy"

Chinese officials and specialists express hope that the United States will reciprocate China's moderate foreign policy by developing closer relations with Beijing and accommodating Chinese interests regarding Taiwan and Japan. But they also recognize that China's peaceful rise has benefits for China even if the United States disappoints Chinese expectations. In particular, Beijing's approach to Asia has greatly expanded positive Chinese influence throughout its periphery. Recent diplomatic and economic initiatives have created a buffer around China that would make it difficult for the United States to gain the cooperation of Asian countries should the United States try to pressure or contain Beijing. In addition, the expanding array of Chinese-backed multilateral efforts and arrangements in Asia acts as a sort of "Gulliver strategy," impeding a more assertive US policy by tying it down in a multitude of multilateral restrictions and constraints.

Thus, rising Chinese influence in Asia is seen to work in some ways against American influence and adds to difficulties the United States already faces in the region. Overall US leadership in Asia is weakened by preoccupations with protracted military and political difficulties in Iraq and Southwest Asia, as well as by concerns about instability or uncertain cooperation in frontline states in the war on terrorism such as Afghanistan, Pakistan, and Indonesia. In addition, the US occupation of Iraq has prompted Asian elite and public opinion to join worldwide complaints against America's perceived unilateralism and dominance in international affairs.

In the context of the Iraq occupation and the war against terrorism, issues in other parts of Asia have tended to receive lower US priority, amid an overall reactive and weakened American posture in the region. In 2002, North Korea broke declared nuclear nonproliferation commitments and reactivated nuclear facilities frozen under the 1994 US-North Korea Agreed Framework accord. Deep divisions within the US government over how to deal with North Korea, and strong differences between Washington and Seoul over policy toward North Korea, hampered an effective US response. China eventually agreed to play an intermediary role that was welcomed by the United States; it organized three-party talks (the United States, North Korea, and China) in 2003 that were followed by six-party talks in 2003 and 2004 (adding Japan, South Korea, and Russia). Little progress ensued, although the Korean situation remained outwardly calm and all parties refrained from serious provocations. A similarly reactive US stance was seen when President George W. Bush on December 9, 2003, responded to the

Taiwan president's moves toward greater independence and rebuked him, warning against efforts to alter the status quo in relations with the mainland.

American Advantages

China's rising influence and other recent challenges to the United States in Asia have weakened and diverted US leadership in the region. Nevertheless, these challenges are balanced to a considerable degree by continuing strengths and favorable trends in Asia for US policies and interests. Indeed, the outlook for US leadership in promoting stability, development, and American values in Asia remains positive.

Despite the preoccupation with Iraq, the Bush administration has adjusted in generally pragmatic ways to unexpected Asian challenges, notably on the Korean peninsula—an area of much more salient concern than Iraq to most Asian governments. While attempting to justify unilateral action in other parts of the world, the Bush administration in practice has sought to deal with the North Korean crisis and other issues in Asia through broad international consultation and engagement. Of course, North Korea's armed power makes American military options on the peninsula more limited and difficult than they were in Iraq; US strategic deployments in Southwest Asia further limit US options against North Korea. North Korea's efforts to develop nuclear weapons continue, and could precipitate sharper divisions between the United States and Asian powers or within the US government. Meanwhile, however, the Bush administration's response to Taiwan's recent assertiveness has broad support in Asia as a sensible approach designed to stabilize a difficult situation.

Despite debate over the size and deployment of US forces in South Korea, the South Korean and US governments have tried to manage the issue without jeopardizing strong mutual interests supported by a continued US military presence. Meanwhile, polls that have shown setbacks for America's image in some Asian countries also show that most of those polled retain overall positive views of American leadership and that clear majorities in Asia agree that their interests would suffer if the United States were no longer the world's dominant power.

Under the Bush administration, the United States maintains open markets despite occasional aberrations—such as moves in 2002 to protect US farmers and steel manufacturers, or official complaints in 2004 about

American job losses to Asia and unfair currency values in China and Japan. Asian governments view the US economy as critical to Asia's economic well-being. Although China is a new engine for regional growth, US economic prospects remain much more important for Asian development. The United States in recent years has absorbed an increasing percentage (about 40 percent, according to US government figures) of exports from China, which is emerging as the export-manufacturing base for investors from a wide range of advanced Asian economies. The US market continues to absorb one-third of Japan's exports. The economies of South Korea, Taiwan, and the ASEAN countries rely on the American market to take about 20 percent of their exports.

Much is written about growing Asian trade with China, and indeed China's share of regional trade is important and expanding. However, US trade surpassed China's trade in 2003 with most major Asia traders. For example, US trade with ASEAN countries far surpassed China's trade with them in 2002. Meanwhile, US foreign direct investment has grown notably in China, but it is still less than in Australia, Hong Kong, Singapore, or Japan.

Despite occasionally strong rhetoric in support of religious freedom in China or condemning political repression in Burma, Bush administration policy has been pragmatic in the promotion of human rights, democracy, and political values in Asia. As the United States has sought allies and supporters in the global war on terrorism, it has moderated its approach in these areas: for example, it did not seek to bring China's human rights conditions before the UN Human Rights Commission in 2003. The adjustment has been generally welcomed in Asia. After the 9-11 attacks, the United States mobilized military, political, and economic power that, at least initially, proved overwhelming to adversaries and duly impressed Asian states. US power contradicted earlier predictions of American decline; indeed, the United States has become more powerful and influential in Asia and the Pacific than at any time since the Vietnam War and perhaps earlier.

Amid criticism by some US nongovernment experts and grumblings in the ranks of the US military, American defense officials have moved ahead with plans to shift US deployments in Asia as part of a global realignment, while sustaining large ground-force commitments in Iraq. The realignment reportedly involves plans to downsize forces in Western Europe and South Korea, to increase the mobility of forces, and to expand the scope of bases and access points while reducing the overall size of bases abroad. On balance, the changes do not appear to alter the prevailing situation in Asia. Some in the region might wish to challenge or confront the United States, and might be more inclined to do so if the United States were seen as bogged down in Iraq. Most, however, remain reluctant to do so given the dangers they would face in opposition to the world's dominant power, with a leadership seemingly prepared to use that power against its enemies.

Meanwhile, the Bush administration has improved US relations with all the great powers in Asia. This strengthens US leadership in the region, and reinforces Washington's ability to deal with crises and regional difficulties. It is rare for the United States to have good relations with Japan and China at the same time. It is unprecedented to have good relations with both India and Pakistan, and with both Beijing and Taipei.

The Balance in Asia

On balance, the advantages of China's moderate approach toward the United States—set forth in China's strategy of "peaceful rise" in Asia— seem substantial for US interests. China's moderation has meant less criticism from Beijing over US policy in Iraq, even though China opposed the war. It has allowed the Bush administration to highlight relations with China as a significant accomplishment. And it has set a positive atmosphere for US-China cooperation on North Korea and the war on terrorism. Any loss of US ability to revert to a policy of containing China seems small in comparison. In the past, Asian countries were unlikely to side with the United States against China out of concern that China might react aggressively; now the Asian governments are loathe to do so for fear of jeopardizing positive benefits they receive from China. In either case, it has long been effectively true that a US containment policy against China would not win much support in Asia.

Since Asian countries have been reluctant to choose between America and China, it would be foolish for the United States to react to China's rise by trying to compete directly and antagonistically with Beijing for influence in the region. A more effective approach would be to build on the US role as Asia's leading power and the region's economic and security partner of choice. Greater activism in the region and sensitivity to the concerns of Asian states going through difficult transitions (South Korea is a good example) also would go far toward improving US influence in this important part of the world.

Given all the difficulties facing the United States at home and abroad, US policy making toward Asia will likely remain somewhat reactive. America is unlikely to come up with as comprehensive and attractive an approach to the region as that pursued by Beijing. China's gains should not be exaggerated, however. So far they amount to less even than those achieved by Japan in the 1980s, when the burgeoning Japanese economy prompted many specialists to argue that Japan was Asia's leader and that American decline in Asia in the face of expanding Japanese economic and political influence would continue.

America's strengths in Asia remain formidable and will grow particularly as the US economy grows and as US military power continues to be seen as serving broad Asian interests in regional stability. Chinese leaders seem to understand this in their acceptance of US leadership in Asian and world affairs, as part of a long-term strategy to develop "peacefully" without upsetting the United States. This understanding represents a sharp reversal from China's post-cold war efforts to wear down the US superpower and create a "multipolar" world. It reflects a clear-eyed adjustment to the realities and asymmetries of power and influence between the United States and China still prevailing in Asia and across the globe.

PART II

Economic Policy and Social Issues

6. The Long March from Mao: China's De-Communization

September 1993

LIU BINYAN

Since 1989, Communist regimes in Eastern Europe and the Soviet Union have collapsed one by one, leaving only China with an apparently flourishing Communist government. China's Communists have not only managed to remain in power, but have even introduced rapid economic growth while maintaining relative social stability during the last few years. How has this been possible? And what is the future of the party, and the China that it rules?

The Roots of Ambivalence

The Chinese Communists (and their Vietnamese counterparts as well) are unique among the world's governing Communist parties in that they came to power only after more than 20 years of bitter fighting. The honesty and high moral standards displayed by the Chinese Communists for their first few years in power starkly contrasted with the darkness and corruption of pre-1949 Kuomintang rule—so much so that all the nearly unbearable problems that had plagued China for so long seemed obliterated overnight. For the Chinese people, the Communists and Mao Zedong became not only great liberators, but the very embodiments of truth, justice, and morality.

The absolute authority and public trust the Communist party enjoyed during the 1950s and 1960s made almost all Chinese eager to join. The best people from every level of society, from the intelligentsia to the workers, became party members and cadres. Even though in following Mao they may have made numerous mistakes (which they have come to regret), many of them had the people's welfare at heart as they waged successive ideological struggles against "erroneous" political lines; large numbers even suffered Mao's ruthless persecution. When Deng Xiaoping rehabilitated the victims of previous upheavals in 1979, the former party members who regained their political rights numbered in the hundreds of thousands; quite a few resumed leadership duties.

Many middle-aged and older Chinese still remember the Communists' outstanding record of political accomplishments between 1949 and 1956. This is largely due to the fact that even after Mao had led the Chinese people into disasters, many party members and cadres stayed true to their ideals and stood with the people in an attempt to mitigate these disasters, or worked to oppose the bad cadres in the party.

This explains why the Chinese frequently view the party with a split perspective. People will occasionally complain, for example, that local magistrate so-and-so (usually a party member) is "very bad and ought to be shot, but the local party secretary is a good person; we like him." Even during the upheavals of 1988 and 1989, when people reviled the party from all sides, they would never have condoned a slogan such as "down with the Communist party!"

Much about the Chinese Communists would be unimaginable in other countries. In its first three decades of rule, the party had no need for a state-security organization like the KGB. During the famine of 1959-1961, which Mao engineered, at least 40 million people died, but there was no rebellion. Far from abandoning the party after it launched the decade-long disaster known as the "Great Proletarian Cultural Revolution," the people actually pinned their hopes on Deng Xiaoping and his clique. Even after Deng decided to unleash an unprecedented massacre in the capital in 1989, the people continued to tolerate the Communist regime.

Compared to their former Soviet counterparts, Chinese Communists are less rigid and dogmatic, and are more interested in obtaining practical results. In pursuing a major goal, they are likely to be more flexible on side issues, and at times even willing to make major concessions or accept faits accomplis that they dislike. People at all levels of the party hierarchy thus often get away with merely feigning obedience to their superiors.

This flexibility extends to China's political mechanisms, which are also slightly more pliant than were those of the Soviet Union. As a result,

Deng's policy of "holding fast to the Four Basic Principles" (which are hardly distinguishable from Maoism) can co-exist with his policy of economic liberalization.* This is the basis for the way Deng Xiaoping and the Chinese people in general behave in society: there are things one can do but not talk about, others one merely talks about but does not actually do. Deng has launched campaigns against "bourgeois liberalization" on four separate occasions, yet the freedom enjoyed by the Chinese people continues to grow.

Depending on their temperament and attitudes, the actions Chinese leaders take in the regions or departments they are in charge of may depart from the limitations imposed by the system. For example, a few months after Mao launched an intensive nationwide campaign of agricultural collectivization in 1956, the secretary of a county party committee in Zhejiang province dared to propose a plan for setting farm-output quotas on the basis not of cooperatives, but individual households (*baochan dao hu*); his superior, the secretary of the provincial party committee, actually implemented it temporarily on a trial basis. (Deng himself dared not fully authorize this system until 1979.)

Similar situations became even more common after the Cultural Revolution. The chaos of that period had brought party activities to a halt for as long as five years; almost all party cadres were stripped of their positions, deprived of their rights, and subjected to ruthless ideological denunciations (which often included physical humiliation and torture). As a result, the will and morale of the Chinese Communist party, previously known for its "iron discipline," were enormously damaged. Different political factions arose within the party, and corruption among party cadres grew significantly, all of which had a devastating impact on the political and economic system in the aftermath of the Cultural Revolution. Considerable liberalization had taken place within the party even before Deng launched his reforms in 1979, which is why there was less resistance within the party to reforms than there was within the Soviet Communist party to reforms in the Soviet system.

These distinctive aspects of Chinese political practice are among the reasons why China's Communists have found their way out of their crises and avoided a total collapse of the system. Since the introduction of economic reforms, the trend toward localization of political authority has

---

* Editor's note: The "Four Basic Principles" to be upheld are: the socialist road; the dictatorship of the proletariat; Communist party leadership; and the leading role of "Marxism-Leninism-Mao Zedong thought."

greatly intensified; local leading cadres can respond to a political crisis by making more independent decisions (which include some concessions to popular demands), thus enhancing local stability and lessening the impact of the crisis. While the overall system remains unchanged, each province and district will gradually become more politically, economically, and culturally diversified.

All this is evidence of a unique and fascinating phenomenon now taking place in China. Though nobody will openly acknowledge it, what is practiced in China today is not socialism but capitalism. Regardless of whether it is Deng himself, his enemies, people who benefit from the reforms, or those who are hurt by them, everyone knows this. Deng's opponents may raise the "anti-capitalist" banner after he dies, but it is already too late.

A Cycle of Corruption

From the very beginning of his economic reform effort, Deng faced a host of problems. The reforms did raise people's standard of living; 800 million peasants were released from semi-serf status as the era of "People's Communes" ended, greatly alleviating popular dissatisfaction with the Communists. But economic liberalization brought with it demands for ideological and political liberalization. Deng's repeated campaigns against "bourgeois liberalization" and his refusal to let the people promote social reform stirred popular discontent and resistance.

The economic reforms and China's opening to the outside during the 1980s gave party officials greater opportunity to abuse their power; resistance to reforms from within the party decreased as a result. But party corruption also gave rise to popular demands for political reform and the introduction of the rule of law, which Deng and his clique had no intention of carrying out.

As the economic reforms progressed, they revealed abuses in the political system ever more clearly. Political reform would necessarily present a threat to the vested interests of the bureaucracy. As the representative of that group, Deng had already shown by the mid-1980s that he had no interest in pursuing even the most elementary political reforms. Without political reforms to improve government efficiency and credibility (and stem official corruption), his economic reforms were inevitably weakened and compromised.

All this culminated in the Tiananmen movement of 1989.

Deng resorted to military force to suppress the pro-democracy movement in Tiananmen Square in order to preserve the Chinese Communist regime. The June 4 massacre and the massive purge that followed badly hurt the forces of democracy, but Deng's own power and prestige, the reforms he had promoted, and the regime itself were also grievously wounded.

In the four years since 1989, the reform process of the previous decade has been almost completely repeated, only faster and more intensely. In many ways, China has come full circle, and has returned to the conditions prevailing on the eve of the 1989 pro-democracy movement.

Corruption among party officials is now much more serious. In 1990, cases of bribery and graft were double what they were in 1989, and these abuses of power have become open and systematic (in the routine operations of party and government organs, fixed prices have been set for various categories of bribes). Cadres at various levels, their children, and people with powerful connections are recklessly plundering the nation's wealth and resources, becoming millionaires or billionaires through trading in stocks or real estate.

China's economy has certainly undergone rapid growth, mainly in the coastal regions, but at a heavy cost. Income gaps have widened alarmingly between the urban rich and poor, between the cities and the countryside, and between coastal and inland regions. In particular, the declining incomes and increasing burdens (including exorbitant taxes, forced contributions, and fines or other forms of punishment) afflicting several hundred million peasants are causing a growing number to resort to violence, which frightens the party Central Committee out of its wits. At the same time, tens of millions of workers at state-run enterprises are facing the threat of unemployment as state-owned enterprises become increasingly uncompetitive and economically irrelevant.

In order to pander to Deng's decrees and in the desire for private gain, bureaucrats throughout China have blindly increased investments without considering the economic impact; at the same time, most state-run enterprises continue to operate at a loss. The result has been a skyrocketing fiscal deficit and the printing of far more money in far greater quantities than planned. Inflation has reached a new peak; many urban residents are panic-buying goods and materials, and a large number of local banks have been forced to suspend operations because of runs on their deposits. These conditions are almost identical to those in 1988—especially the high inflation, which was a direct cause of the 1989 Tiananmen movement.

China has once again reached a crossroads.

A Fifth Asian Tiger?

A peaceful and gradual transition to democracy is still possible in China, and this is what the majority of Chinese hope for. But the death of Deng Xiaoping (generally expected in the next year or two) may remove a major source of China's stability while simultaneously stirring up other forces of destabilization. In 1992, Deng stripped General Yang Shangkun and his half brother Yang Baibing of their influential positions on the party's Central Military Commission, and carried out the most extensive purge of the armed forces since 1949; the resultant dissatisfaction in the military could lead to real problems after Deng's death.

A full-scale civil war does not appear likely. Regional differences in development and local conditions mean that change in China will take place differently in each province and region. Prospects for peaceful change are better in the coastal areas, while varying degrees of disorder appear inevitable in inland areas. In fact, two rebellious outbreaks at the county-seat level have already occurred this year; one, in Sichuan province, involved an estimated 10,000 disgruntled farmers who stoned members of the People's Armed Police.

It is an illusion to think that China can become another Singapore or Taiwan by relying solely on economic growth without political reform and democratization. Those who cling to this illusion ignore two important facts about China:

First, mainland Chinese are different from Chinese living outside the country. More than 40 years of Communist rule have cut them off from Chinese cultural traditions. Mao successfully wiped out the sources of authority that traditionally maintained stability in China and replaced them with the party as the sole authority; that sole authority has now vanished as well. Today the only sources of authority in the minds of the mainland Chinese are their own personal instincts and desires.

At the same time, the Chinese Communists also wiped out social morality and religion, destroyed education, and left the law so compromised that it no longer commands respect. Thus there are neither internal nor external restrictions on the people's behavior. The corruption of party and government officials is driving the corruption of the entire society.

For more than 40 years, Mao pushed the Chinese people toward awakening through actions aimed at creating the opposite effect. Twice he pushed them into hopeless impasses (the 1959-1961 famine and the Cultural Revolution). He stripped them of their freedoms, stifled their hopes, and gave them no choice but to become the party's "docile tools." But precisely because he did his job only too well, the Chinese people have finally awakened from their sleep of several thousand years and realized that they are human beings with a right to defend their individual freedoms and interests and to strive for their individual development. Deng's reforms have further loosened the bonds imposed on the individual.

This is why Chinese society now has such abundant energy, though this energy can be a constructive force or a frighteningly destructive one. The people no longer abjectly obey anyone who tramples on them, which is an enormous and historic step forward. Some Chinese officials complain that the Chinese have become "people of cunning and violence"; this makes a certain amount of sense, in that the people are much smarter now, and much braver. Such Chinese would never accept the kind of autocratic leadership practiced by Singapore's Prime Minister Lee Kuan Yew, nor would they submit to Singapore's coercive social system.

The second major factor that must be kept in mind about China is that Taiwan, Singapore, and Hong Kong do not have anything remotely comparable to mainland China's enormous Communist bureaucracy and its total monopoly on the nation's economy and resources. The Communists' rapaciousness and unrestricted political power, combined with the mutual protection provided by networks of personal connections throughout this bureaucracy, result in criminal behavior that generally goes unpunished.

What China Needs

That the Chinese people have tolerated the rule of a bureaucratic clique since 1989 is partly due to the enormous political pressure it exerts, and partly to the improvements in the people's material well-being during this period. In addition, despite the lack of political freedom, the regime does not generally interfere in people's private lives; in the economic and cultural spheres at least, the scope of individual "liberty" has expanded. In contrast to Mao, Deng has allowed people's lives to become a bit richer, and has also permitted them to be a little happier. A capable person in China now has a much broader range of choices in terms of lifestyles and future prospects. Finally, the social and economic chaos that have followed the Soviet Union's and Eastern Europe's revolutions have led the Chinese to cherish their current stability. Indeed, stability has become Deng's trump card, a card that he uses to intimidate the Chinese people: "If my regime ever falls, China will inevitably fall into chaos and civil war!"

But this impasse is of the Communists' own making. They do not permit an alternative political force to exist legally, or even let people organize themselves for nonpolitical goals; yet their own regime has become so corrupt and incompetent that it cannot even perform the most basic administrative functions.

It will not be long before the people of China see the awful crisis this sort of "stability" is creating for their future. Since 1989 the regime's social control has gradually slackened, which could allow more room for civil society to function for the people's benefit. For the moment, the regime's information blockade prevents people from learning about the struggles carried on elsewhere in China, or gaining an adequate understanding of the regime's current difficulties; they thus have insufficient confidence in their own power to effect change.

But the inevitable power struggles at the top after Deng dies, combined with social disruption brought on by economic crises, will soon force China's intellectuals and the talented people scattered throughout society to realize that they must mobilize themselves, throw off the restrictions imposed by the regime, and organize the people by legal means (based on the civil rights granted to them in China's constitution). This will be necessary in order to defend the rights and interests of the people, satisfy their needs, and protect their personal security and property. The people will have to take over many of the functions that the regime is presently incapable of handling.

This will be a movement by the Chinese people to govern, protect, and save themselves. It is also the only way to re-kindle the people's love for their nation and native land, and change the antisocial psychology and behavior that now results in people venting their hatred of the regime on society at large. (One of the most disastrous consequences of the Communists' total control of China's society and people has been that many Chinese think of their own country as something belonging to the Communists, and that they themselves have no connection to it.) Moreover, a mass self-salvation movement of this kind would gradually teach the Chinese how to live democratically.

A desirable path such as this would allow China to avoid chaos and would transform the Chinese, not into a "cunning and violent" people, but into a constructive force made up of responsible citizens.

7. China's North-South Split and the Forces of Disintegration

September 1993

EDWARD FRIEDMAN

In the 1970s, when the Soviet Union considered Communist China both a major adversary and a dangerous competitor, Victor Louis, understood to be a Soviet intelligence operative, published *The Coming Decline of the Chinese Empire,* a tract prophesying the disintegration of China as a result of "the national aspirations of the Manchu, Mongols, Uighurs, Tibetans, and other non-Chinese peoples. . . ." Today China's media portray anyone who raises the topic of a possible breakup of China as an enemy and saboteur—like Victor Louis, an agent of black propaganda.

On the surface, it does seem that the non-Chinese peoples inside the People's Republic have been reduced to insignificant minorities by waves of Chinese immigrants in what had once been huge non-Chinese regions—Tibet, East Turkestan, Mongolia, and Manchuria. (Tibetans protest this population invasion as cultural genocide.)

In the twentieth century, nationalistic Chinese have tended to take the fate of the Manchus, who conquered all of China in the seventeenth century, as a preview of the destiny of the non-Chinese. To maintain their communal identity, the Manchu kept their northeastern homeland free of female Chinese settlers and maintained Manchu as a national language. Yet nearly 300 years later, the population of what was once Manchuria—known in China merely as the northeastern provinces—is less than 10 percent Manchu, and only a small minority of these can speak Manchu. That Chinese civilization conquers all is the usual conclusion drawn from the Sinicization of the Manchu.

The Chinese view is that in what were once non-Chinese regions, tens of millions of Chinese settlers went to live in inhospitable terrain to block expansionist neighbors: the Russians, Central Asian Muslims, Indians, and Japanese. These settlers are seen as having suffered to make once barren regions productive, and also as having brought with them a superior civilization that Sinicized the indigenous peoples, making China one homogenous people. If this is the case, why even raise the issue of breakup?

One reason is that China cannot escape the global tendencies of the information revolution and the rise of soft technologies. In China, as in Lombardy in Italy, Quebec in Canada, the Breton region of France, Punjab in India, or in the southern states of Brazil, there is an extraordinary resurgence of communalist, or shared identities. There is a desire for a new nation state as people imagine that they would be better off without useless, corrupt, tax-taking, distant, central government bureaucracy. That is precisely how the rulers in Beijing are popularly characterized in China. They know it and they fear the consequences: a breakup of China.

The new international economy based on technologies that can instantaneously penetrate borders welcomes an international culture that subverts Confucianism-Leninism throughout China. Pocket-size shortwave radios pick up BBC and the Voice of America Chinese-language broadcasts, and television satellite dishes are turned toward Taiwan and Hong Kong. The Mao-era national center founded on a monopoly of information and economic autarky is dead, although China's rulers still engage in a fruitless struggle to keep out so-called cultural pollutants from abroad.[1]

Because China's leaders are worried that the country could split apart, they have mounted a propaganda campaign against it. Almost no day goes by without lead stories in the media calling attention to the chaos, killings, and decline that accompany ethnic and nationalist strife around the globe, from the former Yugoslavia and Soviet Union to Northern Ireland, Germany, Czechoslovakia, India, and Africa.

Regional communal identities in China have grown so strong so rapidly that most Chinese are genuinely worried that the toppling of the Leninist dictatorship in Beijing would lead to the disintegration of China, a disintegration in which they would suffer all the privations, pains, and terrors associated with hate-filled civil strife. Anxiety, not affection, holds China together at the end of the twentieth century. The Chinese do not want to end up like the Lebanese or Somalis or Yugoslavs. But can fear long serve as a national glue?

1. Edward Friedman, "A Failed Chinese Modernity," *Daedalus,* vol. 122, no. 2 (Spring 1993).

The Two Chinas?

The central government in Beijing contends that China's post-Mao economic success, understood as an integral part of East Asia's phenomenal growth, is a consequence of the spread of north China's ancient and eternally valid Confucian values throughout East Asia. As the home of these virtues of hierarchal authority, thrift, education, family, hard work, respect for seniors, and submersion of self for the larger good, China, its rulers believe, will surpass the other East Asian countries and become the largest economy in the world by the early twenty-first century. In this vision of the future, the Chinese people will take great pride in a respected, militarily powerful, and politically active nation that will keep Asia free from Japanese or extra-regional domination. China will be the new global center. Such is the nationalism promoted by rulers in Beijing.

This authoritarian, militarist, Confucian nationalist project of the north is challenged by a vision emanating from the dynamic metropolises of south China. The south's alternative to the north's military authoritarianism imagines an open, confident Greater China. (The World Bank has recognized the reality of this project by adding a new statistical category for its collection of economic data, the Chinese Economic Area.) The media inform Chinese that the total investment capital available in mainland China, Taiwan, Hong Kong, Macao, and Chinese communities in Southeast Asia is greater than the foreign exchange reserves available to the Japanese. The south's Greater China, a China that crosses borders, is successfully and fearlessly open to the world. It is a China that celebrates a multiplicity of religious sects and world views, one not constrained by the anachronisms of northern Confucianism, with its denigration of the young, the female, and the commercial—and one not manipulated and glorified by self-serving, parasitic northern bureaucrats. The southern project is not afraid of multiple communities of identity.

Central to the south's vision of a new Chinese national identity is the conviction that the Leninist regime, rather than being admirably responsible for successful post-Mao economic growth, is increasingly an obstacle to China's continuing development. The rural economy was freed not by a decree from Beijing that wisely decollectivized agricultural—as the foreign press has portrayed it—but by local people taking advantage of a small opening and a weakened state apparatus resulting from traumatic Mao-era campaigns. Together these allowed Chinese far from the reach of the center to get around the system. Innovative and entrepreneurial Chinese did so well, despite the rulers in Beijing, that the old fashioned time-servers in the capital finally had to legalize much of what had succeeded so brilliantly in diverse localities.

Reform, however, still has far to go. The old system lingers, a potentially malignant cancer. The frightened old men who rule from Beijing have not legalized private property, and the corrupt Leninist apparatus enjoys the fruits of not permitting peasant households to rent, buy, or sell land. Instead, when a family member dies, moves out, marries in, is born, or finds work elsewhere, permission must be sought from the all-powerful, arbitrary, local village party boss for changes in land allocation, as well as in the imposed state quotas for farm products to be delivered to the state at ridiculously low prices. Consequently, villagers hate the exploitative power-holders. Their belief that an oppressive system remains in place and that a new world is not in the offing is the view of most Chinese. This perspective delegitimating the claims of Beijing is captured in the poetry of Bei Dao:

> The Ice Age is over now.
> Why is there still ice everywhere?

Peeking into the Abyss

Though the government in Beijing and its reactionary authoritarian project are ever more illegitimate, and a southern-based, open image of a Greater China ever more legitimate, no one in China calls for the country's breakup. If the nation disintegrates, it will be because the southern project fails to encompass the communalisms of language, region, religion, and ethnicity that are exploding everywhere.

In fact, one attractive feature of the more open southern world view is that it seems capable of attracting yet more Chinese so that China is not limited to *Zhongguo,* a Chinese state on the mainland, but is open to *Zhonghua,* all who identify with a Chinese nation, including overseas Chinese. If the south's project is a supra-nationalism that is appealing because it is, in part, a super nationalism, why then raise the question of a breakup of China?

Part of the answer lies in the global technological forces undermining the center's control. In addition, in reforming Leninist systems, or in post-Leninist regions, centrifugal tendencies rooted in past and present history are also tremendously reinforced by the economics that accompany reform of the system. Enterprises and regions are thereby empowered, and the economically irrational statist command economy is undermined. Each region then tries to collect its own taxes for local investment and competes against every other region. Unless a new nationalism can reintegrate all China's diverse communities, then disintegration threatens.

Communalist identities and conflicts are heightened by the experience of the Leninist system's inhumanity. In China as elsewhere, communities tied to the capital benefited by keeping down other communities. Local community members therefore view themselves as having martyrs and as having survived because they helped each other out in the face of the alien Leninist system, seen as a foreign, Russian, or Western imposition. The rulers are "them"; the local community is "us." These numerous local communities could become proto-nationalisms as people seek revenge against rulers or release from domination.

China is also experiencing an explosion of communalist identities down to temple sects, secret societies, and lineage associations. Violence and the potential for violence among such groups seem pervasive. An unintended consequence of perverse Leninist irrationalities is that all groups believe themselves to be victims, and find all the rest to be unfairly privileged. Even Tibetans will not be seen as sufferers. Instead, they and other victims of the regime will be imagined as wastrels who have been given subsidies that keep the rest needlessly poor.[2] The irritation among localities has led to the widespread fear that hate-filled, bloody chaos could engulf the country. It is this fear that Beijing relies on for China's continued stability.

The conservative ideologues who rule China are very conscious of and concerned about these disintegrative forces. They are well aware that the idea that China is one homogenous people with a shared culture is nonsense. In fact, what they see everywhere are the differences. Communities mourn differently. They prefer different teas. Cuisines are regional. Most important, it is not even obvious now that Chinese share a culture since they view each other as speaking different languages. Northerners who travel to the south increasingly are confronted by Cantonese who speak Cantonese and Shanghaiese who speak Shanghaiese. Outside the Beijing region, the Mandarin language (the administrative language of the old

2. Edward Friedman, "Ethnic Identity and the De-nationalization and Democratization of Leninist States," in M. Crawford Young, ed., *The Rising Tide of Cultural Pluralism: The Nation State at Bay?* (Madison: University of Wisconsin Press, 1993), pp. 222–241.

empire) is treated like an alien tongue. Northerners complain that they feel as if they are in a foreign country when in southern communities.

Reactionaries contend that only by stepping up Confucian socialization and increasing propaganda for Marxist-Leninist socialism can China overcome its ever more powerful diversities and remain unified. These hardliners clearly do not believe that fear of chaos will prove to be the glue that holds China together. But can they woo outraged communities to ancient verities and a discredited ideology?

The Seductive South

The conventional wisdom has it that the conservative north will win out against the dynamic south because the southern coastal regions have zoomed ahead so fast that the rest of China, resenting the south's wealth, will join together against the region. In this view, most Chinese will respond to the Confucian language of reciprocity and the socialist appeal of economic equality, and therefore unite with the dictatorship in Beijing as it taxes the south, redistributes the region's wealth, and keeps military power out of the southern hands. The south would become a milch cow for a united nation, not a harbinger of a new nation or nationalism.

But there is much evidence that most of China identifies more with the south's project than with the north's. In the hinterlands, museums have been redone that reimagine these regions to be in conflict with Beijing's idea of Chineseness; local people are not part of a Chinese nation working to resist the penetration of foreign ideas, as the ideologically purist, Confucianist-Leninist north would have it. They instead see the local community, and all of China, developing because of open international exchange from the ancient Silk Road to the glorious civilizations of the Mediterranean, the Nile, the Tigris and the Euphrates, and because of a welcoming of Buddhist religion and sculpture. (The south coastal city of Changzhou claims to be the most Chinese city because it has had the longest continuous history of trading overseas.)

In addition, people living in the hinterlands are all too aware that they suffer when they are forced to accept Beijing's state-imposed low prices for their raw materials instead of the south's significantly higher world market-oriented prices. One should not underestimate the large extent to which those in the hinterlands also identify their future and all of China's with the southern project.

In reality, the economically dynamic south has become the source from which China is increasingly re-integrated as an entity. Thirty percent of Hong Kong's currency already circulates inside China. The Cantonese language and southern styles, songs, and customs are spreading north, as is southern investment. Workers come for jobs in the south, send money home from the south, and eventually return with a southern nest egg and a southern tongue. The rise of the south is experienced as benefiting all local communities. It, in contrast to the north, is imagined as friendly to the new communalism.

Before the Cultural Revolution ravaged its economy, Shanghai was seen by Chinese as the best place in the country in which to live. In the late Mao era, with everything decided by narrow political interests, Beijing was viewed as the place that had the greatest opportunities for a good life. But now, in the post-Mao reform era, Chinese pollsters find that people want to live in their own community, with that community enriched by cultural and economic ties to China's future: the Greater China of the southern project. The old center, it would seem, cannot hold.

A Revised History

China's rulers and many foreign analysts contend that the Leninist state is still embraced as the beloved savior of the motherland from Japanese invaders during World War II. The People's Republic is Chinese patriotism incarnate. Profound experiences such as China's war of resistance are seen as having established a difficult-to-change nationalist identity that benefits the government in Beijing, the heir of the liberation struggle. This deep nationalism is said to make for continuity and stability in China in contrast to Eastern Europe, where Leninism was supposedly merely imposed by the Red Army, and thus lacked a nationalist bond to hold the loyalty of the people.

But this concept of Chinese exceptionalism ignores the powerful forces that delegitimate even a nationalistic Leninist system, as in Albania, Mozambique, or Russia itself. The failures of Leninism foster an experience of lost time. A growing number of Chinese see the Mao era as one where time stood still, continuous with the outmoded empire period. The People's Republic was not, and is not, believed to have succeeded as a modern nation. MIT political scientist Lucian Pye has been virtually isolated in his insistence that:

China is really a civilization pretending to be a nation-state. . . . China today is what Europe would have been if the unity of the Roman Empire had lasted until now and there had not been the separate emergence of the separate entities of England, France, Germany and the like.[3]

Pye's view is similar to the long-mocked, but ultimately accurate voices in the field of what used to be Soviet studies, who found the Soviet Union to be the Russian empire refurbished—in other words, a prison house of nations, a political entity that could not hold up against the strong and unyielding urge for independence by diverse communities. Is Pye not right then that China—like Russia, Ethiopia, and Yugoslavia—is an empire that cannot survive growing regionalist communal identities?

Manifest evidence of this coming Chinese identity transformation can be found in the vicissitudes of anti-Japanese nationalism. By the 1990s, Chinese in the northeast saw their rewoven ties to the Japanese economy as a happy return to pre-Leninist growth that had been unfortunately interrupted by economic stagnation and the cultural disruption of Beijing's Leninism. The ruling groups in post-Mao China claim credit for having won beneficial economic ties with Japan, including large aid packages and generous loan terms. Those outside these groups see instead a government selling out to Japan for its own narrow, selfish interests, such as the corrupt deals that enrich the children of the elite but do not benefit Chinese people.

Indeed, Chinese increasingly imagine themselves as a long suffering people who have been continuously betrayed by leaders who did not insist on a large indemnity for Chinese victims of the Japanese massacre in Nanjing or for Japan's Nazi-like medical experiments on Chinese in the northeast, or for the millions of other Chinese victims of Japanese rape, pillage, and slaughter. The anti-Japan slogans that have accompanied virtually every democratic movement in post-Mao China should be understood as anti-regime manifestations, a way of expressing the sentiment that today's rulers of the Chinese state are in fact traitors to the Chinese nation. Zhongguo is suspect today; Zhonghua is the real and future China. A new notion of nationalism, or nationalisms, has already largely replaced the bond that once held Mao-era China together. The old anti-Japanese nationalism has been re-imagined so as to discredit the regime in Beijing.

3. Lucian Pye, "How China's Nationalism Was Shanghaied," *Australian Journal of Chinese Affairs,* January 1993, p. 130.

This delegitimation of anti-Japanese Leninist Confucianism appears in another form when people note that the Soviet troops that invaded northeast China in 1945 at the end of World War II also raped and pillaged. China's Communist dictators covered up their crimes, ignored the suffering of the Chinese people, and allied with the enemies of the Chinese people, again for the benefit only of the party's elite. The new thinking holds that Beijing welcomed Russian rapists and forgave Japanese rapists. Such a regime must be illegitimate; it cannot represent the best interests of the Chinese nation.

This reevaluation, which no longer credits China's rulers for saving the nation in an anti-Japanese war of liberation from imperialism, has gone so far that Japanese scholars can now ask even of Wang Jingwei, previously conceived as China's Pétain and considered the ultimate traitor for having gone over to the Japanese during the war, what alternative did he have? Moreover, the victory of Mao's side is no longer understood as a deep expression of Chinese nationalism. Leninist rule instead seems a mere contingent event, made possible only by external forces such as America's defeat of Japan. Mao thus was lucky; Wang was not wrong.

In another similar and fundamental transvaluation of nationalistic identity, it once was obvious that China's Communists were the carriers of the patriotism of the Ming dynasty, which had overthrown a foreign Mongol imperialism, only to be defeated by the tragic, foreign Manchu conquest. The modern drive to free the Chinese from Manchu rule was often sloganized as restoring the Ming. Patriotism was the Ming, treason the Qing.

Yet by the 1990s Chinese scholars were defending Ming collaborators with the Qing dynasty Manchus.[4] It turns out that the Ming rulers, predecessors and surrogates for the Communist dictatorship, were disasters for the Chinese people. In such a situation, patriots can and must reach out to ally with any groups, even beyond China, to save the Chinese people from parasites parading as patriots.

The Chinese writer Xiao Qian likens the nation to an organism that is murderously sick, its body full of deadly poisons and suffering from constipation. Only diarrhea can get the poisons out; even though this would leave the body weak, it is a price worth paying to escape the continuing tragedy of entrapment in one's own poisons. In short, the militarized, anti-imperialist appeal to a nationalism based on sacrificing everything

4. Wang Hongzhi, *Hong Chenchou zhuan* [*Biography of Hong Chenchou*] (Beijing: Red Flag Publishing House, 1991).

for military power—as with the Opium War, the Boxer Rebellion, and the anti-Japanese war—is rejected.[5]

In like manner, Zhou Bo, in the February 19 edition of the Shanghai newspaper *Wen Hui Bao,* rejects maintaining Mao's militarized anti-imperialism to ward off evils such as those the British brought in during the Opium War. Instead, rulers who isolated China are blamed for making China vulnerable and backward. Only "open dynasties such as the Tang and the Yuan" brought real "national strength and dignity." Pride in a Chinese Ming defeat of foreign Mongols of the Yuan is an error. Parochial arrogance makes for an empty patriotism that kept Chinese impoverished.

Instead of stubbornly clinging to Mao's world view, one should note that Chinese who risked their lives to flee to Hong Kong from coastal Guangdong province in the Mao era, now in an era of maximum openness in south coastal Guangdong, are trying to return home. It was the Guangdong patriot Sun Yatsen who, in the nineteenth century, likewise understood how to revive the nation. The choice for patriots, then, is isolation versus openness, the nativism of the Ming, the Qing, and Mao, or the openness of the Mongols, the Yuan, and Sun Yatsen. A Chinese patriotism that promotes the Mongol Yuan dynasty and has nothing good to say for the fighters of the Opium War expresses an extraordinary transvaluation of values. It regards the proud Confucianist-Leninist authoritarianism of the late twentieth century north as heir and purveyor of empty slogans and real poisons that have kept China poor for centuries and still block a full, albeit painful, opening to what can make all Chinese prosperous—and again make China a great civilization.

To the extent that the notion of a Greater China as an alliance of *Zhonghua*—a coming together of Chinese who escaped the shackles of Leninism by going to Hong Kong, Taiwan, Macao, or Southeast Asia—allows successful economic competition with Japan, the southern project seems most attractive to patriotic Chinese who are still working out their identity in opposition to a successful Japan, but who no longer see China's Leninist dictators as real or successful opponents of the Japanese threat. The increasingly legitimate counter to Japan is the economic power of a southern-based Greater China.

Yet however much southern consciousness spreads, it need not win out. If the lessons of other post-Leninist states have significance for China, they

5. Yi Yueh, "On Diarrhea, Constipation, and Reform—Xiao Qian's Three Political Allegories," *Dangdai* [*Contemporary*], no. 23 (February 15, 1993).

suggest that it will not be easy to knit together a new, democratic confederation of peoples identified with diverse communalist concepts of language, region, and culture legitimated in the wake of Leninist decline. If those lessons from elsewhere hold, Leninism has so poisoned communalist identities that demagogues who can find a popular response to appeals to hates of other communities will likely emerge. That was already the reality of the late nineteenth century Qing dynasty and the early twentieth century republic when the center could not hold and warlords, gangs, and regional satraps violently ruled and ravaged China. It is a frightening alternative to the discredited regime in Beijing. But it may well be what is simmering just below the surface in the boiling caldron of angry communalist identities:

> During the Qing, inter-ethnic conflicts . . . became common between Han and Muslims, Hakka (a minority group of south-east China) and Hoklo (Hokkien-speaking Chinese), and Hakka and Punti (native Cantonese). Ethnic feuds strove to "clear the boundaries" by ejecting exogenous groups from their respective territories. Such ethnic clashes could be extremely violent: a major conflict between the Hakka and Punti in 1856–67 took a toll of 100,000 victims.[6]

Other outcomes, of course, are possible. The southern project could integrate a more open polity. Still, tough northern chauvinists could win out in vicious combat. It is also possible to imagine a succession crisis temporarily resolved by the choice of a regional leader as head of state who is committed to the southern project but who is not from the south coastal area. This could legitimate regional representation and serve as a step toward eventual democratization. Such a course is imagined in China as a gradual but inevitable process, akin to the one that has supposedly already transpired in Taiwan and South Korea. It is taken as the happily shared project of Greater East Asia.

The future is unknown, open, and uncertain. Whatever it proves to be, it will require grappling with the forces that could precipitate the breakup of China.

6. Frank Dikotter, *The Discourse on Race in Modern China* (Stanford: Stanford University Press, 1992), p. 70.

8. The Dangers of Economic Complacency

September 1996

BARRY NAUGHTON

In the past several years the Chinese economy has undergone dramatic growth and structural change. In 1995, for the fourth consecutive year, real gross domestic product grew more than 10 percent, and growth will remain near that mark this year as well. Sometime in 1997, China will reach an important statistical milestone when the proportion of the total labor force engaged in agriculture will slip below 50 percent for the first time, symbolizing the end of China's long history as a predominantly agrarian country. Foreign investment has continued to pour into China; after receiving $28 billion in 1993 and $34 billion in 1994, almost $38 billion in actual foreign investment was recorded in 1995. By most broad indicators, the Chinese economy is doing very well indeed.

Since early 1994, however, Chinese economic policymaking has been stuck in a relatively undistinguished and noninnovative mode. A number of broad policy initiatives have been placed on the agenda, but few decisive actions have been taken, and several general policies have been carried forward from year to year without concrete implementation. The most immediate explanation for the limited policymaking initiative has been the priority the government has given to fighting inflation. Indeed, one of the most important policy successes of the recent period has been the taming of inflation and the achievement of a macroeconomic "soft landing," or gradually controlling inflation without stifling economic growth.

But broader political and economic factors are also at work. Policymaking has seemed less urgent to Chinese leaders because the pace of grassroots economic change has been remarkably rapid; economic growth has been extremely robust; and the Chinese economy has not encountered any especially challenging problems or crises. Under these circumstances, and faced with substantial uncertainty about the effects of their own actions and the direction of the economy, policymakers have found it difficult to mobilize the political will to tackle difficult questions, and have chosen to take a relatively cautious approach to the economy. It may also be the case that the uncertainties of the political transition to the post-Deng Xiaoping era are beginning to inhibit serious attempts to grapple with long-term economic issues. Despite obvious signs of success, then, the current period may turn out to be one in which leaders missed substantial opportunities to consolidate economic reforms and create a much better set of economic institutions.

Certainly nothing in the past two years has matched the flurry of dramatic reform policymaking that marked 1993 and the beginning of 1994. During that fertile period, China passed a series of economic reform milestones. In rapid succession it abolished most of the remnants of central planning and relaxed the bulk of price controls. It gave foreign investors significant access to the Chinese domestic market. At the third plenum of the fourteenth Communist Party congress in November 1993, a program to broadly move to a market economy was officially adopted. Immediately following this meeting, several important reform measures were adopted to regularize China's economic procedures and build substantially more effective institutions. The two most important reforms were the adoption of a new tax and fiscal system and the devaluation and unification of exchange rates. Both of these measures were put into place on January 1, 1994, and each represented a shift from past patterns of Chinese reform policymaking. Previous reforms had usually achieved success only to the extent that they relied on decentralizing authority and resources and liberalizing regulations, and did not require the exercise of substantial new capabilities by the central government. By contrast, the new measures require a more professional and predictable bureaucracy and a modest recentralization of authority in order to achieve ultimate success.

The Downside to Rapid Growth

Since early 1994, we have witnessed the Chinese economy adapting to the reforms implemented between 1992 and 1994, or perhaps more accurately, adapting to the economic dynamism unleashed by those reforms. The torrid growth touched off since 1992 has been extremely positive overall. But certain aspects of that rapid growth have had negative effects. Growth in 1992 and 1993—at 14.1 percent and 13.1 percent, respectively—was unsustainably rapid, and some of this rapid growth represented recovery from the trough of the post-Tiananmen recession. More important, growth in those years was fed by a lax credit policy that contributed to rapid money growth and a severe bout of inflation. As a result, fighting inflation has tended to take priority over other government objectives, and this has tended to produce a cautious attitude toward reform policies. Indeed, the battle against inflation has been a consistent theme in policymaking since June 1993.

At that time, economics czar Zhu Rongji proclaimed an austerity program and announced new restrictions on bank lending amounts and procedures. Some version of this austerity program has been in place ever since. Despite this sustained effort, success in the inflation battle was elusive until recently. Inflation accelerated from 16 percent in 1993 to 25 percent in 1994 (as measured by the urban consumer price index), before moderating to 17 percent in 1995, and only 9.8 percent during the first quarter of 1996. By mid-1996, the regime was on track to achieve its objective of keeping inflation in the single digits. Moreover, the objective of a soft landing had been substantially achieved.

It is worth emphasizing how unusual this successful regulation of inflation is for China. Since the beginning of the reform era in 1978, macroeconomic policy has tended to swing from one extreme to another. Rapid growth phases have led to inflation, causing policymakers to step on the brakes of monetary and credit policy. Overheating was followed by overcooling—sharp and sometimes excessive growth slowdowns. Consistent, steady macroeconomic restraint was the scarcest of all policy outcomes. By contrast, the current cycle has been marked by a prolonged period of moderate austerity that has gradually achieved its objective. That by itself is a significant achievement.

Yet one might wonder why, if austerity has been in place since mid-1993, inflation actually accelerated in 1994, and why it has taken nearly three full years to bring inflation down below the regime's target figure of 10 percent? To answer the latter question, we need to go back to the important reform accomplishments of 1993 and early 1994. Those reforms set off a chain of events that, despite their achievements, gave the regime a scare during 1994 when inflation accelerated. In this respect, the most important reform measures were those in the foreign trade and investment system.

An Embarrassment of Riches

China established a new unified exchange rate at the beginning of 1994, pegged initially at 8.8 renminbi to the dollar. At the time, few Chinese policymakers thought that the new unified exchange rate had any particular long-range significance. China had already devalued the official exchange rate by almost two-thirds between 1980 and the late 1980s, but without establishing an equilibrium value for foreign exchange. At each new exchange rate, demand for foreign exchange exceeded available supplies, yet the government continued to restrict access to American dollars and Japanese yen, even for legitimate export businesses. To get around this awkward bureaucratic system, a secondary market had been allowed to develop in which exporters and importers could swap foreign exchange, with the renminbi trading at a substantial discount from its official rate. Surprisingly, when the official rate was devalued and the exchange rate unified on January 1, 1994, the new rate turned out to be stable and defensible. Access to foreign exchange was substantially liberalized so that by 1996, any foreign trade corporation could purchase dollars upon presenting invoices and shipping documents to a local foreign exchange bank. China has been able to approach current account currency convertibility.

This unanticipated success can be attributed to three factors. First, foreign investment continued to flow into China in large amounts, attracted by newly granted access to the Chinese domestic market. While foreign businesses made most of their investment contribution in the form of machinery or other investment goods, they also contributed money to buy Chinese domestic goods and assets such as land. Thus, the inflow of foreign investment significantly augmented the supply of foreign exchange. Second, foreign-invested export-oriented firms in southern coastal China that had been developing since the mid-1980s continued to increase their exports rapidly but steadily, generating substantial foreign exchange earnings. Third, and most significant, Chinese domestic firms responded vigorously to the new opportunities created by devaluation, and by reforms in the taxation system. These domestic firms (mostly state-owned factories) had borne the burden of the overvalued official exchange rate in previous years, and thus benefited the most from the devaluation of 1994. Moreover, the tax reform adopted at the same time generalized and simplified the refund of value-added taxes paid by exporters. The net result was a huge increase in the incentive to export.

Chinese trade has long been divided into export processing and so-called ordinary foreign trade. Export processing is trade carried out, primarily by foreign-invested firms, under special provisions that allow duty-free imports of commodities used in export production. Such trade has expanded steadily, along with the growing importance of foreign investment in the Chinese economy. However, it was ordinary trade that grew explosively in the wake of the 1994 reforms. Ordinary exports increased 42.5 percent and, responding to the higher price for foreign exchange, imports actually shrank by 7 percent. Quality upgrading had apparently succeeded.

The result was that after 15 years of being in shortage, foreign exchange was suddenly in abundant supply at the prevailing official exchange rate. Exports and incoming foreign investment provided supplies of foreign exchange, while demand for foreign exchange to buy imports remained weak. The abundant supply of American dollars tended to reduce the dollar's price in renminbi; and conversely, the dollar value of the renminbi tended to increase. The renminbi has in fact appreciated slightly since early 1994, and in order to forestall further appreciation the government has bought dollars with renminbi. The result has been a rapid expansion of the government's foreign exchange reserves, which soared from $21 billion to $51.6 billion during 1994, and to $73.6 billion by the end of 1995. The increase in net foreign assets was the main cause of the expansion of the domestic money supply during both years. The flood of newly printed renminbi of course fueled inflation, notwithstanding relative restraint in the growth of central bank credit. This was a kind of embarrassment of riches; the unanticipated success in foreign trade led to a prolongation of inflationary problems in the domestic economy.

The inflationary pressures created by rapid money supply growth were not reflected uniformly throughout the economy. While prices of manufactured goods were stabilized at a relatively early stage, a continuing surge in farm prices kept inflation high. In 1994 and 1995, grain prices were the fastest growing component of consumer prices. This was true even though the grain harvest was mediocre in 1994, but excellent in 1995. Only at the end of 1995 did grain prices really begin to stabilize.

The jump in grain prices appears to reflect an adjustment to the long-term relative scarcity of food in the Chinese economy. Farm prices have been depressed for several years, but as urban incomes have begun to increase, market conditions have finally reached the point where steadily growing demand has led to a surge in prices. Chinese grain prices are now close to world prices, probably reflecting a future in which China will be a significant grain importer and in which Chinese demand for grain, on the margin, will be met from world grain markets. In the short run, the recovery of farm prices is beneficial to Chinese income distribution. For many years, urban income growth has exceeded rural income growth, increasing an already large urban-rural gap. In 1995, by contrast, rural incomes grew 5.6 percent in real terms, slightly more rapidly than urban incomes, which grew 4.9 percent. While this does not begin to close the urban-rural gap, it nevertheless prevents further deterioration.

Tax Reform Disappointment

As the effects of these events rippled through the economy during 1994, policy tended to become reactive and concentrated on the anti-inflation effort. There were also political factors at work. Many in China expected that The People's Republic would enter the World Trade Organization (WTO) as a founding member on January 1, 1995. China's failure to do so triggered something of a conservative backlash against radical reform measures in early 1995. A number of articles appeared in the press arguing for the need to maintain a large state sector and for the importance of management reform as opposed to ownership conversion. This counter-current did nothing to reverse the direction of economic reform, but it may have weakened the resolve of policymakers to solve outstanding problems.

On another front, bold government actions were also hampered by the limited success of the 1994 tax reform. The tax reform has been unable to substantially reverse the erosion of government fiscal resources that has been a persistent characteristic of the entire Chinese reform process. From a prereform level of 35 percent of GDP, state budgetary revenues had declined to only 12.8 percent of GDP by 1993. Tax reform was supposed to stabilize and even increase this ratio, but instead revenue has continued its decline to 10.7 percent of GDP in 1995, with the 1996 budget now projecting a further decline to 9.8 percent of GDP.

The tax reform, however, was not designed solely to raise new revenues. Additional goals were to broaden the tax base, lower peak taxation rates, and create a uniform and fair taxation system. Taxation was to shift to a primary reliance on the value-added tax (VAT), creating a tax structure like those in most Western European countries. In addition, Beijing greatly strengthened its tax collection authority, creating a system in which the central government was the primary tax collector and redistributing revenues among local governments. However, in the initial three years of the reform—through the end of 1996—the central government also guaranteed that no local government would suffer a reduction in expenditures due to the provisions of the tax reform.

The efficacy of the tax reform has been substantially hindered by the ease with which existing firms and local governments have obtained so-called temporary tax exemptions. The tax rate is highest on manufacturing firms, where the VAT rate is 17 percent, although a large number of these firms are able to escape some or all of the tax. Exporters received a full VAT rebate until mid-1995. Many small-scale private firms manage to avoid taxation and many state-owned enterprises have obtained exemptions or delays on full taxation under the claim of short-term financial hardship. Finally, relatively slow progress in setting up a separate central government tax authority—one truly independent from the existing tax bureaus organized under provincial government auspices—has meant that the central government does not yet have full authority to override local interests and achieve compliance. For all these reasons, the tax reform has been disappointing in achieving a substantial revenue increase.

Government steps to deal with this dilemma have been partial and incremental. Most visible have been the steps to tighten tax collection within the foreign-oriented sector. Following on the heels of the dramatic export success, the government has lowered the VAT rebate rate for exporters from the full 17 percent to only 9 percent by the end of 1996. On the import side, the government has tightened import procedures, canceled the tax exemption for foreign-funded investment goods, and moved to limit other exemptions of import duties. These measures will increase the tax take from the rapidly growing foreign trade sector, but at a price; export growth has already begun to fall off, and the long-term impact on China's export performance is difficult to predict. At this time, the government's fiscal and tax reform can be considered a partial success at best.

State Enterprises in Transition

State enterprise reform remains a central and unfinished part of the Chinese reform process. In recent years change has been driven more by external events than by formal reform edicts. Competition from rural township and village enterprises—and more recently from private and foreign-invested firms—has continuously increased, exposing state-owned enterprises to new challenges and eroding their former protected position. By 1995, traditional state-owned industry accounted for only 31 percent of the value of industrial output, and these industries are concentrated in utilities, energy, and manufacturing sectors with substantial economies of scale. A conversion of Chinese industry has occurred, primarily through the entry of new producers and the play of market competition.

Government policymakers have repeatedly tried to develop comprehensive programs for the reform of state-owned industry. The November 1993 party congress continued to rule out large-scale privatization on ideological grounds, but endorsed the adoption of a so-called modern enterprise system, initially on a trial basis. The modern enterprise system essentially corresponds to what would be called in most other countries the commercialization or the corporatization of state ownership. The assets of the corporation are inventoried and revalued and the balance sheet cleaned up. Ownership shares of the corporation are then defined, with the government typically holding most or even all the outstanding shares. A board of directors is established, with seats apportioned to major shareholders. The board of directors then exercises control over the enterprise, including the appointment of managers, and the traditional bureaucratic relations of subordination are supposedly severed. The enterprise is to be freed to pursue economic aims, with government interference restricted to broad policies that apply to all enterprises.

The progress of this experiment has been painfully slow. It was decided in late 1993 that 100 enterprises would be selected for conversion. But by early 1996, only 43 of these firms were actually operating under the reform's provisions (though another batch had recently been approved for conversion). In addition to the modern enterprise system, there are now several thousand "share-holding enterprises" or joint-stock companies, most of them converted state-owned enterprises. The state industries converted to share-holding enterprises typically distribute up to 20 percent of their shares to their own workers, maintain controlling interest in the hands of government agencies, and sometimes sell a block of shares to outside investors. Most share-holding enterprises have, however, been converted by local governments, sometimes without paying much attention to the procedures involved in assessing asset values, allocating ownership stakes, and providing audits and financial disclosure. After a wave of conversions between 1993 and 1994, such joint-stock companies accounted for about 4 percent of industrial output in 1994 and 1995. To get an accurate picture of the size of the remaining state sector, this figure should probably be added to the 31 percent of industrial output produced by traditional state-owned enterprises in 1995, yielding a 35 percent share for the traditional and semi-reformed state sector in that year.

While central government initiatives have been modest, some local governments have moved ahead aggressively. The experience of the small city of Zhucheng in Shandong province has recently attracted attention. City officials transformed all 274 of the town's formerly state-owned industrial and commercial enterprises. By the end of the process, Zhucheng no longer had a state sector, and town officials were instead relying on ordinary taxation revenues from a flourishing economy. The experience of Zhucheng demonstrates that in China, although mass privatization is taboo, substantial conversion of state assets into different ownership forms is in fact taking place.

In the absence of rapid progress in state-owned enterprise reform, the evolution of the sector has been determined primarily by competition and government credit policy. As noted earlier, government credit policy has been consistently restrained over the past couple of years. This has meant that state-owned enterprises do not have access to unlimited bailouts from state banks. While some state industries undoubtedly enjoy preferential access to bank credit, the Chinese government has been unwilling—or perhaps unable—to shelter the entire state sector through a large stream of subsidies. Tight credit and intensified competition have caused extensive difficulties in the state sector and pushed many firms toward painful restructuring. While the number of formal declared bankruptcies has remained small, the number of actual bankruptcies is significant. This can be easily discerned with a look at the numbers on employment.

Despite the extraordinarily rapid growth of the economy, the official urban unemployment rate has steadily increased, from 2.3 percent at the end of 1992 to 2.9 percent at the end of 1995. Moreover, the 5.2 million officially unemployed are only part of the problem. Struggling state firms have also sent home a large number of workers for whom they cannot find regular work. Those workers receive a minimum wage—a kind of enterprise-paid unemployment compensation—that is substantially below the prevailing wage for active workers, but are not required to report to work. Recently, the State Statistical Bureau provided the first official estimate of the number of workers in this category nationwide: 7.25 million as of the end of March 1996. Simply combining this number with the 5.2 million officially unemployed yields an urban unemployment rate of 5.5 percent.

Of course, this does not include the underemployed workers reporting for work in state firms, nor does it include any of the rural under- or unemployed, nor their relatives who have migrated to cities in search of better work. It simply indicates that large numbers of workers are being shed by state enterprises as they struggle to cope with difficult economic conditions.

Recipe for Success?

The Chinese economy in 1996 is the outcome of the interplay of vigorous market forces and rather tepid government policymaking. The progress of tax reform and state enterprise reform indicates that institution-building reforms have proceeded at a modest and in some ways disappointing pace. A similar observation would emerge from a discussion of financial sector reforms—some progress has been made. Government policy banks have been set up to relieve existing state-owned banks of the responsibility to undertake government-directed loans, thus giving them the ability to compete on a commercial basis. Some small competition in that sector has been permitted with new start-up banks and strictly limited foreign participation. But state-owned banks continue to suffer under an immense load of poorly performing loans to existing state-owned enterprises and have not been able to shed completely the need to respond to government requests. Weakness in the banking system is clearly evident, and there may be further financial difficulties down the road.

At the same time, the sheer dynamism of the economy continues to drive institutional development in the right direction, if not at the optimal pace. Precisely because the government does not have abundant financial resources, it cannot afford to waste them in propping up the weakest state-run enterprises. Competition and the opening of the economy are rapidly transforming the most important sectors but institution building lags behind. Leaders may perhaps be forgiven for not seeing the urgency of the institution-building process when the economy is booming. But there is a serious danger of complacency, for some leaders believe that they can shape the future development of the Chinese economy through better management and with the help of a carefully chosen "industrial policy." In fact, the Chinese economy awaits a further round of reform and restructuring in order to begin the transition to a more effective economic system that can productively participate in international cooperation and competition.

9. Rumblings from the Uyghur

September 1997

DRU C. GLADNEY

Three years ago the first rumblings of discontent in northwestern China could be heard in the voices of ethnic and religious separatists in the bazaars of Kashgar and Turfan. Today bombs detonating throughout the region as well as in Beijing have begun to drown out these voices.

On February 25, a bombing in the northwestern border city of Urumqi, the capital of the Xinjiang Uyghur Autonomous Region, left nine people dead. Bombs exploded on two Beijing buses on March 7, killing two people; on May 13 another bomb exploded in a city park in Beijing, killing one person. These bombings, like the more than 30 that occurred last year, are believed to be related to demands by Muslim and Tibetan separatists.

On July 27 the government executed nine members of the Uyghur Muslim minority. The executions followed those of eight Uyghur on May 29 and three other Uyghur in April; all were executed for allegedly carrying out bombings in northwest China. The government has also arrested hundreds of people on suspicion of participating in ethnic riots and separatist activities. At a time when China is still celebrating its recovery of Hong Kong on July 1, many wonder if it can hold on to the rebellious parts of its restive west.

While most analysts agree that China is not vulnerable to the ethnic separatism that split the former Soviet Union, few doubt that should China fall apart, it would divide, like the Soviet Union, along centuries' old ethnic, linguistic, regional, and cultural fault lines. These divisions showed themselves after the collapse of China's last empire in 1911, when its territory was split for more than 20 years by regional warlords with bases in the north and south, and by Muslim warlords in the west.

But China is not about to fall apart—not yet, anyway. The initial rumblings of discontent centered on a desire to see the benefits of the northwestern region's oil and mineral wealth begin to flow back into the region. This desire suggests that if economic and political concerns are addressed by Beijing—along with historical and strategic issues—China can begin to resolve its ethnic dilemma.

A Contested History

First, China must reconsider its long-term historical relations with the people now known as the Uyghur. An understanding of the history of the Xinjiang region is critical to evaluating separatist claims on it, especially since all Chinese histories (as well as many Western histories of China) assume that the region has always been part of China, with the Uyghur a subject people.

Chinese histories notwithstanding, every Uyghur firmly believes that his or her ancestors were the indigenous people of the Tarim Basin, which did not become known in Chinese as Xinjiang (new dominion) until the eighteenth century. Nevertheless, the current understanding of the indigeneity of the present people classified as Uyghur by the Chinese state is a recent phenomenon, one related to Great Game rivalries, Sino-Soviet geopolitical maneuverings, and Chinese nation-building.

According to the historian Morris Rossabi, it was not until 1760 that the Manchu Qing dynasty exerted full and formal control over northwestern China, establishing it as Xinjiang; this administration lasted barely 100 years, falling to a combination of the Yakub Beg rebellion (1864–1877) and expanding Russian influence. The end of the Qing dynasty in 1911 and the rise of Great Game rivalries between China, Russia, and Britain saw the region torn by competing loyalties and marked by two drastically different attempts at independence: the short-lived proclamation of an East Turkestan Republic in Kashgar in 1933 and of another in the northwestern city of Yining (also called Ghulje) in 1944. As Andrew Forbes has noted in *Warlords and Muslims in Chinese Central Asia,* these rebellions and attempts at self-rule did little to unite the politically, religiously, and regionally divided Turkic people who became known officially as the Uyghur after 1934 under successive Chinese Nationalist warlord administrations.

The Communist government's establishment of the Xinjiang Uyghur Autonomous Region on October 1, 1955, perpetuated the Nationalist policy of recognizing the Uyghur as a minority nationality under Chinese rule. This nationality designation, however, masks tremendous regional and linguistic diversity and includes groups such as the Loplyk and Dolans that had little historical connection with the oasis-based Turkic Muslims that became known as the Uyghur. Still, the claims of contemporary Uyghur separatists are based as much on the brief periods of self-rule under Yakub Beg and the East Turkestan Republics as on the earlier glories of the Uyghur kingdoms in Turfan and Karabalghasan.

Uyghur separatist organizations based in Istanbul, Ankara, Almaty, Munich, Amsterdam, Melbourne, and Washington, D.C., may differ on their political goals and strategies, but they all share a common vision of a unilineal Uyghur claim on the Xinjiang region that was disrupted by Chinese and Soviet intervention. The winning of independence by the former Soviet Central Asian republics in 1991 has encouraged these Uyghur organizations in their hopes for an independent Turkestan, although the new, mainly Muslim Central Asian governments all signed protocols with China in the spring of 1996 that they would neither harbor nor support separatist groups.

Though many portray the Uyghur as united around separatist or Islamist causes, they continue to be divided by religious conflicts (Sufi and non-Sufi factions), territorial loyalties, linguistic discrepancies, commoner-elite alienation, and competing political loyalties. These divided loyalties were evident in an attack in May 1996 on the Imam of the Idgah Mosque in Kashgar by Uyghur, as well as the assassination of at least six Uyghur officials last September. It is also important to note that Islam has been only one of several unifying markers for Uyghur identity, depending on whom they are cooperating with. For example, the Uyghur distinguish themselves from the Hui Muslim Chinese (who share the Uyghur belief in Sunni Islam) by saying they are the legitimate autochthonous minority. To contrast themselves with the nomadic Muslim peoples, such as the Kazak or Kyrgyz, the Uyghur might stress their attachment to the land and oasis of origin. In opposition to the Han Chinese, the Uyghur will generally emphasize their long history in Xinjiang. This suggests that Islamic fundamentalist groups such as the Taliban in Afghanistan will have only limited appeal among the Uyghur. Moreover, this contested understanding of history will continue to influence much of the current debate over separatist and Chinese claims to the region.

The Economic Linchpin

Both Beijing and the Uyghur share concerns about the economic impact of conflict in Xinjiang. Since 1991 China has been a net oil importer. It also has 20 million Muslims. If China mishandles its Muslim problems, it will alienate trading partners in the Middle East, who are primarily Muslim. After an ethnic riot on February 5, 1997, in the northwestern Xinjiang city of Yining that left at least nine Uyghur Muslims dead and several hundred arrested, a Saudi Arabian newspaper, *Al-Bilad,* warned China about the "suffering of Muslims whose human rights are violated." Turkey's defense minister, Turhan Tayan, officially condemned China's handling of the issue; China responded that Turkey should not interfere in China's internal affairs. Muslim nations on China's borders, including Pakistan, Afghanistan, and the Central Asian states, though officially unsupportive of Uyghur separatists, may be increasingly critical of harsh treatment of fellow Muslims in China.

Unrest in Xinjiang could lead to a decline in outside oil investment, which is already operating at a loss. Exxon recently reported that its two wells in southern Xinjiang's supposedly oil-rich Tarim Basin had come up dry; the entire region yielded only 3.15 million metric tons of crude oil last year, far less than China's overall 1996 output of 156 million metric tons. The World Bank, which loans over $3 billion a year to China, has invested more than $780.5 million in 15 different projects in the Xinjiang region alone. Some of this money allegedly goes to the Xinjiang Production and Construction Corps (XPCC), which human rights activist Harry Wu has claimed employs prison labor. Already, United States Senate hearings on World Bank investment in Xinjiang have led Assistant Treasury Secretary David Lipton to declare that the Treasury Department will no longer support World Bank projects associated with the XPCC. Growing social and political upheaval may induce international companies and organizations like the World Bank and Exxon to pull out of the region.

At the same time, China's trade with Central Asia is rapidly expanding with the opening since 1991 of direct rail, air, and road links. Energy economist James Dorian has noted that Xinjiang's trade with Central Asia increased from $463 million in 1992 to $775 million in 1996. The end of 1992 saw cross-border trade increase 30 percent, with Kazakstan benefiting the most; China is now Kazakstan's fifth-largest trading partner (China-Kazakstan trade alone totals more than Turkey's trade with all of Central Asia). Xinjiang's top three trading partners are Kazakstan, Kyrgyzstan, and Hong Kong.

The Political and Strategic Dimensions

It is clear that ethnic separatism and foreign Muslim complaints about Chinese policy will have important consequences for China's economic development of Xinjiang. It is also clear that Beijing's relations with bordering nations and with remote internal regions such as Xinjiang and Tibet have become increasingly important not only for economic reasons, but also because of China's desire to participate in international organizations such as the World Trade Organization and the Asia Pacific Economic Cooperation council.

Although Tibet is no longer of any real strategic or substantial economic value to China, it is politically important to China's current leadership to show that it will not submit to foreign pressure and withdraw its iron hand from Tibet. According to Ahmet Türköz, the vice director of the Eastern Turkestan Foundation (which is dedicated to securing an independent Uyghur homeland), since 1981 the Uyghur have worked closely with Tibetans—including the Dalai Lama—to put pressure on China in international forums. Moreover, the elected leader of The Hague–based Unrepresented Nations and Peoples Organization, a group originally founded on Tibetan issues, is Erkin Alptekin, the son of the late Uyghur nationalist Isa Yusup Alptekin. These international actors cannot force China to change its policies, any more than the annual debate in the United States over the renewal of China's most favored nation status can. Nevertheless, they do influence China's ability to cooperate internationally. As a result, China has sought to respond rapidly, and often militarily, to domestic ethnic affairs that might have international implications.

Finding Solutions

Continuing the legacy of Deng Xiaoping's many crackdowns on separatist movements in the borderlands (he led the 1959 invading army in Tibet) no longer makes sense in a country trying to open itself to world markets and global expectations. Post-Deng China must go beyond its former two-pronged border-area policy of political repression coupled with economic reinvestment. Not only has erecting a "steel Great Wall"—to use regional party secretary Wang Lequan's term—failed to keep separatists out of Xinjiang, but it can no longer hide China's problems from the world.

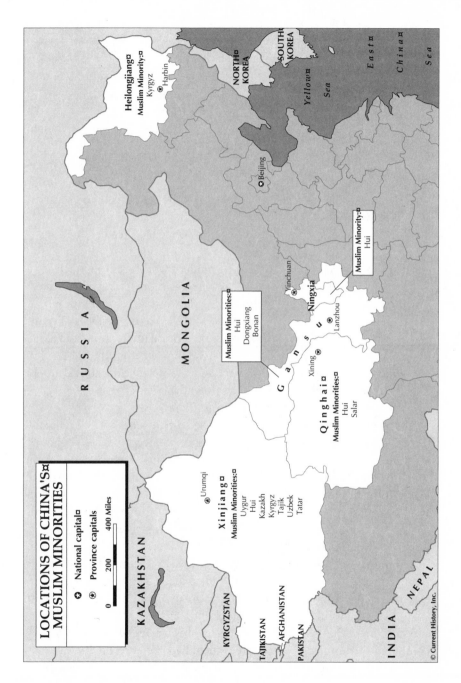

LOCATIONS OF CHINA'S
MUSLIM MINORITIES

National capital
Province capitals

0   200   400 Miles

KAZAKHSTAN

KYRGYZSTAN

TAJIKISTAN

AFGHANISTAN

PAKISTAN

INDIA

NEPAL

RUSSIA

MONGOLIA

Xinjiang
Muslim Minorities:
Uygur
Hui
Kazakh
Kyrgyz
Tajik
Uzbek
Tatar

Urumqi

Qinghai
Muslim Minorities:
Hui
Salar

Xining

Gansu

Lanzhou

Muslim Minorities:
Hui
Dongxiang
Bonan

Yinchuan

Ningxia

Muslim Minority:
Hui

Beijing

Heilongjiang
Muslim Minority:
Kyrgyz

Harbin

NORTH
KOREA

SOUTH
KOREA

Yellow
Sea

East
Sea

China
Sea

© Current History, Inc.

111

China's are the last Muslims under communism. With the independence of the largely Muslim nations of former Soviet Central Asia, the end of the war in Bosnia, the Israeli-Palestinian rapprochement, and even the recent peace accords with Muslim separatists in Chechnya and the Philippines, world Muslims have turned their attention to the Uyghur. The Chinese leadership should note that support for the Bosnian Muslims was the only issue on which the Iranian, Saudi, and Turkish governments could agree. Turkish Defense Minister Turhan Tayan recently told China "that many living [in Xinjiang] are our relatives and. . .we will always be interested in those people's welfare." China can begin to address its ethnic problems by reassessing its freedom of religion policy, especially for Muslims and Tibetan Buddhists (and Catholics as well). China can no longer say to the world that it has a "freedom of religion" law guaranteed by the constitution yet continue to arrest monks, harass priests, shut mosques, and closely monitor religious activities. The modern world sees too much.

Economic development must also become more evenly distributed. Chinese economists admit that despite 30 years of state subsidies for border areas, the minorities living in the interior and western provinces have incomes that are as much as 15 times lower than those in the south and along the coast. Minorities in general still have the shortest lives, the poorest living conditions, the worst health care, and the lowest educational levels. This is despite official "preferential treatment" policies that were designed to assist minority development and integration.

These policies, which include increased birth allowances (generally three children to the Han majority's allowance of one), tax relief, economic assistance, political representation, and educational opportunities, have benefited the minorities, but they have not raised the minority standard of living in the border regions and they have not allowed minorities real access to political power. While the National People's Congress has heavy minority representation, the Communist Party—where real power lies—is primarily Han. There is no first party secretary in any minority region who is a minority. On a recent sudden stopover in Urumqi from Europe, Deputy Prime Minister Qiao Shi, President Jiang Zemin's primary rival, emphasized not minority preferential treatment but an "iron hand" against separatists who would "split the motherland." His visit was followed by the announcement that ten Uyghur youths had been arrested for the February bombing in Urumqi, and that eight of them had been executed.

Regional development must directly benefit local inhabitants. Most Uyghur claim that if profits from energy and mineral development remained in Xinjiang, their incomes would equal those of Guangzhou (Canton) residents. Skilled and high-tech jobs in the industrial and energy sectors often go to Han, who are better connected and better educated. The free market has also led many of China's "floating population" of an estimated 100 million people to flood minority areas, seeking quick profits from cross-border trade and purchasing cheap raw materials. In the classic colonial model, unprocessed agricultural and animal products flow out from provinces like Xinjiang at reduced rates while manufactured goods are sold at a premium in the borderlands.

The Chinese have much to be proud of, especially the many accomplishments of Deng's generation. Patriotism need not be exclusionary; after all, many of China's citizens, though not Han, are proud to be Chinese. In Urumqi, Uyghur residents cheered the triumphs of the 1996 Chinese Olympic gold medalists as loudly as the Han. As they have in the past, the Uyghur will support a policy that benefits them even as it contributes to the rest of the country. Few believe, however, that the current two-pronged policy of economic development and political repression will satisfy these demands.

10. Beijing's Ambivalent Reformers

September 2004

BRUCE J. DICKSON

China's leaders have been exceedingly cautious about embarking on extensive political reforms, and not without good reason. There is no guarantee that reform efforts will succeed, or that China will be better or more easily governed as a consequence of reform. There is certainly no guarantee that the Chinese Communist Party will survive as the ruling party if it initiates fundamental reform of the political system.

The leadership is acutely aware that even good intentions can have disastrous consequences: when Soviet Communist Party leader Mikhail Gorbachev launched his reforms in the Soviet Union, he did not envision the collapse and dissolution of his country, and yet that was the result. Even though the immediate causes of the Soviet collapse are not as salient in China (economic stagnation, separatism, populist leaders, Gorbachev himself), the country's leaders are concerned that political reform could lead to the same fate. With few examples of authoritarian parties sponsoring democratization and surviving as the ruling parties of their countries, the Chinese Communist Party is still searching for a suitable role model to emulate.

What kinds of reforms are necessary to keep the party in power, and what reforms would jeopardize its tenure? These are questions that bedevil the current "fourth generation" of leaders just as they did their predecessors. Both Deng Xiaoping and Jiang Zemin, leaders of the second and third generations, respectively (Chairman Mao, of course, was the first generation leader) believed that economic modernization had to precede political change, and took the Soviet collapse as a cautionary tale. The current leadership, symbolized by party General Secretary Hu Jintao and Prime Minister Wen Jiabao, has not made its full intentions clear, but it has not yet shown any inclination to experiment with bold political reforms.

Even though China has not experienced the kinds of democratization that most observers have in mind when they look for signs of political reform, the party has implemented various modest reforms in recent years. Some are designed to allow the party to implement its policy agenda more efficiently. Others aim to make it more responsive to a changing society, or at least appear so. All are designed to perpetuate the Communist Party's rule, not necessarily to make China more democratic.

Adapting the Party to the New Agenda

At the beginning of the post-Mao period, Deng Xiaoping and other reformers recognized that their goal of modernizing China's economy with "reform and opening" (*gaige kaifang*) policies could be undermined both by remnant Maoists, who did not support their policies, and by veteran cadres, who were not qualified to carry out reform even if they supported it. For their economic reforms to be successful, therefore, they changed the party's policies regarding recruiting of new members and appointments of officials. After removing the Maoists from their posts and easing the veteran cadres into retirement, they transformed the composition of the cadre corps and rank-and-file membership.

At all levels, party members and officials have become on average younger and better educated. To make the Communist Party younger, leaders assured that roughly two-thirds of new recruits each year were no older than 35. To prevent local officials from remaining in office indefinitely, the party instituted a two-term limit on all posts and required officials to retire once they reached a certain age and were not promoted (65 for provincial-level officials, younger for lower levels of the bureaucracy).

The emphasis on education is even more apparent. Whereas less than 13 percent of party members had a high school or better education in the late 1970s, by the time of the sixteenth party congress in November 2002, the figure had risen to 53 percent. Within the central committee—which comprises the party's top 150 to 200 leaders—the proportion of those with a college degree rose from 55 percent in 1982 to 99 percent in 2002. Improvements in the education qualifications of local officials from the provincial to the county level were even more dramatic: in 1981, only 16 percent had a college education; 20 years later in 2001, 88 percent did.

The current generation of leaders is often referred to as "technocrats," meaning they hold bureaucratic posts and have technical backgrounds in the sciences and engineering. As Li Cheng has noted in the *China Leadership Monitor*, all nine members of the Politburo's standing committee, the very top elite of the party, are technocrats, as are eight of the ten members of the State Council, China's cabinet. Below this top level, however, the growing dominance of technocrats has abated. According to Li, the proportion of technocrats on the central committee dropped from 52 percent at the fifteenth party congress in 1997 to 46 percent at the sixteenth party congress in 2002. Similarly, among provincial party secretaries and governors, the proportion of technocrats has declined from about 75 percent in 1997 to only 42 percent in 2003. Moreover, none of the provincial leaders appointed after March 2003 (the likely candidates for the fifth generation of leaders) are engineers. For this younger generation of leaders, educational backgrounds in economics, the social sciences, humanities, and the law are increasingly common.

While it is dangerous to infer political preferences from academic backgrounds, this change in the composition of local leaders is a trend worth following. Many observers have predicted that the technocratic background of fourth generation leaders makes them more disposed to practical problem solving than bold experimentation. But the next generation of leaders comes from very different formative experiences. They have different educational backgrounds, have had greater exposure to international influences, and have enjoyed deeper experience in local administration. They may be more inclined to not just make the political system work more efficiently but to change it to make it more responsive to societal demands.

For these leaders, the key political event was not the Cultural Revolution (they are too young to have had their careers affected by those tumultuous years between 1966 and 1976 as previous generations of leaders did) but the popular demonstrations of 1989. The challenge facing the party is not to undo the mistakes of the Maoist period or to achieve rapid economic growth, but to prepare the political system for the consequences of modernization. How the party addresses this challenge will largely determine whether China will become more democratic, and more important, how systemic change may come about.

The best example of the party's change in recruitment strategy is the proportion of workers and farmers in the party. In 1994, they comprised 63 percent of all party members; by the end of 2003 their proportion had dropped to 44 percent in a party that had grown to over 68 million members. In less than 10 years, these representatives of the proletarian vanguard had become a minority in the Chinese Communist Party. The party now focuses on educational credentials and professional accomplishments in its recruitment strategy. Increasingly, that has meant turning to the urban entrepreneurial and technological elites.

These changes in the composition of the rank-and-file party members, local officials, and top leaders were designed specifically to promote economic reform. In this regard, the party reform was certainly successful. Over the past 25 years, China's economy has grown by 8 percent annually, lifting per capita income from $190 in 1978 to $960 (according to the World Bank, using current dollars) and shifting the bulk of economic activity from agriculture to industry, commerce, and services, and from the state sector to the nonpublic sector. Rapid economic change has also led to the emergence of new social groups, and the party has switched from excluding them from the political arena to actively incorporating them. It has co-opted these new elites by recruiting them into the party, appointing them to official posts, and creating corporatist-style organizations to integrate state and society.

The Rise of the Red Capitalists

In August 1989, soon after the end of popular demonstrations in Tiananmen Square and elsewhere, the Communist Party imposed a ban on recruiting private entrepreneurs into the organization. Party leaders were concerned that the economic interests of businessmen conflicted with the political interests of the party. This was not just Marxist paranoia: several prominent businessmen publicly supported the Tiananmen demonstrators and later fled the country to avoid arrest. Although the ban remained in place for more than 10 years, it was not very successful in keeping entrepreneurs out of the party. As I noted in my recent book, *Red Capitalists in China: The Party, Private Entrepreneurs, and Prospects for Political Change*, local officials had an incentive to reach out to entrepreneurs even if central leaders disapproved. Creating economic growth is now a key criterion for career advancement, and throughout the 1990s most economic growth and job creation came from the private sector.

Because of this, local officials in some communities—but by no means all—began to recruit successful entrepreneurs into the party despite the formal ban. The percentage of private entrepreneurs who belonged to the party—a group known as "red capitalists"—grew from around 13 percent in 1993 to more than 20 percent in 2000. Not all were new party members, however; most red capitalists had been members before going into business, but about one-third were co-opted after becoming successful businessmen. Orthodox Marxists harshly criticized the emergence of red capitalists and warned that it would spell the demise of the Chinese Communist Party.

As the economic clout of the private sector has grown, the political roles filled by private entrepreneurs have also increased. In addition to being members of the party, many entrepreneurs also belong to local party committees, the major decision-making bodies in China, further integrating them into the political system. At the sixteenth party congress in November 2002, entrepreneurs were among the delegates for the first time, although none were named to the central committee. When China's legislature, the National People's Congress, met in spring 2003, 55 entrepreneurs were selected as deputies. Entrepreneurs have been asked to serve in local legislatures in even larger numbers: over 17 percent of entrepreneurs belong to local people's congresses, and 35 percent belong to local people's political consultative conferences, a body designed to allow discussion between the party and other local elites. Many have been candidates in village elections, and most of the successful candidates are also party members, showing the party's desire to keep all political participation under its control.

In addition to bringing new social strata into the political arena, the party has also developed institutional ties with a variety of new social organizations. These groups are designed to be the party's bridge to society, allowing it to monitor what is occurring without directly controlling all aspects of daily life. China has tens of thousands of civic and professional organizations and hundreds of thousands of nonprofit organizations, such as private schools, medical clinics, job-training centers, and community groups, that provide a variety of social welfare services.

This vast number of organizations may create the foundations of a fully developed civil society, but at present they do not enjoy the kind of autonomy normally expected to be found in the groups that compose a civil society. All organizations must be formally registered and approved, and have a sponsoring governmental organization. They are also not supposed to compete with each other for members or for governmental approval. Where more than one similar group exists in a community, they may be pressured to merge or disband. These restrictions on social organizations suggest a corporatist logic to state-society relations, with controls over which organizations can exist and what kinds of activities they can engage in.

At the same time, many of these new groups are unlike the Communist Party's traditional "mass organizations," such as the All-China Federation of Trade Unions, which are seen by their nominal members as tools of the state rather than representing members' interests. Many professional organizations are not simply transmission belts for the party line, but instead are able to provide tangible benefits for their members. As Scott Kennedy shows in his forthcoming *The Business of Lobbying in China,* a variety of business associations have sprung up, often industry-specific, organized from the bottom up, and active at lobbying the state and in some cases unilaterally setting industry standards and regulations. These associations are more autonomous, more assertive, and less interested in simply representing the state's interests. This may complicate the party's strategy of creating new institutional links to monitor and control the private sector, but at present these business associations limit their activities to issues within their sphere and are not involved in larger public policy issues.

That behavior remains the key to success for both individuals and organizations: do not stray into political matters, and do not challenge the Communist Party's monopoly on political power. While much has changed in China in recent years, this basic political rule has not. Yet most of these new organizations are more inclined to succeed within the existing boundaries than try to change them. This also is a function of civil society: not just to challenge the state, but to find ways of working with the state to pursue common interests. Most writing on contemporary China focuses largely on the conflictual nature of civil society, but the potential for cooperation is just as important and certainly more prevalent today.

Courting New Elites

As economic development created a more complex society, with new social strata that did not fit neatly into old class categories, third generation leader Jiang Zemin and his colleagues recognized that they relied on these new elites to maintain rapid economic growth and could not continue excluding them from the party. Beginning in early 2000 and culminating in his speech on the eightieth anniversary of the Chinese Communist Party's founding on July 1, 2001, Jiang laid out a new definition of the party's relationship with society, which became known as "the important thinking of the 'Three Represents.'" According to this formulation, the party no longer represented only farmers and workers, its traditional base of support, but now also incorporated, first, the advanced productive forces (referring to entrepreneurs, professionals, high-tech specialists, and other urban elites); second, the most advanced modern culture; and third, the interests of the vast majority of the Chinese people.

This was a very inclusive definition of the party's role, and while often ridiculed as an empty slogan, it indicates a serious effort to update the party's relationship with a changing society. It acknowledged that what brought the party to power in 1949 was substantially different from what the party faces in the twenty-first century. If the party's guiding ideology no longer fit China's economic and social conditions, then the ideology needed to be updated—but not abandoned altogether. The party still goes to great lengths to show how its ideology remains consistent with its Marxist origins, even if China's few remaining ideologues believe the party has already abandoned its traditions and betrayed its revolutionary goals.

After Jiang's Party Day speech in 2001, in which he recommended lifting the ban on recruiting entrepreneurs and other new social strata into the party, and after the sixteenth party congress in 2002, when the "Three Represents" was added to the party constitution, large numbers of these "advanced productive forces" were expected to join the party. That did not happen, but it is not clear why. It may have been that local officials were not enthusiastic about this new policy and resisted implementing it. While some local leaders had ignored the ban on recruiting private entrepreneurs into the party, other leaders adamantly believed that capitalists did not belong in the Communist Party.

After the "Three Represents" became official party doctrine, a small number of cities was chosen to experiment with recruiting members from among these new urban elites. The public media did not report on the results of these experiments, indicating little progress was made. The party's organization department issued new directives on recruiting private entrepreneurs in 2003, but the message was ambiguous. Local party committees were advised not to be so eager to recruit new members that they lowered the standards for party membership, nor so strict that they did not let in any. Without clearer guidelines, the adoption of the "Three Represents" slogan was not fully integrated into the party's recruitment strategy.

However, the lack of progress may have been due to declining interest among private entrepreneurs themselves in joining the party. The number of red capitalists has continued to grow in 2003—up to 30 percent of entrepreneurs were party members—but most of the growth has come not from new recruitment, but from the privatization of state-owned enterprises. As these enterprises were converted into private firms, their former managers, almost all of whom were party members, became owners of private firms, automatically becoming red capitalists. Other entrepreneurs, however, seem to have lost interest in joining the party. Some claimed that they did not want to belong to a party that seems increasingly corrupt. Others did not want to be subject to party scrutiny of their business practices.

In a more general sense, party membership has become less valuable for many entrepreneurs. When the party was more ambivalent about the private sector, membership was useful for promoting business interests, such as securing loans, finding new investors, limiting outside competition, and above all protecting them from predatory actions of local officials. Reports of the confiscation of private property and financial assets remain common, showing that many local officials are more concerned with profiting from the private sector than promoting it. As the party's commitment to the private sector grew, and the interests of businessmen became better protected in party policy as well as laws and regulations, party membership became a less valuable commodity for private entrepreneurs. Still, the slowdown in co-opting entrepreneurs into the party—which seemed to be the main motivation behind the "Three Represents" in the first place—remains something of a mystery.

Even so, in the years after 1978, the party has steadily become younger, better educated, more professionally experienced, and more diverse as the farmers and workers, the traditional mainstays of the party, have been replaced by entrepreneurs, high-tech specialists, managers, and other new social strata. These changes have reinforced the commitment of party members and officials to the "reform and opening" policies. As a result, party adaptation has been generally successful by one measure: the changes have allowed the party to pursue its new goals more efficiently. However, a more challenging test of the party's adaptability is whether it is responsive to the changing wants and needs of society, and here the results have been more ambiguous.

Restoring Balance

Under the leadership of Jiang Zemin, the Communist Party had a distinctly elitist orientation, emphasizing the first of the "Three Represents": the advanced productive forces, which are primarily the urban entrepreneurial and technological elites. In recent years, private entrepreneurs in particular have become more assertive in seeking political and legal protection of their economic interests, and the party has been very responsive to their interests. To further symbolize the party's commitment to the private economy, in November 2003 it decided to revise the state constitution to protect private property and to promote the interests of the private sector.

This increasingly close relationship between the party and the private sector has created the widespread perception that the benefits of economic growth are being monopolized by a small segment of the population while the rest of the Chinese people are being left behind. Many Chinese now believe that economic success is based on personal connections with party and government officials, not individual initiative or quality work. As people come to believe that the benefits of the economic reform policies are unfairly distributed, the legitimacy of the party's policy of letting some get rich first is jeopardized.

In response to this perception, the new leadership of General Secretary Hu and Prime Minister Wen has shifted the focus away from the elitist orientation of the Jiang era to the third of the "Three Represents": the interests of the vast majority of the Chinese people. Hu and Wen, along with many others, concluded that the pendulum had swung too far in recent years, favoring the elites over the general population. They now want to create a new image for themselves and the party. This can be seen in Hu's speech on Party Day in 2003. Like Jiang just two years earlier, Hu concentrated exclusively on the "Three Represents." But whereas Jiang had emphasized the advanced productive forces, Hu mentioned the new social strata only once in passing. Instead, he focused on the "fundamental interests of the vast majority of the people," a phrase he repeated 13 times. In doing so, he was not rejecting an important symbol of the Jiang era, but he was reinterpreting it to signal a shift in priorities.

Hu and Wen have done more than simply speak on behalf of the majority. They have also shown their support—or at least their sympathy—for the disadvantaged in their public appearances and activities. During the 2003 Chinese New Year, Wen visited and shared a meal with miners. During the 2003 SARS crisis, Hu and Wen visited SARS patients in hospitals. They fired the minister of public health and the mayor of Beijing for covering up the extent of the epidemic. On World AIDS Day in December 2003, Wen visited and shook hands with HIV/AIDS patients, the first top leader to recognize China's AIDS crisis. In January 2004, the Communist Party issued a new policy directive on improving rural conditions that included policies aimed at alleviating income inequality. The Hu-Wen team has also tried to alleviate regional inequalities by promoting development in the northeast rustbelt and the less developed western provinces. This effort was begun under Jiang but expanded under Hu and Wen. Experiments with local elections, also started under Jiang, have continued with the fourth generation. In recent years, there have been elections for party secretaries, township leaders, urban neighborhood committees, and other positions.

Mixed Signals

Along with hints of change came signs of the enduring features of the political system. The doctor who exposed the SARS cover-up and became a national hero, Jiang Yanyong, was taken into custody by military officials in June 2004 and held for six weeks for advocating a reassessment of the official verdict on the 1989 Tiananmen demonstrations. Although the extent of the AIDS crisis has been gradually but not yet fully acknowledged, HIV/AIDS victims still rarely get the treatment they need and official culpability in the spread of the virus has yet to be admitted, much less punished. AIDS activists, most notably Wan Yanhai, have been harassed and imprisoned, and reporters who have tried to expose the policies of local governments that allowed the virus to spread have been fired and their stories suppressed. Residents of "AIDS villages" in rural Henan, where the AIDS virus has spread widely through blood donations that use unsanitary practices, have been beaten, arrested, and had their homes destroyed for seeking medicine and financial assistance from higher levels of government, for meeting with journalists to publicize their plight, or for attempting to gain the attention of investigating groups visiting China from the World Health Organization.

Efforts by top leaders to compensate the disadvantaged continue to be hampered by the failure of local leaders to act on new initiatives. For example, Wen may order local leaders to pay iou's and unpaid wages to specific individuals in specific cases when they come to his attention, but similar cases that do not get singled out are rarely addressed. Local governments are themselves often starved of cash and cannot be as generous and proactive in identifying and addressing the many injustices that exist in their jurisdictions. And candidates in local elections are still either Communist Party members or independents; no new political parties have been allowed to form, and there has not even been official discussion of such a possibility. Efforts to create the China Democracy Party went for naught, as petitions to register the party were denied and the activists who were behind the effort were arrested and sentenced to jail terms of more than 10 years.

At the same time, Hu and Wen seem determined to shift away from the elitist orientation within the party. There is now frequent media coverage of Politburo meetings. Hu reported on the work of the Politburo to the most recent central committee meeting in fall 2003, and lower-level party committees are also expected to give regular reports to the bodies that formally elected them. Hu also canceled the annual meetings in the resort city of Beidaihe, which have traditionally been held each August to decide major policy and personnel issues. Because they are more informal than Politburo meetings and central committee plenums, they have been frequently used by senior party leaders to influence decision making, even after these officials have formally retired from office. The decision to cancel the meetings gives greater emphasis to the formal meetings in Beijing, and may curtail the informal influence of retired elders.

These changes are designed to promote the transparency and accountability of top-level decision making and to give greater weight to formal processes over informal politics. While the party has described these changes as improving inner party democracy, a dubious claim to be sure, they should at least be recognized as creating greater institutionalization in the Chinese system, which by itself would be a generally positive trend.

But these changes occur within clear limits. Reports on Politburo meetings reveal little beyond the topic under discussion and the theme of Hu's remarks to the group. Work reports by themselves do not provide for much accountability, and in any event the central committee only "elected" the Politburo after top leaders agreed among themselves who would belong to it. And media coverage of the November 2003 central committee plenum highlighted again the party's secretive nature. Although the media reported that the central committee had approved major constitutional revisions, they did not report on the content of those revisions. Speeches were given by top leaders, but the texts of the reports—including Hu's report on the work of the Politburo—were not published.

These mixed signals are the result of several factors. First is the leadership's ambivalence about pursuing any one course exclusively, with the danger that concessions to some individuals or groups may be used as a precedent for others to make claims against the state, or might raise expectations that more expansive political reforms are being considered. Second is the fragmented nature of political authority in China. Not all actions are the result of coherent decisions by unified leaders; they are also the result of different parts of the state taking actions that other parts of the state, and other leaders, may be unaware of or even oppose. Third is the consequence of political decentralization. Policies announced in Beijing are not immediately or even inevitably implemented by local governments. Finally, the transition from the third to the fourth generation of leaders is still incomplete. Jiang retains his post as chairman of the Central Military Commission, the Communist Party's top body for military matters, and continues to intervene in domestic and foreign policies—he was reportedly behind the detention of Dr. Jiang (no relation). Hu and Wen, perhaps recognizing that time is on their side, have not directly challenged Jiang's interventions even when they run contrary to the new leaders' preferred direction. Which of these causes is behind each zig and zag is often difficult to determine by outside observers and even by the victims and beneficiaries of these steps and missteps within China.

Benevolent Leninists?

While many no longer believe Marxism remains a relevant doctrine in contemporary China, there is no doubt that Leninism remains the guiding influence in the political system. There is still no organized opposition of any kind, and no public lobbying for policy change is visible outside the economic realm. But for those who do not choose to challenge the Communist state—and this involves the vast majority—the party is increasingly less pervasive and less intrusive. This is not to suggest that the party is seen as legitimate, much less popular. But it points to a fact that is often overlooked in most criticisms of China: although freedoms of all kinds are sharply delimited, and not well protected by law, it is nevertheless true that the degree of mobility, expression of ideas, and access to information is increasing, not contracting. When compared to the freedoms enjoyed, even taken for granted, by citizens of democratic countries, this progress seems halting and minuscule. But when compared against China's own past, the changes are dramatic.

Whether they will be sufficient to forestall popular demands for more significant change, and to prolong the Communist Party's tenure as China's ruling party, remains a key question in Chinese politics. In short, it is still not clear if we are seeing a more benevolent form of authoritarianism or signs of more significant political reform yet to come.

11. China's New Exchange Rate Regime

September 2005

BARRY EICHENGREEN

On July 21, 2005, China unexpectedly revalued its currency, the renminbi, raising its value by 2.1 percent against the US dollar. At the same time, it altered the fluctuation band that limits the daily movement of the exchange rate to 0.3 percent by redefining it in terms of a basket of foreign currencies rather than simply the dollar. And it announced that henceforth the People's Bank of China, the central bank, would allow the exchange rate to be more heavily influenced by market conditions.

These decisions came at the end of two years of intense foreign criticism of the country's exchange rate peg, most notably by the United States. Was this in fact a very uncharacteristic Chinese concession to foreign pressure? Were officials in Beijing swayed by congressional threats of tariff retaliation if they did not act? Or was the decision to alter the currency regime in China's own interest?

Splitting the Difference

Answering these questions requires understanding how economists think about currency issues. The theory of "optimum currency areas" provides the obvious jumping-off point. This theory suggests that countries that experience business-cycle expansions and contractions at different times from the rest of the world will want a more flexible exchange rate, since they will need to tailor monetary policy to domestic needs. In contrast, export-dependent economies with weak financial systems will want a less flexible exchange rate, since currency volatility could threaten both financial stability and export growth.

Here we immediately see the dilemma confronting the Chinese authorities. While China's exceptionally rapid development subjects it to distinctive business cycle risks, the country also has a high export to GDP ratio and a weak financial sector. Splitting the difference suggests a moderate increase in currency flexibility, which was precisely the decision taken on July 21.

This framework also suggests that, with the passage of time, China will want to move in the direction of even greater flexibility. Eventually, Beijing will address the problems in its banking and financial system, and a stronger financial system will enable it to cope more easily with additional exchange rate volatility. With time, domestic demand will become more important; grassroots insistence on higher living standards will make this so. And economies less dependent on export demand demonstrably prefer a more flexible exchange rate.

Greater flexibility will allow the authorities to more effectively steer the economy. It will prevent domestic interest rates and financial conditions from being dictated by interest rates and financial conditions in the rest of the world, since investors will have to worry not only about the level of interest rates, but also about a possible future change in the exchange rate. Flexibility will become still more important as China's banks are commercialized and stakes are sold to foreign investors, rendering less effective the past practice of managing monetary conditions by issuing instructions to financial institutions.

Sequencing the Market

Another factor that entered into China's decision to alter its currency regime was the need to correctly sequence its monetary and financial reforms. The central conclusion of most economic thinking on the topic is that exchange rate flexibility should precede capital account liberalization (that is, the removal of restrictions on the flow of foreign capital into and out of a country). The idea is to avoid opportunities for currency speculators to make, in effect, one-way bets. Situations where the exchange rate can only move one way, so speculators run no risk of making losses, force authorities to abandon their exchange rate commitment under duress, and at considerable cost to their policy credibility.

If the capital account is opened first, large amounts of liquidity may flow in, creating the specter of a financially disruptive credit boom and fanning fears of a socially disruptive inflation that can only be headed off by revaluation. Alternatively, large amounts of liquidity may flow out, draining reserves unless the authorities devalue the currency.

In contrast, if exchange rate flexibility precedes capital account liberalization, this creates losses in the event that expectations of revaluation or devaluation are disappointed, thereby avoiding one-way bets and discouraging currency speculators from all lining up on one side of the market. This is one of the principal lessons of the 1997–1998 Asian financial crisis, which was aggravated by the fact that many Asian countries opened their capital accounts before moving to greater exchange rate flexibility.

That China has now taken a modest step in the direction of greater flexibility is reassuring in light of the measures taken in the past year to liberalize its capital account. Already the capital account is sufficiently porous that large amounts of portfolio capital are attracted by expectations of rapid economic growth and currency appreciation. The authorities' capacity to insulate the economy from overheating (by inter alia instructing the banks not to lend) is increasingly limited by the ability of that finance to circumvent the banking system entirely. Greater exchange rate flexibility will not eliminate risks associated with overheating, but it should attenuate them.

Equally, there is already considerable scope for disruptive capital outflows, which could destabilize the country's weak banks in some future scenario where there is a slowdown in growth, new problems surface in the financial system, or there is a serious diplomatic or military dispute with the United States. The authorities may then be tempted to support the exchange rate and the banks by intervening in financial markets, purchasing domestic currency with the foreign reserves of the central bank. Both theory and evidence suggest that this would be a losing battle even for a central bank with $1 trillion of reserves; this formidable war chest is nothing compared to the resources that can be mobilized by the markets.

This observation also points to the principal lesson of the literature on exit strategies from fixed exchange rates: countries should exit from a peg while growth is strong, capital is flowing in, and expectations are for appreciation. Exiting under duress is almost always costly. It forces the authorities to reluctantly abandon their stated commitment to defend the peg, contradicting previous policy statements and diminishing their credibility. Recent economic thinking also suggests that a nondisruptive exit to flexibility is easier to engineer when at least some capital controls remain in place. This permits the authorities to move at a time of their own choosing, and any disruptive financial fallout is lessened.

It is thus worrisome that Beijing still shows a preference for intervening heavily in the foreign exchange market to limit currency fluctuations. The weightiest argument against curtailing that intervention now is that it is first necessary to further develop financial markets and instruments with which banks and firms can hedge against the risk of sudden changes in the exchange rate, thereby preventing exchange rate volatility from undermining financial stability and growth. And, according to the authorities in Beijing, it is necessary to proceed further with the relaxation of capital account restrictions to develop those markets.

Hedging foreign currency exposures on financial markets is impossible when the capital account is fully closed, since regulations prohibit banks and firms from buying foreign assets to offset their foreign liabilities. At the same time we know, for all the reasons enumerated earlier, that a large country with an open capital account should embrace some degree of exchange rate flexibility. The degree of capital account liberalization in practice being a continuum, there must be an intermediate stage in the process at which it is optimal to move from a peg to a more flexible exchange rate. In effect, the question boils down to: At exactly what point in the process of capital account liberalization should the country begin to move to greater exchange rate flexibility?

Why China was Ready

A number of reasons explain why the Chinese authorities were correct to conclude that this point had arrived. In particular, they were correct to think that limited flexibility would not destabilize the banking system. To be sure, China's banks are still burdened by a legacy of nonperforming policy loans, information systems are inadequate, and internal controls are lax. Fixing these problems should be an urgent priority. That said, it is not clear that these problems will be significantly aggravated by a limited increase in exchange rate volatility.

It is not as if the banks have large foreign exposures that will become vastly more difficult to manage. Because China's outward investment was constrained in the past by a combination of factors that included capital controls, the banks possess limited foreign-currency-denominated assets.

Capital controls and financial regulations have limited the accumulation of foreign-currency-denominated liabilities even more strictly.

The main risk to the banks lies in the danger that export growth and growth generally will slow sharply. Slower growth will make for more non-performing loans, and slower export growth will make for more nonperforming loans in the export sector. A substantial (double-digit) revaluation might have had this effect on growth, given the relatively low (single-digit) profit rates in the export sector. But this was not the decision taken this July. Rather, it was for a modest 2 percent revaluation and a limited increase in the variability of the exchange rate.

In any case, there are reasons to think that any given increase in exchange rate volatility will have a smaller impact on exports and investment than China's dependence on foreign markets would otherwise suggest. Export enterprises not only sell final products abroad, they also buy manufacturing inputs abroad. Consequently, their costs and revenues move in the same direction when the exchange rate fluctuates (economists refer to this as a "natural hedge"). In addition, a large share (by some estimates, a majority) of Chinese exports is accounted for by foreign investment enterprises. These foreign owners and joint venture partners are in a favorable position to hedge against currency fluctuations. They can invest in a diversified portfolio of production locations or in financial assets whose returns vary negatively with the profits of Chinese export enterprises, since they are not prevented from accumulating assets abroad by China's capital controls.

Were exchange rate volatility to rise immediately to very high levels, that would be a different story. But this is not what anyone foresees. The currency's movement will continue to be limited by the central bank. The bank will lean against the wind, pumping liquidity into the market if the exchange rate shows a tendency to appreciate excessively, and selling foreign assets into the market if there is the danger of a currency collapse.

By providing this liquidity, the central bank in effect supplies the hedging services required by the export sector. This is precisely the situation in other emerging markets that operate a managed float despite the retention of capital controls. India is a good example of a large, export-oriented emerging market that has successfully reconciled currency flexibility with the maintenance of capital controls through heavy management of the exchange rate. There is no reason why China cannot do likewise.

Abandoning the Band

Only time will tell how freely the authorities will permit the exchange rate of the renminbi to move. That there is no change in the official bandwidth, only a statement that the currency will henceforth be guided more by "market conditions," is in fact compatible with no increase in variability. There are many examples of emerging markets that officially pursue managed floats but in practice operate what amounts to a de facto peg.

If this is what China does, then domestic interest rates will become more tightly linked to foreign interest rates as the capital account opens further. This will make it harder for those responsible for macroeconomic management to tailor money and credit conditions to domestic needs. A rigid exchange rate will also heighten risks in the financial sector by encouraging lenders and borrowers to underestimate the danger of foreign exposures. If, on the other hand, the new regime really represents a shift toward greater flexibility, then it will be a step in the right direction on all these grounds.

From this standpoint the decision to retain the 0.3 percent daily fluctuation band is the most problematic aspect of the reform. As China further strengthens its financial system and diversifies its demand, it will want to allow the currency to fluctuate more freely. As it moves toward a market-based financial system and acquires a more conventional monetary-policy transmission mechanism, it will wish to adopt a form of inflation targeting as the anchor for monetary policy. It will thus have to widen the fluctuation band or drop it entirely.

However, repeated changes in monetary regime, including changes in foreign exchange market intervention rules, heighten uncertainty about the future. They raise questions about the consistency of the authorities' policy commitments and they diminish the credibility of policy. For planning purposes, producers need to be able to anticipate how the authorities will react to new information about the state of the economy. If that reaction is going to be different sometime in the not too distant future, the stabilizing impact of current policy will be less.

A 0.3 percent daily fluctuation band is not a binding constraint at the moment—when the problems of the financial system, the importance of export demand, the weakness of conventional mechanisms for monetary transmission, and the maintenance of residual capital controls all militate in favor of limited flexibility. But it may well bind five years from now, when the authorities will want a more flexible rate. If speculation about whether China will revalue is now replaced by speculation about how quickly it will relax or abandon its fluctuation band, stability will suffer.

Rebalancing the Economy

A 2 percent appreciation of the renminbi, even accompanied by appreciations of other Asian currencies, is too small to have much impact on the pattern of global imbalances. But a 7 percent of GDP current account deficit like that which the United States is currently running is patently unsustainable. This deficit (the difference between the goods and services that America imports versus what it exports) will have to be cut by more than half in order to stabilize net claims on the United States as a share of global wealth. And substantial exchange rate changes will be needed as part of that adjustment (and this is on the optimistic assumption of 6 percent nominal income growth in the United States).

Mainstream economic models suggest that a real effective depreciation of the dollar of at least 20 percent will be needed to reduce the US current account deficit to 3 percent of gross domestic product. Assume that half of this adjustment should occur in the next year, while the other half can occur the year after that. For simplicity's sake, we can take US trade with Europe and Asia as of roughly equal importance. Then the 10 percent fall in the dollar's effective exchange rate that must occur in the next 12 months can be accomplished by a 15 percent appreciation of Asian currencies against the dollar and a 5 percent appreciation of the euro against the dollar.

Europe's competitiveness and growth will be hurt by the euro's further appreciation against the dollar but more than cushioned by its fall against the Asian currencies. Still, treating trade shares with the two regions as being of equal importance for purposes of our back-of-the-envelope calculation, the euro's effective rate depreciates by 2.5 percent. The negative impact on profitability and growth in Asia is similarly moderated by the fact that the appreciation of Asian currencies is less against the euro than the dollar. Again, with trade shares of equal value, the effective appreciation of Asian currencies is 12.5 percent.

This simple arithmetic is a reminder that the problem of global imbalances has not been solved by China's 2 percent revaluation and that further appreciation of the renminbi will be needed to help rebalance the world economy. Otherwise, when investors come to the sudden realization that

US deficits are unsustainable, the dollar could fall with a crash, forcing the US Federal Reserve to raise interest rates sharply and precipitating a global recession.

Conservatively estimating profit margins in the export sector as 6 percent and noting that imported content accounts for half of the value of exports suggests that Chinese exporters might just be able to tolerate a 12 percent appreciation. Of course, how easily they do so will depend on how quickly they succeed in cutting costs. This will also be critical for whether the second part of this process of global adjustment, involving an additional 10 percent decline of the dollar, can be smoothly reconciled with continuing Chinese (and global) growth.

The unavoidable conclusion is that global rebalancing requires additional currency flexibility on China's part. But there is also a danger: hot money inflows may accelerate in anticipation of the renminbi's further strengthening. This makes it all the more essential that Chinese authorities allow the currency to exhibit greater volatility. Only the presence of a two-way bet—that is, only the possibility that the renminbi can fall as well as rise from day to day—will prevent currency traders from all lining up on one side of the market and thereby limit speculative inflows. This is another reason why the decision to retain the currency band was a mistake.

The 2 percent revaluation and commitment to greater exchange rate flexibility announced on July 21 were important first steps. Greater flexibility will help the Chinese authorities tailor monetary conditions to domestic needs. The revaluation is a modest Chinese contribution to resolving the problem of global imbalances. But definitively resolving that problem will require considerable further appreciation of the renminbi-dollar rate. So, too, effectively managing domestic monetary conditions and averting the danger that China will be overwhelmed by speculative capital flows will require considerably higher levels of exchange rate variability than officials have shown a tolerance for so far. China's exchange rate system is a work in progress. Notwithstanding all the attention attracted by the dramatic decisions this July, that process has only started.

PART III

Domestic Politics and Governance

12. Is Democracy Possible?

September 1995

MERLE GOLDMAN

D espite the June 4, 1989, crackdown on the Tiananmen demonstrators, China can no longer be described as a strictly authoritarian or totalitarian country. One political scientist, Kenneth Lieberthal, calls China's government a "fragmented authoritarianism." Another, Harry Harding, terms it "consultative authoritarianism."

There is no question that the reforms carried out from 1978 to 1989 by paramount leader Deng Xiaoping and his disciples Hu Yaobang and Zhao Ziyang moderated the harsh authoritarianism of the Maoist era. Now, after several decades of authoritarian rule, rapid growth rates, and a semimarket economy, many intellectuals, reform officials, Western governments, and businesspeople believe that China will follow the same route as its ethnic and Confucian neighbors in Taiwan and South Korea and move along a democratic path similar to that of its East Asian neighbors. But how realistic is that scenario?

Dissident Voices in the Legislature

Although conventional wisdom holds that China has had economic reform but no political reform, this is in fact not the case. During the reform decade, China's Leninist political system began to change in subtle but unprecedented ways. Since the late 1980s, there have been elections for local congresses in which there have been more candidates than positions. Although candidates have to be approved by the party, the party's official choices do not always win. Sometimes the party refuses to allow elected candidates to assume their positions, but in the countryside peasants have often voted incumbents out of office in recent years and the party has gone along with their choices.

By allowing peasants to replace unpopular local cadres with leaders of their own choosing, the party hopes to achieve stability in the country-side. Even after the 1989 Tiananmen crackdown, this practice continued. It is estimated that by the early 1990s nearly one-third of the local people's congresses had multicandidate elections. Equally unprecedented were the multicandidate elections for the party's Central Committee in 1987. In that election delegates to the thirteenth party congress voted out of office a number of old revolutionaries who had been obstructing Deng's reforms.

The National People's Congress, the rubber-stamp legislature of the Mao period, has become in the Deng era a forum for voicing dissent on important issues. Its debates on the bankruptcy law in the 1980s were tel-evised to the nation. Only three years after Tiananmen, one-third of the legislators voted against or abstained from voting on building the Three Gorges hydroelectric dam, a project pushed by the party leadership. At this year's NPC session, about one-third of the parliament's nearly 3,000 deputies voted against or abstained from voting on one of President Jiang Zemin's candidates for vice prime minister. In addition, a meeting of the Guangdong delegation during the congress issued a demand for the reha-bilitation of deposed General Secretary Zhao Ziyang, who had been ousted for urging a more conciliatory approach to the 1989 demon-strators.

The National People's Congress became a forum for expressing dissent in the mid-1980s, when it was headed by the revolutionary elder Peng Zhen. Though conservative on political reform, Peng used the NPC to re-strain reformers in the Politburo's Standing Committee, the ultimate deci-sion-making body. The potential role of the NPC as a check on party leaders is demonstrated by the fact that even after Peng retired in 1988, it continued to function as a forum for expressing disagreement with the leadership's policies. However, over the years the political tone of the two institutions has been reversed. Today the Standing Committee is domi-nated by more conservative officials and the congress by more reformist officials. Public dissent on party decisions in China's supposed legislature was unknown in the Mao era. The NPC is becoming a legislature in prac-tice as well as in name—which was one of the institutional changes pro-posed by China's political reformers before June 4.

More Voices, Different Views

A freer press is another qualitative change from the Mao era. Beginning just before Deng's official takeover of power at the third plenum of the eleventh Central Committee in December 1978, the media began to open up. It has published debates on fundamental political issues such as the rule of law, freedom of the press, a system of checks and balances, universal human rights, and exchanges between advocates of democracy and advocates of neoauthoritarianism. As long as the participants did not challenge the leadership or the party directly, these discussions, with some brief interruptions, peppered the media. Scores of semiofficial and nonofficial newspapers, journals, and book series were published. Although they had to be officially registered before publication, they presented alternative and sometimes divergent views from the official position.

After June 4, the regime sought to return to the harsher authoritarianism of the pre-Deng era and imposed much tighter censorship. But it had difficulty as long as China continued its economic reforms and remained open to the outside world. Moreover, the burgeoning middle class created by the economic reforms had spawned a lively popular culture that has blossomed outside the party's control. Sinologists Orville Schell and Geremie Barmé have described the efflorescence of nonofficial literature, art, and music in the 1990s.[1] Most popular are semipornographic works of literature and art, rock music, television comedies, and call-in radio talk shows that discuss everything from sexual relationships to environmental pollution. This popular culture is very much influenced by that in Hong Kong, Taiwan, and even Japan.

Although popular culture offers an alternative to the official party culture, it is tolerated because it does not directly touch on political issues. And its escapist quality not only reflects the party's desire for an apolitical culture, it also mirrors the overwhelming desire of the urban population after June 4 to stay away from politics. Nevertheless, this new culture indirectly subverts the party's control by promoting values totally alien to mainstream traditional Chinese and Marxist-Leninist emphasis on obedience and conformity. Although ostensibly nonpolitical, popular culture

1. Orville Schell, *Mandate of Heaven* (New York: Simon and Shuster, 1994), pp. 280-427; Geremie Barmé, "Soft Porn, Packaged Dissent, and Nationalism: Notes on Chinese Culture in the 1990s," *Current History,* September 1994.

could in time lead to ideological and political pluralism as change is pushed from the bottom up.

China is now tied into the international community to a much greater degree than even before the 1949 revolution. The Chinese have foreign contacts through travel, telephone, e-mail, fax machines, and direct personal connections with their Chinese brethren overseas. These sources, along with the newly wealthy Chinese entrepreneurs, provide nonparty funding for new journals, newspapers, and films. In 1993 it was estimated that over 2,000 new newspapers and journals had been launched since 1990. With the growing number of media outlets, the party finds it difficult to monitor their growth or their content. Moreover, the emergence of thousands of private booksellers and scores of private schools (permitted since 1994) makes it virtually impossible for the party to sustain even the relatively loose control over intellectual and cultural life that it had in the 1980s.

Petitioning the Courts—and the Party

At the same time, more overt challenges to the party are increasing. Individual Chinese are confronting government officials and local cadres through the courts. Ironically, around the time of the crackdown, the party passed the Administrative Litigation Law, which codified the procedures under which ordinary citizens can sue for infringement of rights. In the spring 1993 issue of *Daedalus*, William Alford describes how Chinese are bringing suit against officials and party organizations for legal transgressions, defamation of character, improper seizure of property, and abuse of power, and they seek official apologies, compensation, and injunctions.[2]

Legal actions have ranged from well-known writer Wang Meng's lawsuit against the party journal *Literary Gazette* in 1991 (for publishing a letter attacking one of his short stories as critical of Deng Xiaoping) to ordinary people protesting human rights violations. Wang's case never came to court, but just the threat of his suit effectively curbed the party's criticism of him. In fact, a book about the case, implicitly favorable to Wang, was published soon after. In another case, the philosopher Guo Luoji, who had been transferred from Beijing University to Nanjing University in 1982 for criticizing party officials in the late 1970s, was forbidden to teach or go

2. William Alford, "Double-Edged Swords Cut Both Ways: Law and Legitimacy in the People's Republic of China," *Daedalus,* vol. 122, no.2 (Spring 1993).

abroad after he expressed support for the 1989 student demonstrators. Guo responded by instituting legal proceedings against the State Education Commission and Nanjing University's Party Committee for depriving him of his rights.

Since the judiciary remains under party control, intellectuals generally lose their suits or their cases are ignored. Actions brought by budding entrepreneurs against local cadres for interfering with business activities, however, have been more successful because the party wants to use the legal system to spur the economy. Nevertheless, although the courts did not accept their cases, Wang Meng's suit ended his harassment in the pages of the *Literary Gazette*, and Guo Luoji was eventually allowed to go abroad. Just the threat of legal actions against the party may sometimes result in the desired effect for well-known intellectuals, but it can result in even more repressive treatment for lesser known political activists.

Dissidents purged for their views and activities in the 1980s and imprisoned for their participation in the spring 1989 demonstrations have begun to find their voices again after nearly five years of silence. The most outspoken have been those released from prison in 1993 and 1994 to help China in its bid to win the 2000 Olympics and to help secure President Bill Clinton's delinkage of China's most favored nation treatment from human rights issues. Shortly after their release the dissidents resumed their demands for democratic reforms. And unlike before June 1989, when the elite intellectuals had little to do with student and former Red Guard pro-democracy activists and workers, elite and nonestablishment groups have joined together in various political activities.

Their major activity has been to petition publicly party leader Jiang Zemin and Qiao Shi, the head of the NPC, for reform. Though petitioning leaders resembles the Confucian practice of literati memorials to the emperor, the sponsorship of recent petitions by a coalition of high-level intellectuals and nonestablishment political activists makes their protest qualitatively different. This new political collaboration of disparate social groups resembles the political coalitions that eventually led to the 1989 revolutions in Eastern Europe.

The most publicized petition, issued on May 15, was signed by a group of China's most prestigious intellectuals, including scientists from the Chinese Academy of Sciences, former Red Guard political activists, and China's most famous student leaders. It urged an end to persecution for holding differing viewpoints and the release of those imprisoned for their political and religious beliefs, including Tibetans and Christians. In addition, it also called for a repeal of the designation of the spring 1989 demonstrations as "counterrevolutionary." The willingness of China's intellectual elite to join with nonestablishment political activists suggests that they now have a more realistic understanding of the need to work with other social groups if China is to move in a democratic direction.

Parallels with Taiwan and South Korea

Some of the changes under way in China today are reminiscent of the early steps toward democratization in Taiwan and South Korea. These two countries also began with multicandidate balloting, the election of nonofficial candidates, and a more open culture and media. Despite these similarities, important differences exist. While Taiwan's and South Korea's democratization demonstrates that there is no intrinsic cultural value or historical legacy that prevents China from becoming a democracy, China may follow a path that is longer and more twisted than its neighbors in reaching that goal.

The 1989 protests in Beijing and in almost every Chinese city, during which massive numbers of people from all social classes joined the student demonstrators, revealed that China was becoming an increasingly pluralistic and restive society. But the crackdown that ended the movement showed how much of the autocratic Leninist political system remained intact. Deng had reinvigorated the economic reforms in 1992 by his symbolic trip through the special economic zones, but his purpose was not to expedite the political reforms, as some Western observers had hoped— it was, instead, to forestall the need to introduce them. Although economic reforms may gradually subvert the Leninist system, this does not necessarily mean that China will then move in a democratic direction.

There is no question that intellectuals and students today have more freedom to pursue their academic work, and that most people feel less restrained in their personal lives than even before June 4. Nevertheless, it is still risky to challenge the party and its leaders publicly and in an organized fashion. When former Red Guard Wei Jingsheng, imprisoned in 1979 for 15 years for questioning the party's willingness to reform politically and for calling Deng a dictator, expressed more moderate views just months after his release in 1993, he was reimprisoned. Recently released leaders of the

1989 demonstrations who signed the petitions have been continually harassed. While the elite intellectuals have not yet been detained by the authorities, they too have been questioned and some are under police surveillance.

Those former Red Guards who participated in the 1978–1979 Democracy Wall movement have been treated most severely. The persistent repression of intellectual dissidents, as well as independent trade union organizers and Tibetan and Christian religious leaders, shows that even this most modern of twentieth-century Chinese governments will not countenance any political opposition and is determined to suppress any unofficial political organizing.

In South Korea, several opposition leaders (intellectuals, labor union leaders, and Christians) were also arrested early in that country's movement for democracy, but others were allowed to organize. Similarly, while some advocates of Taiwan's independence were imprisoned in the earlier decades of the Kuomintang rule, a few others continued to organize politically. Consequently, when these countries permitted competitive elections—South Korea beginning in the late 1940s and Taiwan in the 1980s—members of opposition parties were able to compete for office and gain political positions and dominance in certain regions. These elections may have begun as democratic façades to please South Korea's and Taiwan's American patrons or domestic critics, but in time they gained credibility.

In China there are eight small, supposedly "democratic" parties, but they are under the direct control of the Chinese Communist Party. Therefore, even if the Communist Party had stepped down in 1989, as the most militant protesters demanded, no independent organization or group of alternative leaders was waiting in the wings to replace it. And every effort to organize an alternative has been crushed by the party.

Equally important, China currently lacks the social preconditions for democracy found in its East Asian neighbors. While reforms in South Korea and Taiwan have produced greater social and geographic equality, China's reforms have led to increased inequalities, especially between China's interior provinces and coastal areas, and between workers in stagnating state industries and those in the dynamic nonstate economy. In addition, South Korea and Taiwan began their reforms with nearly 100 percent literacy and maintained that level after the reforms were instituted; China's literacy rate has fallen in recent years as peasants have found it more beneficial to keep their children working on the farm instead of sending them to school. Moreover, while the bureaucracies in South Korea and Taiwan were filled with officials trained in the United States and Europe, China's Western-trained technocrats have barely penetrated the Communist Party's bureaucracy, now dominated by Soviet-trained leaders such as Jiang Zemin and Li Peng.

Taiwan and South Korea also were predominantly middle class societies. It is estimated that the emerging middle class in China already numbers about 100 million people. This new class could serve as the social base for China's democratic movement. Some members of the new middle class were active in the spring 1989 demonstrations. They ranged from the small vendors who dispensed free refreshments to the demonstrators to Wang Rannan, the former president of the Stone Group, China's largest nonstate computer company. Wang provided the copiers, faxes, cellular telephones, and printers that fueled the demonstrations. In the late 1980s he had also funded a think tank that tried to introduce political reforms into China. But after the crackdown, he and his associates escaped abroad. Other members of China's new middle class have since turned away from political action and now devote themselves to making money. Some claim that they prefer the supposed stability of an authoritarian system, so long as they make money, to the uncertainties of a democracy.

While China's middle class is growing, it comprises less than 10 percent of the country's more than 1 billion people. Furthermore, it is quite different from the South Korean and Taiwanese middle classes. Although the South Korean and Taiwanese states play a much greater role in the economy than the state does in Western nations, the middle class had some degree of autonomy even during the most authoritarian periods. In China, the 1949 revolution eliminated the autonomy of every group, including the middle class, as the party extended its control over all aspects of life. Even as China has moved to a semimarket economy, much of the entrepreneurial activity has occurred with the permission of party officials. Thus, the middle class is growing, but few of its members can function independently of the party.

Taiwan and South Korea also developed civil societies during their democratization. While the Chinese state has retreated from direct involvement in China's economic life and the Chinese people now express themselves in many voices on a large number of issues, few of these voices can publicly express political ideas that diverge from the party line. Consequently, the key social forces that fostered democracy in Taiwan and South Korea, as well as in Eastern Europe, have not yet fully developed in China.

The forces opposing democratization in China remain strong. Although the revolutionary elders who are determined to maintain the party's Leninist structure are dying off quickly, a new conservative force—the elders' sons and daughters, and the economic and technocratic bureaucrats—wants to maintain its positions and interests at all costs. Like the elders, this group calls democracy a divisive force. Many took the neoauthoritarian side in the debates of the late 1980s, which called for China to maintain an authoritarian government as it developed a market economy; democratization would come only after the economic reforms had produced a relatively large middle class that could support such a government. Because this approach was associated with deposed party leader Zhao Ziyang and some of its advocates participated in the 1989 demonstrations, it was rejected after June 4.

The new conservatism has taken neoauthoritarianism's place. Its supporters are from the same social groups as the new authoritarians, and they too insist that China is not ready for democracy because it does not have a large enough middle class. But unlike the new authoritarians, who sought to decrease gradually the state's involvement in the economy and society, the new conservatives want to recentralize state control over the economy and the country—especially the richer, more independent southeast coastal region—in order to strengthen the regime's power and increase revenues. The decentralization and regionalization that have accompanied China's move to the market, however, may have progressed to the point that it is impossible to reimpose centralized control.

The regime and its ideologues have also increasingly emphasized nationalism. Antiforeigner, especially anti-American, sentiment was expressed openly by ordinary people as well as officials when China lost its bid in 1993 for the 2000 Olympics. As the vitality of Marxism-Leninism-Maoism has waned because of its association with the destructive policies of the Mao era, along with China's move to the market, and the worldwide decline of socialism, the regime is pushing nationalism and a Singapore-like Confucianism as unifying ideologies. The revival of Confucianism, however, may be a double-edged sword. While officials stress its authoritarian and hierarchical elements, some intellectuals see it as potentially supporting democratization because it calls for criticism of those who abuse power.

Democratic by Default

It is unlikely that the rule of a few old men can guarantee the stability that China's increasingly pluralistic society desires. Perhaps democracy's greatest attraction is that it provides procedures that can create a degree of order and predictability. When the current collective leadership begins to encounter troubles—as it will—its superficial unity may disintegrate and chaos may threaten. Then its authority based on the promise of stability will be undermined.

Moreover, neither nationalism nor a renewed Confucianism is likely to hold China's diverse, decentralized regions together. A form of federalism may be the only political arrangement that can unite Beijing with its increasingly independent provinces—and effectively incorporate Hong Kong as well as Taiwan someday. Federalism, which is implicitly a representative form of government, may be the most feasible structure for maintaining Beijing's hold over its constituent parts.

Even more threatening to the party is the widespread anger with rampant corruption in the party and government bureaucracies. Although the leadership has launched campaign after campaign against corruption—including purging top leaders in the Beijing party government—the effect has been negligible. Legal action and exposure in the press may be the only ways to curb corruption and moderate social discontent. Perhaps nothing frightens a Chinese official more than chastisement in the press. Using the courts to defend individual rights and the media to expose corrupt officials will not necessarily produce an independent judiciary or a free press in China, but it may allow some protection for individual or group rights and may make the press more independent and critical of abuse of power.

Democratization may thus evolve in China not because of choice, but because of necessity. With a much larger, more pluralistic society, and with a more entrenched Leninist structure, it may take much longer for China to democratize than the several decades it took Taiwan and South Korea. Nevertheless, the possibility of the emergence of some form of democracy in China in the first half of the next century is not unrealistic. The shape Chinese democracy takes is likely to be different from than its neighbors. Already some of that shape may be seen in the political changes of the reform decade. But whatever form it takes, it will be uniquely Chinese.

13. The Leader in the Shadows: A View of Deng Xiaoping

September 1996

LUCIAN W. PYE

Perhaps never in human history has an established society gone through such a total transformation—without a war, violent revolution, or economic collapse—as did China with the ending of Mao Zedong's reign and the emergence of Deng Xiaoping as paramount ruler. The leitmotiv of Mao's China was orthodoxy, conformity, and isolation; a whole people walking in lockstep, seemingly with only one voice, repeating one mindless slogan after another. All Chinese appeared to be united in a state of egalitarian autarky. To have read one newspaper was to have read them all; to have heard one official's briefing was to have heard them all.

In amazing contrast, Deng's China was a congeries of elements, not an integrated system at all. Regional differences suddenly surfaced. Some urban centers vibrated to the currents of international commerce, its youth in tune with the latest foreign fashions, while the great rural masses reestablished bonds with their ancient folk cultures; and nearly everybody rejoiced over the ending of Maoist orthodoxy and politics by mass campaigns. Above all, economics and politics seemed to adhere to different rules, so that there was openness here, controls there. All the different voices saying different things made it hard to hear any one authority giving vision and guidance. As the people scrambled to look after their private selves, corruption seeped in, and while the government did not seem really to expect people to obey all its orders, it also acted erratically, sometimes cruelly.

Politics in Mao Zedong's China was theater, and there was constant drama, albeit in a tiresome Chinese style. The chairman was a master manipulator of public sentiments. Political life was an incessant stirring of emotions, as the whole society careened first in one direction and then another. But in the implementation of public policy, Mao's record was unimpressive, except for the appallingly cruel treatment of people. No other Chinese ruler matched him in the number of people killed, banished from their homes to rural exile, imprisoned in the gulags and in the caste-like categories of class identities, and starved in policy-produced famines.

In modern times the Chinese have proclaimed one "revolution" after another, but with only modest actual progress or change; with the more humble label of "reform," Deng's rule brought a real revolution. Yet in Deng's China there was no visible leader, no conductor, indeed no orchestra. Everyone of course knew the name of the paramount leader, but he rarely made a public appearance. State policy was, however, extraordinarily beneficial to the Chinese people. China experienced genuine economic progress: living standards dramatically improved, people became freer to move about and attempt to better themselves, and instead of hearing only empty promises they could begin to see substantive advances in their lives. China at last began to take on some of the appearances of a modern society, albeit a less developed one.

The Magician . . .

The changes seemed nearly miraculous, and it is therefore understandable to ask how far Deng Xiaoping should personally be credited. It must be acknowledged at the outset that it is far from easy to arrive at firm answers about Deng's eventual status, especially because he chose to operate in quiet ways often out of the public eye. Deng was like the Chinese magician who, in his unassuming manner and dress, is no different from his audience and whose prattle suggests that he is as surprised as the audience at the wonders taking place—not at all like the Western magician who is as much the center of attention as the feats he performs. The extraordinary and dramatic changes in China would seem to have called for a larger-than-life charismatic leader-magician who could project his persona to captivate the imagination of a whole population. Yet Deng rarely appeared in public and almost never used the mass media personally.

There was something strange, almost unnatural, in Deng's approach to television. First he brought it to China so that more than 560 million people could watch it every day. But then, during the years he controlled the state's propaganda apparatus and had an urgent agenda for change, he unaccountably shunned using what is manifestly the most powerful technology yet invented for mobilizing public opinion. Imagine what a Gandhi, a Nehru, a Nkrumah, or any other modern national leader trying to educate his public would have done if he had the reach of China Central Television available. Western political consultants would have advised Deng to exploit vigorously his access to television to get across his message of change.

The potential payoffs from television that Deng had earlier denied himself were dramatically demonstrated in January 1992, when he was persuaded by his *mishu,* or faithful secretary, Wang Ruilin, and his two daughters, Deng Nan and Deng Rong, to make a trip to southern China during which he briefly appeared on television. The act electrified the entire country, suggesting to the Chinese that politics had again been turned around, and the way was opened for the publication of a spate of articles praising more economic liberation and reform. It seems undeniable that at any time in the late 1980s and early 1990s Deng could have severely set back his political opponents by openly attacking them with the novel power of television, but he never made such a public move. If he truly wanted to overwhelm the so-called "hard-liners," his leftist enemies, and open the way to uninterrupted reforms, why had he not years before mounted a concerted campaign in the new electronic medium, thereby mobilizing the Chinese people who were craving progress?

The reason is simple: Deng was behaving like a conventional Chinese political leader. This apparent self-denial was only peculiar from a Western point of view. What Deng did was totally normal according to standard Chinese practices. The great leaders of traditional China were all supposed to have unassuming manners and private virtues, and none of the oratorical skills or the heroic posturing of Western leaders. China does not have the finger-pointing, sword-waving, horseback-riding statues that can be found throughout parks in Western cities. Deng's quiet approach to leadership conformed to important norms in traditional Chinese political culture, a political culture that was shaped by the role model of mandarin-bureaucrats and semidivine, superman emperors, leaders who operated out of sight, secretly, behind the scenes.

To understand Deng's accomplishments in the context of Chinese culture it is necessary to start with a paradox: although Deng Xiaoping was the paramount leader during what has been China's most revolutionary period of change, his style of leadership was more traditional than that of other recent Chinese national leaders. Deng's behind-the-scenes leadership and his nonuse of television were indeed extraordinary examples of the supremacy of culture over structure and rationality in responding to new technologies.

In all cultures the mystique of authority rests on the illusion that rightful leaders are somehow different from the mass of people. The magic of authority resides in the mind of a public eager to show deference to its leaders. With cunning wisdom, the world of Chinese officialdom long operated on the principle that the best way to exploit such fantasies of omnipotence was to keep top leaders largely out of sight.

The Chinese logic that, the greater the leader the more invisible the personage, contributed decisively to the total failure of the Chinese to develop the arts of oral persuasion as nurtured and admired first in Athens and Rome and then in parliaments and congresses. Modern Chinese national leaders risked diminishing their aura of greatness by speaking publicly, an activity generally left to lesser figures who could not hope to raise their prestige by engaging in the shrill shouting and barking that passes for oratory in China.

Deng's refusal to mount the political stage and exploit the manifest powers of modern mass media technologies thus conformed to a long-standing Chinese tradition. But it was not just the Chinese people who assumed that they knew all that was necessary to fathom Deng's goals, values, and political methods. China-watchers in the West also claimed to understand this nonpublic man. Deng's image as a superman was most vivid for those who were the most removed from the realities of his rule. Like Gorbachev's, Deng's popularity was greater with Westerners than with his own people. *Time* magazine twice chose Deng as its Man of the Year even though the magazine's editors could provide no empirical evidence that he had actually caused what they found good in China at the time, or that he believed what they thought he believed.

. . . and Invisible Puppeteer

Since Deng Xiaoping did not operate as a public figure, people had to assume that his greatness lay in his ability to manipulate events from behind the scene, much like a puppeteer. But how did he do it?

Seeing the man in person provides no clues. He enters the room at the slow, unanimated pace at which great authority is expected to move in China, the exact opposite of the vigorous American politician or executive.

He is surrounded by his assistants, all of whom seem a head taller. It is said that he is five feet tall, but that is surely an exaggeration. He awkwardly greets his guests; his handshake is limp, without life, almost as though the nicotine stains had taken all the strength from his fingers. As he settles into an overstuffed chair his sandaled feet barely touch the floor, and indeed hang free every time he leans forward to use the spittoon. His provincial Chinese haircut brings out the contours of his skull to make his head seem even bigger than it is, an impression that is exaggerated because he appears to be almost without a neck.

He doesn't bother to communicate any emotion. Even when he throws back his head for a ritualized, cackled laugh there is no sign of real feelings. As a host he makes a feeble pass at being jovial, but he is not warm; indeed, he seems oblivious to the uses of charm. When he speaks of enemies, such as the Soviet Union or the Gang of Four, it is without animus but straightforward and low key. He is known to rattle off statistics in the manner of Chinese cadres who strive to suggest by extreme precision that they are in command, or at least that they have good memories. He has an atrocious Sichuan accent that makes his words slur together in a gargle. Like Mao, who in his old age became unintelligible to all but his faithful interpreters, Deng in his last years usually has his aides at hand—primarily his daughter—to make his utterances into intelligible communications.

To the observer he reveals not a hint as to how he was able to manipulate people and lead a huge nation. There are few signs of liveliness of mind, of wit or humor, and no sustained, systematic pursuit of ideas; only cryptic remarks, shorthand indications of opinions, or dogmatic assertions of policy.

People come away from meeting Deng Xiaoping with different reactions. Not surprisingly, many are convinced that they have discovered that what they wish for China is also what Deng wants. For some, however, the most lingering impression is the absence of any signs of affect, no hints as to his understanding of how emotions work. What he has to say is straightforward enough, but there is no attempt to reach out and win over others by the bonding powers of sentiment. Equally, there is no attempt to awe his audience, or to capture its imagination. One could call his approach businesslike; it is, however, not surprising that former Secretary of State Henry Kissinger, who was peculiarly sensitive to the workings of personal chemistry in diplomacy, concluded that Deng was a "nasty little man."

Deng did not physically communicate the secret of his greatness because the mystique of what was special about him could not be seen. But by doing almost nothing to cultivate his public image or persona, Deng went well beyond the traditional avoidance of public posturing by Chinese leaders. It was not that he discouraged any suggestion of a cult of personality; he actually seemed to work at creating his anonymity. He rarely attended any of the grand international meetings where he could have rubbed shoulders with other world leaders. In contrast to Mao, Deng managed China's foreign affairs with a less personalized form of diplomacy.

Within the sphere of China's leadership, he could easily have been the prime minister or party chairman after the removal of Hua Guofeng from those posts, yet he chose to be merely a deputy prime minister, a designation that created awkward protocol problems for the world of diplomacy, precisely because everyone knew that he was in fact the supreme leader. And eventually, presumably to gain even greater power, he abandoned all posts and offices to be just a common citizen who also happened to be China's paramount leader. As such he must have been the most powerful private person in all of Chinese history. But any formal office would have limited his powers. People were thus free to imagine him as being truly omnipotent, far more in command than if his powers were only those assigned to a particular person or job.

By not having a formal rank and office, Deng also was able to avoid accountability. With no assigned post and no set responsibilities, risk taking became possible. This puppeteer was truly invisible, for he did not appear to have his hands on any recognizable levers of power, and was happily freed from all the customary standards for evaluating performance. How could one criticize someone who was an elderly private citizen, who played bridge with his cronies twice a week, went swimming regularly, happily chain smoked, and played with his grandchildren every day? But in the end accountability could not be entirely avoided, and when things did go wrong, such as the Tiananmen massacre, for example, Deng became the target of diffuse and equally unbounded blame from both foreigners and Chinese.

Climbing the Greasy Pole

To understand how this seemingly ordinary and unassuming man could have so dramatically changed the lives of nearly one and a quarter billion people, it is helpful to begin by asking how he became paramount leader in the first place. He was neither popularly chosen nor legally designated. Instead, several factors in Chinese political culture helped produce a vague and indeterminate process that without much turmoil yielded the unarticulated consensus that Deng Xiaoping should be China's supreme decision-maker after Mao.

Deng's elevation was furthered by the extraordinary and instinctive deference the Chinese give to old age and seniority, a propensity underlying the Chinese tendency to have a semipermanent gerontocracy. By merely being one of the Communist Party elders, a Long March veteran, a colleague of Mao Zedong, Zhou Enlai, and all the other heroes of the party, Deng was enveloped by the aura of unchallengable authority and thus automatically anointed a leader.

The authority of age reinforced the Chinese manner of not distinguishing between status and power. People with high status are simply powerful figures, regardless of their formal positions or offices. Therefore Deng's status as the senior Great One meant that his views and preferences had to be respected over the views of those who merely had official positions; and the power inherent in status ensured that there could be no real retirement for those who were known to be important.

In speculating about Deng Xiaoping's ultimate place in Chinese history one needs to keep in mind that Chinese respect for age is, in a peculiar way, countered by a powerful cultural propensity to give only lip-service respect to the dead while easily ignoring their last wishes, if those happen to be inconvenient. A culture without a strong legal tradition has no way of enforcing the last wills of the deceased, and in China it was enough merely to show ritual respect to the spirit of the dead. Furthermore, the Chinese rule is, "Speak no ill of the elders—until after they die."

The treatment of Mao confirmed this rule. He was totally above criticism until his death, and then it became commonplace to fault him, especially for his last years when he was, ironically, the elder beyond criticism. With few exceptions, Chinese heroes honored in life are seen after death to be flawed men with feet of clay. In other cultures time seems to work to enlarge the reputation of deceased heroes, but in China the popular images of Sun Yat-sen, Chiang Kai-shek, and Mao Zedong have all shrunk with time. This helps to explain the Chinese paradox of having living leaders who are larger than life but of not having an established pantheon of great heroes. (Deng will almost certainly be criticized after his death since he had few endearing qualities.)

Deng's rise to power was facilitated by the situation in China after Mao's death. He benefited from the two most profound but paradoxical legacies of the Cultural Revolution. That decade of horror shattered whatever illusions the Chinese had about the potency of ideology; above all, it left them profoundly cynical about Marxism. Yet it also taught the Chinese that the dangers of anarchy were very real and intensified their deeply held cultural fears of *luan,* or disorder. As a consequence, they wanted an end to ideological politics but they also remained fearful of unpredictable change and hence sympathetic to heavy-handed authoritarianism, even to the point of tolerating and rationalizing the need for repression. This distinctive combination of attitudes provided the basis for legitimacy for the Deng era. The Chinese people had clearly had enough of grand collective visions and were ready to focus on private concerns, but at the same time they wanted political stability and public order. For the authorities this meant they needed to keep their own power struggles muted, but it also gave them justification to use force to repress political dissent.

Deng caught the Chinese public's imagination by becoming leader at a time when all Chinese wanted to rid themselves of the memories of the Cultural Revolution. Nobody associated with the horrors of that awful period of Chinese history could have effectively ruled the country. Once Deng, who had been a prime target in the Cultural Revolution and sent into exile, was rehabilitated and back in Beijing, he was universally seen as an innocent and victimized comrade, and thus a deserving hero who was also remembered as a leader during the "good years" before the "lost decade." His son Pufang had been permanently crippled by the Red Guards when he was thrown from a fourth floor window at Beijing University. Deng's younger brother committed suicide for being related to the "Number Two Capitalist Roader."

With revulsion over the Cultural Revolution dominating public sentiments, it did not take much skill for Deng to push aside those who were close to Mao when the chairman plunged the country into disaster. Deng could go about quietly removing, first, the hapless Hua Guofeng, whose claim to leadership rested solely on Mao's mumbled words, "With you in charge, I'm at ease." Then it was equally easy to purge others such as Wang Dongxing, the head of Mao's bodyguards, Wu De, the mayor of Beijing, and anyone else tainted with bad memories from the Mao era.

The Chinese public welcomed Deng's businesslike style of speaking whatever was on his mind. After Mao's hyperbole and the decades of Aesopian language on the part of all Chinese leaders, it was as though a window had been opened to let in fresh air when Deng spoke out. He did not seem to have a hidden agenda, and he was not trying to be clever. At last there seemed to be a degree of honesty and down-to-earth common sense in China's political language. But over time, as Deng settled in as paramount ruler, his language did revert occasionally to the old Communist mode. He began to make preposterous boasts about Chinese socialism surpassing the advanced industrial countries while slipping more and more into cryptic slogans for guiding the country's business. (After the collapse of the Soviet Union, Chinese officials had to try to make sense out of Deng's dictum that "One cold war is over, two new ones have started.")

As the reforms began to take shape under his formal guidance, Deng seemed to be operating without a set plan or a complete vision of what he wanted for China. Rather, he was primarily responding to the universal desire of the Chinese people to escape from the stifling effects of Mao's rule. All Deng had to do was to revive one of Mao's epigrams, "Seek truth from facts," and add his own, "Practice is the sole criterion of truth," to be seen as heralding a new day for China. The Chinese had had enough of impossible dreams, and as they came out of their times of folly they were jolted into an awareness that China was not leading the world into the wonders of communism but rather stumbling far behind not only the West but all its Asian neighbors.

Authoritarianism Tempered with Anarchy

Deng thus became the symbol of the times at a moment in history when China had to break out of its isolation, abandon its absurd ideological rhetoric, and let in a little common sense. While this process was taking place, Deng benefited from the Chinese mystique about leadership. Following the imperial tradition, the Chinese assume that there is always a superior figure responsible in a vague way for whatever is happening in the country, and even in nature. The emperor figure is ritualistically bound to the country's fate, but not in the precise and indelible way greatness is established in Western cultures. The Chinese measure of greatness is limited almost entirely to private virtues, not public skills.

But why was Deng's traditional Chinese approach to leadership so effective in the post–Cultural Revolution environment? The nonpublic leadership style of the mandarin-bureaucrat was designed to be effective when there was an entrenched bureaucratic state and a society hierarchically ordered and well established. Post–Cultural Revolution China, in contrast, was in a state of disorder because Mao had disrupted the party and the government and had shattered public institutions.

Paradoxically, two key features of Chinese culture made the mandarin-administrator's role an effective one even in such chaotic circumstances. First, the period of disorder had left the public intensely anxious to find stability and order, and for the Chinese this meant seeking hierarchical arrangements. People wanted to know who they should look up to for guidance and thus they needed a clear sense of who was superior and who was inferior. Second, their reaction to their anxiety was to adhere ever more strongly to their basic communitarian or group-oriented values—that is, they wanted to belong to some sheltering group. This combination of seeking out their assigned group or collectivity and, once in their offices, factories, schools, neighborhoods, or communes, of spontaneously arranging themselves in their proper hierarchical slots, meant that a remarkable semblance of order was restored in record time immediately after Mao's death. People who only a year or so before had passionately clashed with each other were now able to work together.

Deng's basic approach of not trying to command and control totally but allowing a great deal of independence and autonomy, and above all delegating authority, were what China needed. The people could feel that even though they could not see him at work, Deng as their paramount leader was in full control. The public mood and the objective circumstances in China when Deng came to power were ideally suited for the restoration of the basic essence of the traditional Chinese style of government. The topmost leaders could solemnly proclaim an ideology that required only lip service; lesser officials could freely practice feigned compliance (and as long as they did not challenge the ideology they could do what they thought best for themselves and their communities); and the masses could pursue their own interests as they operated in their small groups. In a phrase, it was a form of authoritarianism tempered with anarchy.

The Master Administrator, Chinese Style

Deng's approach to government was that of the behind-the-scenes manipulator, the master administrator. To the Western mind, imbued with the principle of rule by law, the concept of an administrator suggests careful attention to regulations, details, processes, procedures, and forms, while remaining impersonal, unreachable to special pleading and totally task oriented. In China, coming out of a very different mandarin-magistrate tradition, the ideal administrator, while possessing some of these qualities, was primarily the skilled master of human relations. The key to manipulating power was knowing how to read human character so as to spot individual strengths and weaknesses, with the ability to control subordinates, manipulate superiors, and play off equals.

Confucian mandarin-administrators could build guanxi networks, or webs of personal ties, while always pretending to observe propriety according to a moralistic ideology. When they turned their attention outward to deal with the public they followed two somewhat contradictory rules of behavior. They were expected to be benevolent toward the people and sensitive to their basic wishes and desires. They were also called on to be personally involved in the punishment of wrongdoers. Unlike the Western bureaucratic administrator, the Chinese mandarin had to prove himself capable not just of ordering penalties but of actually supervising extremely harsh forms of torture.

In following the Chinese administrative tradition, Deng was the master of the insider's art of personnel management. As for his approach to the public, Deng was sensitive to the people's wishes: he understood their craving for economic progress and improvements in their material well-being. He knew that people wanted a better life for themselves and their families, and that they would respond enthusiastically to material incentives. But in the Chinese tradition he also accepted the need to be ruthless in administering punishment if necessary.

Throughout his career Deng cultivated an image of toughness, of being anxious to make hard choices, to take on challenges, to prove that he was not afraid of a fight. Westerners generally find it difficult to reconcile Deng's sympathy for the people's welfare with this posture of toughness. Deng gained a reputation for it early, while carrying out the land reform program, by urging peasants to kill landlords because, as he said, once they had blood on their hands they would be loyal to the party. In intraparty struggles he had the reputation of being the hard-headed, aggressive investigator of misdeeds and of standing up to the Soviet leadership in polemical battles. And, of course, there was his "Three Don't Be Afraids" speech during the Tiananmen crisis in which he told the Politburo that it should not be afraid of foreign opinion, public reactions, or the shedding of blood.

It was the way in which he played the insider's game that made Deng the quintessential Chinese administrator. He understood that power resided in the management of officials. Yet Deng was also almost unique among Chinese leaders in his understanding that it was possible to delegate responsibilities while staying in total command. His distinctive leadership style was to find the right person for each job and then to step back and allow the appointee to perform, a very untraditional Chinese practice. It was second nature for him to leave lesser officials to work out problems on their own. Mao's style was that of reigning and ruling; of withdrawing from daily operations for long periods, but then coming in and troubling himself with all manner of petty details. Deng rarely intervened in details, except in the making of personnel appointments. Thus, much of the specifics of the economic reforms can be credited to Prime Minister Zhao Ziyang, and the cultural opening to General Secretary Hu Yaobang. All these characteristics of Deng as the behind-the-scenes administrator suggest an extraordinarily self-confident and secure personality.

The Limits to Pragmatism

It has been conventional to summarize Deng Xiaoping's political philosophy with the single term: pragmatism. Deng earned the label largely because of his often quoted statement that, "It doesn't matter whether the cat is black or white as long as it catches mice." This suggested that he was unencumbered with ideological constraints and thus would be able to focus on efficiency as his guiding principle. To a large degree this was a fair judgment as far as economic policies were concerned. By restoring the reign of common sense and abandoning the more egregious follies of Mao's economic policies, Deng did preside over a transition to a more efficient economy. Certainly he was not ideologically troubled by the differences between the public and the private sectors of the economy; the rule was simply "getting rich is glorious."

But even in the economic realm there were limits to Deng's pragmatism. He replaced the elitism of ideologues with an equally elitist view that technocrats had almost magical powers to bring about economic development. One can read Deng's *Selected Works* and find no evidence that he appreciated the true functions of markets and entrepreneurs, or even the basic rationale for price reform. What one finds instead is his strong faith in technocrats, technology, and people's preoccupation with material betterment—all of which could be consistent with continuing the state enterprises while trying to make them more efficient. In this respect Deng might properly be classified with some of the leaders of the developing East Asian countries, from South Korea to Singapore, who found a positive role for state intervention in speeding up economic development.

There were other significant limits to Deng's pragmatism. The most important become self-evident when the division between economics and politics is taken away. Politically there were certain values Deng would not sacrifice for the sake of economic efficiency, the most important being the organizational integrity of the party and its monopoly on political power.

This still leaves open the question of Deng's motivations about political power. Did he have only a "pragmatic" objective of power for power's sake? Or did he have a more "sacred" mission for which he felt it essential to monopolize all power? The more one probes for hints of Deng's real political objectives, the more it seems that he was in many ways surprisingly ambivalent about change for China.

Deng wanted to see China wealthy in a materialistic sense and strong internationally, but he also feared that China could be robbed of its essence and contaminated by foreign influences. Deng's ambivalence was thus similar to that of the first generation of Chinese reformers who, in the nineteenth century, formulated the idea of adopting Western technology while preserving essential Chinese values. Their formula was that values could be categorized as either *ti,* which are "essential" and hence Chinese values, or *yong,* which are merely "utilitarian," and thus useful. But in Deng's case there was one critical difference: the ti he would protect from the "spiritual pollution" of "bourgeois liberalism" in building his "socialism with Chinese characteristics" was in fact already a foreign import, Marxism-Leninism. Like the turn-of-the-century reformers who thought it possible to welcome Western technology while preserving Confucianism, Deng believed it possible to have economic development based on Western capitalistic methods while preserving in the political realm the Four Cardinal Principles of Marxism-Leninism.

The *ti-yong* formula never worked for precisely the reasons that the conservatives who opposed the 1898 reform movements had pointed out: it is impossible in practice to separate values arbitrarily and to erect a wall between the mental state that goes with understanding modern technology and the sociopolitical sentiments of modernity. Indeed, the formula had it the wrong way around; modernization calls for the acceptance of universalistic values associated with the world culture, though adapted to local, parochial conditions. The *ti* has to be the universal values, and it is the *yong* that should be related to Chinese realities. Deng's goal of seeking "socialism with Chinese characteristics" may turn out to be a half-step in the right direction in that it acknowledges that the universal should be a foreign import that can be adapted to Chinese conditions. Maybe, as the bankruptcy of socialism sinks into the Chinese consciousness, the formula will be changed again, to "modernization with Chinese characteristics," which might finally put China on a firmer path to progress.

Deng in the Chinese Pantheon

What is Deng's likely place in history? His ultimate standing will depend on what happens next in China. It will be decisively influenced by the immediate reactions at the time of his death and the more long-term prospects of his policies. In the short run much will depend on whether his successor chooses to establish his own legitimacy by identifying himself with Deng—as Hua Guofeng sought to identify with the memory of Mao—or whether he will seek to distance himself from his predecessor, as Deng did when he made the Gang of Four the sole villains for all the horrors of the Cultural Revolution, thereby shielding the system itself from fundamental criticism.

With respect to more long-range developments, events in China could go in quite different directions. It is entirely possible that Deng's efforts to realize economic progress without political liberalization will not work, and that political change will indeed come about. If this were to happen, history would record that Deng opened the way to forces he could not regulate. He would then take his place alongside Gorbachev: two men who started processes that went beyond their control and who consequently will be seen as somewhat failed leaders. Deng's successor might then become China's Yeltsin.

It could turn out that authoritarian repression will continue in China despite economic advances. This would seem to be Deng Xiaoping's preferred course, but if this should be China's fate, then it would again be Deng's successor who would be acclaimed by history; he would be the one who had defied the predictions of modern social science and kept China in an unnatural state of sustained repression.

Between these extreme developments there is the not at all unlikely possibility that China will continue to experience significant economic growth but only limited modifications to its repressive political system. There might be a revival of the concept of "neoauthoritarianism" as a form of "soft authoritarianism" that is compatible with continued modernization and in which Deng's successor would play the role of dictator rather than tyrant. If this were to happen, judgments about Deng's ranking in history would differ according to whether he is viewed through the perspective of economic progress or that of human rights. He would be praised in one regard and damned in the other.

The most confident overall judgment one can make of Deng Xiaoping's place in history is that he will be seen as the man of the moment during a transition decade in China's slow progression to modernization. He was the man on the spot when the Chinese were ready to turn their backs on the Maoist road to modernity. He was also wise enough to tolerate half the changes progressive Chinese craved: those that gave China substantive economic progress. The changes he refused to tolerate were the political freedoms essential for building a civil society. In the annals of history there is only a small chapter devoted to those who have advanced economic progress. The big chapters are reserved for those leaders who brought political freedom and security to their people.

14. Village Elections: Democracy from the Bottom Up?

September 1998

TYRENE WHITE

D uring President Bill Clinton's state visit to China in late June, his itinerary included a trip to a village outside Beijing whose leaders were elected by popular vote. For both the Chinese and the Americans planning the president's trip, the village stop was potentially very useful. China could use the visit to highlight its progress in promoting and implementing grassroots democracy, and to suggest the possibility of an expanded agenda of political reform. President Jiang Zemin could also use this public event to silence domestic critics of the grassroots initiative and possibly build momentum for further reforms.

The United States could use the village tour in precisely the same fashion. By exposing a skeptical American audience to signs of incipient liberalization and democratization in rural China, President Clinton might be able to increase domestic support for his trip and deflect his many critics. The village tour could be used to reiterate what has become one of the central themes of Clinton's foreign policy: the importance of freedom and democracy to economic vitality and political stability in the twenty-first century.

As it turned out, the village visit was completely overshadowed by live coverage of a joint presidential news conference and Clinton's question-and-answer session with Chinese students at Beijing University. Yet its inclusion on the itinerary was the logical culmination of a decade-long process that has transformed an obscure rural political reform into a widely touted democratization project with international and foreign policy implications. How and why did this transformation come about? And how do grassroots elections work in the context of continuing Chinese Communist Party rule? Whose interests do they serve?

Managing Dissent

In the mid-1980s, when China's economic reforms began to take off, the country's rural institutions were breaking down. The reforms had begun to undermine the state's monopoly of economic and political power, and many local cadres saw more profit in working their own fields or starting sideline businesses than in carrying out difficult jobs such as collecting taxes and enforcing birth control. Peasants grew bolder in their resistance to authority, especially as price inflation, tax increases, and corruption began to erode the economic gains of the early 1980s and incomes began to stagnate or fall. Meanwhile, local governments sometimes ran out of money to buy peasants' grain and dared to hand out IOUs instead. Predictably, relations between peasants and cadres, and between cadres at higher and lower levels, grew tense, and skittish party leaders in Beijing began to worry about the prospect of rural unrest.

It was in this context that the foundation for village-level elections was established. In 1986 and 1987, heated debate took place on a draft law on grassroots organization called the Organic Law of Villagers' Committees. Adopted on a trial basis by the National People's Congress (NPC) in June 1988, the law attempted to address the problems of village-level organization and township-village relations by establishing a system of village autonomy (cunmin zizhi) and self-management.

The bill was designed to clarify the legal status of the village, which is not a formal level of government (the township, a level above the village, is the lowest official level of government), and to limit the rapacious tendencies of township and county governments to extract as much as possible from villagers to fund local development projects, pad budgets, and boost salaries. By declaring villages to be autonomous and self-managing, supporters of the bill hoped to establish a sound basis for village organization, and to temper the power of township officials by setting clear limits to their authority and defining village obligations explicitly.

If villages were to have any chance of achieving meaningful self-rule, however, they needed leaders who were empowered to defend village interests while still carrying out those unpopular and thankless tasks—collecting taxes, enforcing birth control—that villagers resisted but the state required. This legitimacy could come only through some form of popular representation or election. To that end, the trial law called for the creation of:

- villagers' councils (comprised of all adults or a representative from each household),
- villagers' representative assemblies (comprised of delegates nominated and elected by the villagers), and
- villagers' committees (comprised typically of about five elected village leaders).

Despite intense opposition from conservative county and township cadres—who feared the new law would erode their power over village leaders—the bill took effect in 1988, only to be derailed by the 1989 democracy protests and crackdown. In the repressive climate that followed, conservatives tried to repeal the law, only to find that they were blocked by Peng Zhen, a conservative party elder who had been instrumental in navigating the law through the NPC. Peng was convinced that village autonomy would stabilize the countryside and thereby strengthen, rather than weaken, party rule. In late 1990, a party central directive endorsed the trial law, and in 1991 it began to be enacted in a variety of locations across the country.

The law's implementation over the intervening years has led to the establishment and election of village assemblies, the public posting of village finances, and the drafting of village compacts that cover rules and regulations on all aspects of village life and state policy. What has earned the law so much attention at home and abroad, however, is the practice of direct elections of village officials every three years. While the shadow of Tiananmen still hung over China in the early 1990s, few in or out of the country took much notice of the rural reform, assuming that the countryside was a conservative backwater that served as a brake on democracy, or that any elections under Communist Party rule had to be a sham.

Spreading the Word

The office in the Ministry of Civil Affairs (MCA) charged with the implementation of the village autonomy law, the Department of Basic-Level Government, worked steadily and methodically to establish model sites for villagers' autonomy in every province in the country, cultivating close ties with local authorities who were receptive to the program and attempting to win over those who were not. By 1992, contact with the Ford Foundation's Beijing office had translated into an initial cooperative agreement that allowed the MCA to bring foreign advisers and scholars to China, and to send members of the office staff to the United States for brief investigatory visits. That same year, the National Committee on U.S.-China Relations hosted an MCA delegation and introduced the visitors to the operations of local government in the United States. From this beginning the MCA office began to draw increasing media attention at home and abroad, as reporters started to investigate village self-government on their own, or with the assistance and cooperation of the MCA.

Throughout the early and mid-1990s, as international contacts, scholarly interest, and media attention escalated, the process of village elections became institutionalized in many areas. Although foreign observers, especially in the United States, were skeptical about how democratic the elections were, reporting on the topic began to shift as the shadow of 1989 receded and as more information about the electoral process became available. Chinese officials provided access to a wide variety of village election sites, including some that were exemplars of fair and competitive elections and others where elections had clearly been orchestrated by local party leaders. This gave outside observers the opportunity to gain a balanced view of the reform and draw their own conclusions. By the mid-1990s, officials who had confined themselves to the language of "villagers' autonomy" after the Tiananmen crackdown began to speak more openly about "grassroots democracy," and foreign observers, while remaining circumspect and cautious in their appraisals, began to acknowledge that village elections showed real democratic potential, even if that potential was rarely fully realized.

As Sino-American relations plunged to their nadir in the wake of the Taiwan Strait crisis of 1996, and as conservatives in Washington and Beijing pressed to gain the upper hand in domestic policy debates, those on each side seeking to avoid a breach in the relationship began to marshall evidence to support a policy of constructive engagement. By 1996 and 1997 that evidence included documentation of progress in implementing rural elections in Chinese villages, documentation that was leading even skeptical observers to appreciate the Chinese effort, however imperfect and limited it remained.

It was by this path that village self-government made its way into the seemingly distant world of foreign policy and Sino-American relations. In a landscape littered with conflicts over trade, human rights, and security issues, the grassroots democratization project is a rare piece of terrain on which Chinese interests and American values seem to converge.

How to Think about Village Elections

Village elections may aid Sino-American diplomacy, but are they useful and meaningful to Chinese villagers? Answering that question requires critical examination of some of the claims made about village elections.

Village elections are conducted democratically.

Although the Chinese press consistently makes this claim, it is true only by the narrowest definition of democracy. If by democratic one means that China's villagers get the chance to cast a ballot, then the elections are indeed democratic. If, however, one means that the candidates for village leadership have been democratically selected in a transparent process that meets with villagers' approval, and that elections to each post are competitive, or at least potentially competitive, then many—perhaps most—village elections do not yet qualify as democratic.

There is no question that hundreds of millions of rural residents now have the opportunity to vote for their village leadership team, a group that usually consists of a village chairman plus several deputies.[1] But specific election methods vary a great deal from place to place. All regions are supposed to conduct their elections according to the Organic Law of Villagers' Committees, but this still leaves ample room for provinces, municipalities, counties, and even townships to draft laws, regulations, or guidelines that specify local election procedures. In many regions local people's congresses have drafted laws or regulations, while local branch offices of the MCA have their own set of administrative regulations. This process may eventually lead to a set of harmonized procedures in individual provinces (units equivalent in population to large European nations), but for now there continues to be substantial variety in how the elections are conducted.

The one feature most areas have in common is that the number of people on the ballot exceeds the number to be elected by at least one, thus cre-

---

1. Estimates of the proportion of China's 930,000 villages that has held elections range from a low of one-third to nearly two-thirds. This means that roughly 300 million to 600 million villagers have been exposed to the electoral process.

ating a small element of competition. Villagers are asked to vote for a slate of leaders (for example, choosing five out of six or seven candidates), and may also be asked to indicate which individual on the slate they prefer as village chairman. A step beyond this is direct competition between two or more candidates for the post of village chairman, with the rest of the leadership team selected from a group of nominees that exceeds the total number to be elected by one or two. This type of competitive election first appeared in northeast China during the initial round of elections a decade ago, and was picked up quickly by other regions, such as Fujian and Hebei provinces, which have been leaders in implementing competitive elections.

Just as important as a competitive ballot is the issue of how nominees are selected. The Organic Law allows for several methods of nomination, including indirect nomination by a villagers' representative assembly, or direct nomination by any group of 10 villagers. Because such public forms of nomination can intimidate villagers or be manipulated by local party officials, some areas have recently moved to a new method of nomination called *haixuan* (literally, election by sea), in which all villagers are allowed to write the names of candidates they would support on a secret primary ballot. Then a process of public winnowing occurs until the two or three most popular candidates have been selected for the final ballot.

No matter what method of selection is used, the test is whether villagers are satisfied with the candidates who emerge, and with the process that produced them. Some provinces and regions score better on this test than others, and there can be wide variation even within the same county on how the nomination process is conducted. Interference by party and government officials at the township and county levels, or unlawful manipulation of elections by corrupt village election commissions, has led some villagers to lodge formal complaints demanding the voiding of election results. If the complaints are a sign of continuing attempts to rig elections, they are also a sign of the growing sense of empowerment some villagers feel in the face of such abuses.

Village elections are designed to prop up a repressive regime.

It is true that the Chinese Communist Party turned to village elections in the hope that they would ease tensions and create the stability that would assure unchallenged party rule. But village elections cannot be labeled a sham merely because they serve the party; they are a sham only if they do not serve the interests of villagers by making local leaders more accountable. On this point the early evidence, although partial and incomplete, suggests that many villagers believe the elections give them an increased stake and a voice in village politics. According to MCA data, voter turnout is high, including participation by absentee ballot, and roughly 20 percent of incumbents are defeated in each round of elections.

Still, it is also true that where local party officials are determined to control an election they may succeed in doing so, especially if no one in the village complains or the officials have powerful allies at higher levels. As a general proposition for all of China, however, the statement that village elections are a sham is false. The fallacy here lies in assuming that the Chinese Communist Party is one uniform, monolithic authority, when in fact it is not. If China's economic reform has given us a strange, hybrid economic system, it has also given us a strange, hybrid communist system, one in which local power, prestige, status, and money are no longer monopolized by the Communist Party. If the party were monolithic, the villagers' autonomy law would not remain controversial in some quarters. Inland agricultural regions continue to drag their heels on implementing meaningful, competitive elections, while coastal areas in northeast and southern China work to improve the process by requiring campaign speeches, ensuring full secrecy in the balloting process, eliminating proxy voting, and providing absentee ballots for residents working outside the village.

The assumption that party power is inconsistent with meaningful elections underestimates the importance of local party sanction and support for getting the process right. Where elections have been successfully implemented and where nomination is fair and competition fully integrated, the county-level party secretary is usually a strong supporter of the process, setting the tone for township and village party leaders. So while it is true that party interference can crush all meaning out of the elections and turn the process into a sham in some locations, it is equally true that a supportive party leadership at the county and provincial levels can restrain township and village officials who might otherwise skew the election results their way.

The best indicator of a democratic process is the defeat of candidates who are party members.

This is one of the most common and most misguided assumptions that foreign observers make when evaluating village elections. Certainly it is important to know that non-party candidates can not only run for election, but sometimes win, turning out incumbents who are party members. This provides outside observers with added assurance that the electoral process is reasonably competitive and fair. Viewed from the point of view of China's villagers, however, the defeat of an incumbent who holds party membership may or may not be a good thing for the village, for several reasons.

First, what villagers want is what most people want in a local leader: someone who is honest, competent, capable of improving the local economy, and efficient and thrifty with tax money. They also want someone who will defend their interests in the face of pressures from county and township officials. Depending on local circumstances, local politics, and the merits of the candidates for village chairman, villagers may choose the candidate who is a party member as their best option. They may calculate that party membership will work in the leader's favor, or that his personal or family ties with township and county officials (or, even better, factory managers) will mean more jobs for villagers in township enterprises and greater economic development opportunities. Although party membership no longer carries the clout it once did, it can sometimes be seen as an asset, not a liability, where village interests are concerned.

Second, while party members voted out of office will learn one kind of democratic lesson, those voted into office may learn another. Assuming there is open and fair competition from nonparty candidates, party members who must stand for election and reelection may begin to experience in a new way the tension between their roles as party members and as representatives of their village interests. As a result, what the party gains in legitimacy from winning elections it may lose in internal discipline as village leaders resist the implementation of orders that cut against the grain of village interests. Conversely, but equally positive from the vantage point of villagers, local party branches filled with members who must stand for re-election may become more responsive to village needs and interests and less arbitrary in their rule.

Finally, in some rural villages, the party, whatever its limitations, may be the only force that can restrain the power of a strong local clan or village faction that has come to dominate village life at the expense of the weak and vulnerable. From abroad, the party is easily perceived as the only political bully on the block. But other bullies have emerged in recent years as the power of local party branches has declined. For example, complaints are already being heard about attempts by clans to dominate local elections by engaging in intimidation and vote buying. In villages where this is the case, a strong and uncorrupted party presence would be a welcome improvement, especially if it could eliminate clan violence and break up criminal gangs. In short, the diversity and complexity of contemporary village life and politics are easily overlooked by those who see the Communist Party as the only threat to China's prospects for liberalization and democratization.

China is another Taiwan in the making, building democracy out of authoritarianism.

It is true that Taiwan's experience of first introducing elections at local levels has been noted and studied by Chinese officials, and that China's decision to begin at the grass roots echoes that experience. Yet the differences between the two are so great, and the trajectory of the People's Republic still so uncertain, that any attempts at comparison are entirely speculative.

One of the most important differences at this stage is the scope for elections in China as opposed to Taiwan. When the ruling Kuomintang (KMT) began to implement local elections in Taiwan in 1950 and 1951, it simultaneously introduced elections at the village, township, city, and district levels for positions on local councils. Like the Communist Party in China today, the KMT did not allow organized political opposition, and there was wide variation in the quality of the election process, with central and local KMT officials resorting to an array of methods to defeat, intimidate, or co-opt nonparty candidates.

The difference is that elections were not confined to the bottom of the political hierarchy, as they are in China today. The result, for China's village leaders, is that they alone have been elected to serve, while the government leaders they must answer to are appointed, and then confirmed by local people's congresses. Meanwhile, county and township officials, who are not subject to electoral politics, and with their careers, incomes, and bonuses in the hands of other unelected authorities, find themselves increasingly at cross-purposes with village cadres who live in intimate contact with their electorate and are subject, to some degree, to public accountability. Their instinct is to resist village elections altogether, or to manipulate the process in their favor to ensure the election of compliant local leaders who will make their lives easier.

No Going Back?

In the run-up to the fifteenth party congress in September 1997, the issue of extending elections to the township level was debated at senior levels and tentatively endorsed by President Jiang Zemin. And on June 10, 1998, shortly before President Clinton's trip, a Communist Party Central Committee circular announced the party's intention to "make active efforts" to extend elections to the township level. The fears and uncertainties raised by this prospect, however, appear to have forestalled the creation of a timetable for implementation.

Yet unless China moves quickly to extend the electoral process upward to the township and county levels, forcing state officials to face the same public scrutiny beginning to fall on village leaders, the contradiction between the two political cultures will grow sharper. In the end, the fate of China's experiment in grassroots democracy may hinge on whether Beijing will commit itself to extending the process upward. The risks to the regime in moving forward will be tremendous. But after promoting grassroots democracy for a decade and allowing democratic elections to take root in the countryside, the risks of retreat might be just as high.

15. An All-Consuming Nationalism

September 1999

MICHAEL DUTTON

When tens of thousands of students took to the Beijing streets this May to protest the American bombing of the Chinese embassy in Belgrade during the NATO air campaign against Yugoslavia, Western journalists expressed consternation. After years of waiting for the return of student protests and the reawakening of the democratic desires of June 1989, the events of May 1999 came as something of a shock. Here was an undeniably popular protest movement that did not chant the familiar demands for democracy and human rights the West wholeheartedly endorsed. If anything, the message of this crowd was radically at odds with the spirit of June 1989. Indeed, it seemed to reinforce the anti-Western rhetoric of the Chinese Communist Party rather than proffer a version of the West as China's future.

Here was an outburst suggesting that, on some issues at least, the Communist Party was more in touch with its constituency than were the Western journalists. But it seems that the streets of Beijing are host to quite a few popular protests that do not match this Western way of seeing. The other major protest story out of Beijing this year involves an organization known as Falun Gong. Far from being advocates of Western-style democracy, Falun Gong promotes a particular type of Chinese health and spiritual exercise regime known as *qigong*. Despite its tenuous connection to politics, the meteoric rise of the group, the fanaticism of some of its members, and its resemblance to what the party labels "heretical reactionary religious sects" have made Falun Gong appear as a threat. Suffering local-level harassment, Falun Gong responded this April by organizing 10,000 members to demonstrate outside the leadership compound in Beijing known as Zhongnanhai.

These protesters did not issue demands but instead adopted the traditional method of petitioning the emperor against injustices committed by lower-order officials. The emperors responded with anger, labeling this group the most serious challenge to party power since 1989. Both the style and the content of Falun Gong's protest, however, are light years away from the 1989 dissidents. In other words, neither the anti-American protests of May following the embassy bombing nor the Falun Gong blockade of Zhongnanhai in April followed the script the Western media imagined for the past decade or raised the demands journalists thought the Chinese populace should want.

Since 1989 the great hope of the West has always been the Chinese democratic dissident. Each arrest, expulsion, or problem suffered by the dissidents has received extensive coverage in Western news reports. Most recently, when 13 activists formed a democracy party and were arrested, the headlines in the West highlighted their plight as part of the ongoing struggle for human rights in China. While few would doubt the newsworthiness of this event, its prominence in the face of other equally compelling stories was but another telltale sign of a type of journalism motivated by both a desire for change in China and by selling copy "back home."

Undoubtedly there is a limited interest in things Chinese "back home" in the West. Yet far from trying to broaden horizons, post-1989 Western journalism on China seems as committed as its readers to this narrow focus. In general, this results in finding only the Chinese economy or human rights issues newsworthy. These two areas are judged important because they are thought to be the fault lines along which significant news will be made.

Thus China is represented endlessly in Western accounts as a dynamic or faltering economy or as a human rights and democracy problem. It is along these two narrow vectors that China has become familiar and important to Western readers. The result, in terms of selling news about China in the West, is a self-fulfilling prophecy. It is, quite literally, bad news. Moreover, by continuing to focus on human rights and economics, to the virtual exclusion of other news, Western journalists have tended to overestimate the appeal of the West within China itself in the post-1989 era. In truth, human rights and economics are two of a diminishing number of domains in China where, albeit for different reasons, the high valuation of the West common in 1989 remains largely unchallenged.

In the case of economics, the reason for this Western dominance lies with the nature of the discipline itself. Of all the social sciences, economics especially craves a scientific and universal status. Thus, while Chinese humanities and social sciences have increasingly developed under the influence of various forms of cultural neoconservatism that have themselves turned on the centrality of indigenous Chinese knowledge, economists have continued to rely on and advance universal (read Western) formulas.

The democracy movement's influence is different. Its democratic commitments are largely shared by Western journalists, as is its opposition to the Communist Party. In the post-Tiananmen era, this movement's arguments appeared not only moral, but readily understandable to a Western audience. Most of all, they appeared newsworthy.

The sea-change in values since 1989 is more opaque. First, the emergence in the 1990s of a form of "nostalgic nationalism" among former radical intellectuals is difficult to explain in any simple newsworthy manner. Where once dissidents could be described by the familiar language of Western political science, the new nostalgic nationalists cannot; their focus is on traditional Chinese knowledge, not Western imports. Second, the emergence of this nostalgic nationalism makes it more difficult to tell the story of the struggle between the party and the people in a simple fashion. This nationalism's arguments seem to confuse the battle for human rights and democracy in China—either because they are baffling to non-Chinese sensibilities, as is the case with Falun Gong, or because they seem to concede too much to the party by stressing the importance of non-Western solutions. Put simply, this new nationalism does not fit into the general categories used by Western journalists to approach news about China.

The Distorting Image

Western journalists and editors—and also, one suspects, the majority of their readers—still seem to view China through the lens of 1989 and the imagery of the man and the tank. Although this imagery may no longer be on show, it is no less dominant for Westerners. Indeed, if anything, as it has moved off the television screen and into our heads, its importance has grown, shifting from being merely a photographic image about China to being a subconscious paradigm through which to view China. As a binary opposition of good and bad, the man-and-tank image has helped frame most of "our" understandings of contemporary Chinese politics in the post-1989 era.

This is strange given that, with a different semiotic coding, one might mistake the man-and-tank methodology for the much-maligned "two-line struggle" of Maoism. After all, the logic of the man and the tank reproduces the same sort of simplicity of argument as the Maoist two-line struggle between the revolutionary and the reactionary. While Maoism was pilloried in the West for the dogmatism of its approach, few seem to object to the more recent, liberal Western version of this two-line struggle. Moral righteousness and the television-screen evidence from 1989 seem to conspire to keep this analogy in focus. As it has shifted from television image to subconscious paradigm, it has fueled a bifurcated image of Chinese street politics. On the one side are the freedom-loving ordinary people; on the other, the evil, corrupt, and authoritarian Communist Party. How could one argue against this when the evidence is summed up so convincingly by the 1989 footage? Yet when the streets filled with overtly political protesters after the 1999 bombing of the Chinese embassy in Belgrade, this binary opposition had gone. After all, how can one speak of two lines when both party and people seem to be speaking with one voice?

Left without its now-familiar trope, the West could understand the anti-American protests of 1999 only by crying foul. These protests were "orchestrated," or, more politely put, "party sanctioned." Either way, the meaning was clear. The protesters were being manipulated by the Communist Party for its own ends. The problem with this reading, however, is that it is beside the point. Manipulated or not, the popularity of the protests against the bombing was beyond doubt, the rage vented by the crowd, genuine. More significantly, the demonstrations were a sign of much broader changes taking place both on the Chinese streets and in the intellectual salons. The popular anti-Americanism was but a jingoistic expression of a new nationalism sweeping the country. While the events of May are the most political expression of this change in attitude, signs of it have been literally everywhere—from the resurrection of traditional belief systems expressed through organizations like Falun Gong to the market craze for things Chinese and traditional. Blinded by the logic of economic reform and by an intuitive belief that democracy was all-important, Westerners read these signs as individual events rather than as indications of a growing shift in Chinese attitudes.

Chinese responses to such disparate events as the 1993 decision to make Sydney, not Beijing, host of the 2000 Olympics or to America's blocking of China's entry into the World Trade Organization in 1999 are markers on a trail that show increasing popular disenchantment with the West. The resurgent nationalism was captured most dramatically in 1996, when right-wing Japanese elements claimed Fisherman Island (Diaoyu dao) for Japan and established a lighthouse on it. When the Japanese government did not respond, university students from Shanghai, Beijing, and other Chinese cities angrily demonstrated, forcing the Chinese government to negotiate with Japan and to calm the anger of patriotic students.

In popular literature, signs of this growing culture of nationalism were also clearly on show. From the widespread acceptance of Harvard Professor Samuel Huntington's culturist thesis ("the clash of civilizations") to the success of the populist 1996 bestseller, *China Can Say "No,"* one can discern a growing awareness of cultural difference and alienation from the West. These examples may be extreme, but they highlight the changing mood of China since 1989. With the exception of the most recent and striking expression of this "Chineseness," namely Falun Gong, a new nationalistic sentiment is enveloping the intellectual scene just as the products of this nostalgia are emerging in the marketplace.

Neoconservatism's Rise

Intellectually, the roots of this retro trend lie in the events of 1989. At that time liberal intellectuals viewed the past as something to be overcome. Democracy could be achieved in China, they argued, only if the vestiges of the country's feudal past were eradicated. By 1986 opponents of feudal relics could be roughly divided into two camps. The liberals argued for immediate democracy to sweep away the remnants of the past. Adherents of this view looked to the West for the model of what China could be. The other side, which was dominant by the end of the decade, argued that China was not ready for democracy. Rather, it needed a period of enlightened neoauthoritarian rule to force the economy to develop to "maturity," which would then supply the conditions for full political democracy.

The significance of this neoauthoritarian school, however, was not its familiar developmental argument but its geographic reorientation of the debate. Where Chinese liberal intellectual discourse had turned to Western models that would eliminate the vestiges of feudalism, the neoauthoritarian focus shifted the debate toward Chinese problems that required solutions. Its arguments tilted the emphasis away from Western political theory and back toward an examination of Chinese cultural conditions.

This neoauthoritarian-inspired tendency to reexamine China's culture and tradition was further reinforced by the changed political climate in post-Tiananmen China. The Stalinist freeze after 1989 made intellectuals wary of overt political comment. Generally, most employed an age-old method of protest by returning to the classics—known in Chinese as the Jia-Qian style after the emperors Jia Qing (1796–1821) and Qian Long (1736–1795).

As intellectuals adopted the Jia-Qian style of work, their own research interests began to change. They developed a different appreciation of their culture's past, its diversity, and its greatness. No longer were they interested in sweeping away the past to make way for the new and the Western. By the mid-1990s, anything new had to be appropriate for Chinese conditions.

Illustrative of this process was Lu Mingzhuo's article in *People's Daily* in July 1996. Arguing that Confucianism was at the heart of Chinese culture, Lu held that a program of Confucian moralization would benefit the nation and form a stable harmonious political order that would produce conditions aiding the development of a market economy. While the appearance of this article refocused debate on the value of Confucianism, other tendencies pushed thinking in a slightly different direction but still reinforced this interest in China-centric research.

One of the intellectual winds that blew scholarship in an Eastern rather than Western direction emerged after the appearance in 1994 of Yang Dongping's *City Monsoons: Beijing and Shanghai's Cultural Spirit.* Yang compared Beijing and Shanghai cultural expressions and suggested that these two cities had unique and important differences. This work sparked a series of publications on local and provincial cultures, and the term "area research" (*diqu yanjiu*) came into being. Area research was China-centric, highlighting the cultural complexity and differences within China as well as the fundamental differences between China and the West. In focusing on difference in the era of globalization, this school of thought helped reinforce another trend also gaining intellectual ascendancy at this time: nation studies (*guo xue*).

Nation studies focused on historical questions of the Chinese nation and civilization. By tracing the cultural uniqueness of China back to its great traditions, this school placed emphasis on Chinese value systems. Like area research, nation studies emphasized appreciation and appropriation of China's past, not importation of foreign models. These trends joined with others to form a new, more disparate tendency that became known as neoconservatism.

Thus, while the dominant intellectual trend in 1989 had led to the West, the neoconservative intellectual trend 10 years later pointed to the past. This new appreciation of the past has become known as the "second culture craze." In this new intellectual climate, most interest focused on those academics who had become familiar with Western scholarship but nevertheless recognized the centrality and greatness of China's traditions. They were thought to offer an appreciation of how to institute change in harmony with Chinese traditions.

What had begun, in part, as a forced retreat from politics now led to a new political appreciation of the past. This new generation of scholarship highlighted the greatness of the past and valorized Chinese tradition and civilization. It formed the intellectual bedrock upon which a resurgent nationalism was built. Indeed, some neoconservative voices have even suggested that it is Chinese traditional culture that will lead the way in the Asia-Pacific region and possibly the world in the twenty-first century.

This resurgent nationalistic intellectualism is markedly different from the views of the 1989 dissident or intellectual who looked longingly to Western models. In both cases, however, the values and trends inaugurated by intellectuals have tended to spill out onto the streets. In 1989 this had tragic consequences; in 1999, much less so. Indeed, the newfound nationalist nostalgia has gained a street voice not simply through the events of May 1999 or the actions of Falun Gong.

Culture for Sale

Out on the street and always ready to make a buck, the entrepreneurs of the new China have launched a neoconservative drive of their own. Where once the street signs beckoned with transliterated Western shop names, today the trend is to indigenize. An entire series of teahouses have sprung up sporting traditional Chinese names such as Ziyige (Purple Arts Pavilion), Fudao (The Way of Happiness) and Xinlong (New Dragon). Even Nike is arm-wrestled off the street by Li Ning in this battle of wills. (Li Ning was an Olympic gold medalist who became a brand name for a highly successful local line of sports clothes that rivals Nike and other imported sports labels.) Like their intellectually pontificating brethren, the Chinese neoconservative street entrepreneurs are delving deep into history to support this new fashion trend.

An entire niche for the nostalgia industry has sprung up. The result is an endless trail of products pumped out to keep alive this fad of the past. From Emperor Kang Xi to the late great Chairman Mao, money is being made on this retro revival. As with the neoconservative intellectual trends, little seems to tie together these disparate array of products other than their reference to, and indulgence of, China's past. While various fads abound, one of the strangest must surely be the resurrection of Mao and the Cultural Revolution as sales icons. Like the current neoconservative intellectualism, this street-level retro trend began shortly after Tiananmen, an effect of contemporary Communist Party initiatives.

Short of heroes and low on symbolic capital, the party tried to resurrect the movement's boy scout, Lei Feng. Alongside this youthful figure was a newly airbrushed image of the chairman. Mao, the newspaper *Law Daily* blithely stated in 1990, had come to replace Sartre as the pinup boy of young intellectuals in China's universities.

Strangely enough, by 1992 this blatantly self-interested lie launched a market craze. With the half-dead Deng in the south of China promoting the idea of capitalism, the very dead Mao in the north became an icon. Suddenly the Mao craze began to grow; by 1993 it appeared unstoppable. The state sponsored a birthday bash for Mao on the 100th anniversary of his birth, and the people joined in with alacrity. By the end of the year, approximately 11 million new posters of the born-again chairman were said to have been sold.

Meanwhile, on another street corner, party-inspired hawkers were busily selling the new disco version of "The East Is Red." Even operas by Mao's wife, Jiang Qing, were making a video comeback. By this stage, however, the party propaganda machine was outflanked by the advertising agent. That business took over party business should hardly come as a surprise. After all, the Communist Party has not had a lot of experience marketing its "product."

Unfortunately for the party, in an era in which commodification reigns, form, not content, rules. Markets will accept any content—even revolutionary content—as long as it is offered in a sellable form. In these terms, the significance of the party's post-Tiananmen gambit for power by promoting its image through the process of commodifying its iconography seems problematic. All its marketed party artifacts, while revolutionary in content, ended up carrying a different subconscious message. The new message of these "red" items was ultimately that commodities fulfill desires. Content could and would change as fashion dictated, but this message about the worth of commodities would remain intact and, like a dripping faucet, would slowly eat away at the granite face of what remained of Chinese socialism.

Thus, as the Mao craze faded into a general fad for nostalgia, the revolutionary was once again forced to struggle with the "reactionary." This time around, however, the fight was over market share. As the advertising art posters of pre-liberation Shanghai—selling everything from beer to perfume—were resurrected, it was as if the revolutionary operas of Jiang Qing were being forced to struggle against her former self, the femme fatale actress Lan Ping. By 1996 the prerevolutionary past seemed to be winning out over the revolutionary icon.

Whether it is the revolutionary or reactionary past being resurrected, nostalgia is now big business. This nostalgia of the street feeds into a nationalism that grounds the philosophies of the neo-conservatives just as it lines the pockets of those entrepreneurs who exploit it as a niche market. Under the rule of the Communist Party, we are witnessing the unruly transformation of China into a commodity culture and, as this new world of merchandising unfolds, the old world is remembered. Yet the irony of this turn of events does not stop here. Even more revealing is that this newfound attention to the past brought on both by neoconservative thinking and the nostalgia industry seems to be developing as quickly as the physical signs of that past are disappearing.

Hammering Away at the Present

Nietzsche once remarked that the great leaders of the future would philosophize with a hammer. In the case of China, it is with a jackhammer. But this transformation of the landscape is taking place at such a pace that it seems difficult to philosophize.

The good static ordering of the traditional city has been completely reorganized by the rapacious boom of capitalism and the development of technology. Within a decade, an unprecedented transformation has reconfigured the urban landscape and transformed traditional forms of life. The almost religious dedication once shown to the three devotions during the Cultural Revolution (devotion to Mao, to the party, and to socialism) gave way to a new materialism that, by the early 1980s, turned on a desire for the "three wheels" (a bicycle, a sewing machine, and a watch).

As the training wheels of a new and nascent form of consumption, the three wheels helped turn a national mind-set once fixated on the political realm. What emerged was the first signs of overt consumer desire. As the training wheels come off, a new and more indigenous form of consumption takes hold. The land that once produced nearly 20,000 variations of the Mao badge and simultaneously reduced the variety of consumer goods by 21 percent now hosts 40,000 different advertising agencies and an endless array of consumer products, including the revalued Mao badge. As this consumer revolution that enveloped the cities snakes its way to remote parts of the countryside, local practices are also revalued as commodity trinkets.

Herein lies the magic of consumption and the dynamic behind a growth in local forms of nostalgic nationalism. As it does, the mantra of Western social science—that China's economic reform will lead to political reform—remains in place. The content of these reforms appears in ways that we no longer recognize as absolute mirrors of the Western developmental road. Chinese acceptance of this seems to cause disquiet outside China, yet it is, if anything, a sign that the process the West so readily encouraged has finally begun to take root.

16. Understanding Falun Gong

September 2000

RICHARD MADSEN

The basic facts about the Falun Gong affair in China are generally known among the American reading public: On April 25, 1999, approximately 10,000 members of this movement staged a peaceful protest in front of the Chinese government's leadership compound in Beijing. The government responded on July 22 by outlawing the movement, charging that it was an "evil cult." A massive vilification campaign ensued that led to the arrests of many Falun Gong members.

In the spring of 2000, several dozen top leaders, including an air force general and a judge, were publicly sentenced to long prison terms. (Li Hongzhi, the movement's founder, now lives in the United States, which refuses Chinese government requests for his extradition.) Thousands of lesser leaders and ordinary practitioners have been more quietly prosecuted. According to the Information Center for Human Rights and Democracy, a human rights group based in Hong Kong, about 5,000 members have been sent to labor camps and about 300 tried and sent to prison. Several dozen have died or committed suicide in police custody. Nonetheless, Falun Gong members continue to stage regular peaceful protests in sensitive public locations such as Tiananmen Square, even though such demonstrations inevitably lead to their arrest.

But even sophisticated followers of international affairs understand very little of these facts. Western media do not even know how to name the movement. Falun Gong and Falun Dafa are two Chinese names for the movement. After tinkering with various translations of these names, the press just transliterates the Chinese sounds. Unsurprisingly, there is widespread confusion about how to classify it. Members of Falun Gong say that it is not a religion. International human rights advocates, joined by most of the Western media, call it a religion and see the Chinese government's suppression of the movement as a violation of religious freedom. The Chinese government calls it a "cult," which places it outside the Chinese constitution's protection of religious liberty. These confusions of classification are symptoms not only of relatively obvious differences in political ideologies but also of more subtle variations in cultural traditions between China and the West.

A "Practice" or a Religion?

To help make sense of the issue, let us start with a translation of the movement's names. Falun Gong literally means "Dharma wheel practice." As seen by those Falun Gong members whom I have met, it is indeed primarily a practice, something one does rather than something one believes. The practice involves a series of five exercises. Four are performed standing and involve stretching various parts of the body and moving one's arms in circular motions around the body. The fifth is performed sitting in a lotus position and involves focusing the mind in meditation on a visualized wheel spinning within the core of the body.

The purpose of these exercises is to channel and harmonize the *qi* that is supposed to circulate through the body. Qi is a kind of vital energy; theories about its flow and function are the basis of traditional Chinese medicine. For thousands of years, Chinese have practiced various exercises devised to regulate qi. These exercises are called *qigong* and are believed to prevent and cure illnesses, induce a general state of vigor and well-being, and extend life. Many forms of qigong have been devised by various masters. In the 1980s, an explosion of interest in qigong occurred that saw the rise of many different qigong masters, each propagating a particular form of practice, often making extravagant claims about its efficacy, and sometimes making a good deal of money in the process. To some degree, the Chinese government encouraged the development of qigong to show the world the scientific value of indigenous Chinese medicine. By the 1990s the government had become concerned about unlicensed qigong practitioners and moved to control them.

Falun Gong is a form of qigong developed in 1992 by Li Hongzhi, a railway official with no particular spiritual or medical training. One advantage Falun Gong has over other forms of qigong is that its exercises are relatively simple, can be learned quickly, and can be performed anywhere, making it ideal for people living busy lives in modern cities. Most Chinese see qigong as a form of health practice rather than a religion. They aim to improve their lives in this world rather than to achieve an afterlife. It seems reasonable for Chinese Falun Gong practitioners, therefore, to claim that they are not practicing a religion. Such a claim, however, draws on a deep structure of cultural assumptions subtly different from those in the West. Chinese traditions assume a profound interpenetration of matter and spirit, body and soul. To bring health benefits, the physical exercises of qigong must be accompanied by moral cultivation. For Falun Gong, for example, the virtues to cultivate are Truth (*zhen*), Benevolence (*shan*), and Forbearance (*ren*). And moral cultivation involves spiritual exercise, a way of focusing the mind. Like most qigong practitioners, Falun Gong members do not make a clear distinction between physical and spiritual healing. Thus, from a Western viewpoint, most forms of qigong look more like religion than medicine.

Falun Gong looks even more like a religion because of its use of folk Buddhist discourse to interpret its physical-spiritual healing exercises. The other name for Falun Gong is Falun Dafa, which literally means the "Dharma Wheel Great Dharma." *Dharma* is the Buddhist term both for cosmic law and for the doctrines taught by the Buddha that reveal the law. (Thus, although the two names are almost interchangeable, Falun Dafa emphasizes the movement's doctrinal aspects, while Falun Gong emphasizes the practices.) The Wheel of Dharma is an important concept referring to cycles of birth and death. Religious masters in China are expected to write doctrinal treatises. Following in this tradition, Li Hongzhi, Falun Gong's founder, has written lengthy books about the laws of the cosmos.

Falun Dafa can be seen as part of the long tradition of Chinese folk Buddhism. A hallmark of this tradition was that one did not have to be a celibate monk to fully practice Buddhism. Also, laypeople could be authoritative developers of Buddhist doctrine. This tradition has led to a bewildering variety of folk sects, which were usually syncretistic blends of Buddhism and folk religion. Often the teaching of these sects had a millenarian element, a belief that this world was hopelessly corrupt and would come to an end. Some of these teachings inspired massive rebellions, like the White Lotus Rebellion at the end of the eighteenth century. Falun Dafa draws on this folk Buddhist tradition and, although the published writings are not clear about this, it may even encourage some of its members to believe in an imminent end of the world.

Falun Dafa gives these folk Buddhist traditions a superficially modern twist. It uses imagery from modern science, especially astronomy, to represent its cosmic laws. The qi of the universe is a circular spinning force. It leads planets, galaxies, and the entire universe to spin in circles. The wheel of dharma is a literal wheel of energy that rotates within each properly exercised human body and connects the human person to the rotation of the cosmos. Among the Falun Dafa practitioners I have met are Chinese scientists with doctorates from prestigious American universities who claim that modern physics (for example, superstring theory) and biology (specifically the pineal gland's functioning) provide a scientific basis for their beliefs. From their point of view, Falun Dafa is knowledge rather than religion, a new form of science rather than faith. Their belief can be seen as in continuity with understandings of folk Buddhism in the Chinese cultural tradition. That tradition did not have a word directly corresponding to the Western term "religion." It simply named a variety of teachings, which were not about supernatural faith but about various ways of understanding the realities of the world.

Or Cult?

The Chinese tradition did have ways to distinguish between "orthodox" and "heterodox" teachings. According to the rationalistic scholar officials who controlled the imperial Chinese state, many folk Buddhist sects were heterodox (*xiejiao*). Holders of power in imperial China employed this term in fluid fashion to label teachings that they deemed a threat to social order. A teaching was heterodox not so much because of its intellectual content but because of the practical consequences that might flow from it. Thus, folk religious practices were basically ignored by the Chinese state as long as they kept people acquiescent to the political order, but were labeled as heterodox when they seemed to contain seeds of rebellion. It is precisely this traditional vocabulary of heterodoxy that the present Chinese government has revived to denounce the Falun Gong.

The English translation the government now gives to this traditional word for heterodoxy is "cult." Falun Gong, the government claims, is an "evil cult" that threatens society. As such it is not entitled to the protections given to genuine religions. But is Falun Gong a cult in the sense given to the word by Western scholars of religion? Usually, Western sociologists use the term to refer to a new religion, often founded by a charismatic leader, as distinguished from a sect that has broken from an established church and claims to be a purification of that church's teaching. When such cults practice beliefs widely at variance with mainstream culture, they sometimes organize themselves into closed groups that totally dominate their members' lives. On occasion such cults have led to violence, in the form of mass suicide or terrorism. The general public naturally sees such cults as a "social problem" and supports ways to control them, within the limits of basic protections of religious freedom. An Asian group that closely fits this common Western understanding of cult is Japan's Aum Shinrikyo, which carried out a sarin nerve gas attack on a Tokyo subway in 1995. Chinese government officials compare the Falun Gong "cult" with Aum Shinrikyo and the Branch Davidians in the United States. If the comparisons were apt, many measures taken by the government to suppress Falun Gong might seem justifiable by international human rights standards.

Although it does resemble the standard definition of a cult, Falun Gong does not closely fit the definition. It is, as we have seen, not so much a new religion as a recognizable variant of widespread qigong practices. Its leader is seen as a charismatic figure with extraordinary levels of insight, but most founders of Buddhist and Daoist sects in Asia—even of groups considered quite mainstream—are considered by their followers to have extraordinary spiritual capacity. Finally, most Falun Gong members are well integrated with the rest of society. For many, Falun Gong practices are attractive precisely because they do not take an undue amount of time and do not interfere with work or ordinary social life.

Some of Falun Gong's claims will seem incredible, even bizarre, to secular people, especially Westerners. For instance, Falun Gong members claim a kind of clairvoyance through a "third eye." Some, like Li Hongzhi, claim that they can levitate. But Falun Gong is by no means the only group to make such claims, and indeed it seems in continuity with a wide spectrum of Chinese religious practices. Though perhaps near the outer edge of the normal spectrum of Chinese indigenous spiritual practices, Falun Gong does not seem to go far enough over that boundary to be considered a cult.

The Government's Response

Regardless of whether it is a cult, can Falun Gong reasonably be considered a threat to Chinese society? The Chinese government claims that it keeps people from seeking appropriate medical treatment and has therefore been responsible for many deaths. The government also claims that Falun Gong's leaders are frauds who have swindled followers out of a great deal of money. Yet the level of social harm caused by Falun Gong's beliefs in the efficacy of prayer over medicine seems no greater than that alleged of religions like Christian Science. The accusations of fraud are similar to those that could be made by secular skeptics against any religious leaders accepting donations from followers who had come to believe in things unseen. A government could be justified in prosecuting specific documented abuses, but by international standards protecting the right to religious freedom, it could not reasonably suppress an entire group such as Falun Gong. In any case, Falun Gong has a strong presence in Hong Kong and Taiwan (along with adherents scattered around the world, including the United States) and is not seen as a serious social problem in these places.

Why has the Chinese government mobilized vast resources to crush the Falun Gong? The answer has less to do with the strangeness of its doctrines than with the effectiveness of its organization. Falun Gong has adapted traditional Chinese organizational practices to create a tremendously supple organization. A decentralized network of local groups linked through cadres of leaders are in contact with their counterparts at different levels of the network. This form of organization was long used by peasant rebels throughout Chinese history—and by the Chinese Communist Party during its insurgency in the 1920s and 1930s.

The traditional ways of communicating through face-to-face contact have now been supplemented by use of modern information technology. At a time when Internet use was just beginning in China, Falun Gong developed surprisingly sophisticated web sites. Although all such sites based in China have been closed down, the organization maintains several outside China and on July 1, 2000 launched a radio station, which is based in the United States and broadcasts daily into China.

The Communist Party has enough historical memory to know an effective organization when it sees one, and enough common sense to know that in its current bloated, bureaucratic, and corrupt incarnation, it no longer has such a structure. Thus any organization like Falun Gong, no matter what the content of its ideology, would be considered a threat to the Communist regime. The Chinese legal system forbids any independent associations. This means that, despite formal freedom of religious belief, no freedom of religious association exists. All churches and congregations must be registered with the government and are subject to its control. Religious believers who find this unacceptable, including "underground"

Christians who refuse to practice their faith in government-registered churches, are subject to prosecution. In connection with the campaign against the Falun Gong, prosecution of all such groups—whether folk religious, Buddhist, Christian, or Muslim—has been stepped up. Falun Gong was singled out because it was one of the most successful of these groups, one of the largest, one of the best organized and strategically placed.

Who Belongs—and Why

It is difficult to know how large Falun Gong is. The movement's leaders claim between 50 million and 100 million members worldwide; the Chinese government says only several million belong. Besides being influenced by obvious power interests, the claims are also affected by how one defines membership. Many people, perhaps, have practiced some of the Falun Gong exercises without being deeply committed to the organization.

Clearly, Falun Gong has a sociological profile that the government finds alarming. Unlike many potentially threatening religious movements in China today, Falun Gong is not comprised of people from rural areas or people at the margins of urban society. Some of its leading members have been high-ranking officials in the Communist Party, government, police, and military. At a time when economic reforms are producing increased inequality and a huge discontented population of laid-off workers and rural migrants, the regime must find it extremely threatening to have an unreliable repressive apparatus. Thus it would urgently want to root out any independent group that had gained significant allegiance among members of that apparatus.

Why would people with good positions in urban China be attracted to Falun Gong? The answer seems to be generational. Falun Gong seems to gain its greatest following among people in late middle age. After suffering through the horrors of the Great Leap Forward in the late 1950s and the Cultural Revolution in the 1960s, many in this age group nonetheless rose through seniority into middle and even upper levels of the state apparatus. Now they are being pushed aside. Some are being laid off as state-run industries try to streamline themselves in a more competitive "socialist market economy." Others hold on to their jobs but see themselves becoming increasingly irrelevant because they had never learned the technical skills necessary to succeed in the new economy. Many members of this generation are beginning to face health problems but are losing many of

their entitlements to medical benefits because of government retrenchment. They have been disillusioned by the failures of state socialism yet
have no way to escape from it. One reaction is complete cynicism, which
leads to the corruption so rampant in China today. Another response is attraction to groups such as Falun Gong, which promise physical health and
moral rehabilitation.

Most members practiced Falun Gong precisely because they saw it as an
apolitical response to their trouble. After the June 4, 1989 crackdown, political mobilization seemed too dangerous. But Falun Gong has drawn them
into politics in unexpected ways. It is unclear why the group's leadership
dared to challenge the government by organizing the April 1999 demonstration. The demonstrators were protesting an article that had appeared
in a Tianjin magazine warning about the danger of cults. In the United
States, a religious group offended by such an article might aim its criticism
at the author or the magazine in which it was published. But in China, especially among the older socialist generation, the government is held responsible for slanderous articles in the press—even if government
propagandists have not written them, the government is responsible for
preventing their publication through its powers of censorship.

But if Falun Gong wanted to express its grievances to the government,
why not do so in a quiet way, rather than stage an unlawful demonstration
in one of the most sensitive spots of China at a time when the government
was nervously anticipating the tenth anniversary of the Tiananmen crackdown? The answer is that the leadership of Falun Gong was either extremely naïve or megalomaniacal and that significant numbers of followers
were unquestioningly loyal to this leadership. In any case, the government
must have felt that if Falun Gong could get away with such a demonstration, other groups would become similarly emboldened—with dangerous
consequences for a brittle regime that cannot accommodate any independently organized dissent.

Thus, in July 1999 the government not only banned Falun Gong but
launched an old-fashioned, all-out political campaign against it. Within a
few weeks, a notoriously inefficient government had published a series of
thick books detailing Falun Gong's alleged abuses. Researchers at universities and academies of social science were called together for day-long
meetings and told to organize exposés of Falun Gong. (I saw a document
presented by the public security bureau at one such institution outlining
Falun Gong's flaws and instructing the researchers to use their knowledge
to fill in the details. So much for objective scholarship.) Criticism and

self-criticism sessions were held at all levels of society to expose Falun Gong members and force them to recant. For months, most of the print and broadcast media were devoted to exposés and denunciations of Falun Gong. Arrests were made and show trials held.

Nevertheless, a steady stream of Falun Gong members continues to demonstrate and court arrest within China. The government crackdown may even be a benefit to Falun Gong. Like many other qigong movements that have been allowed to develop in China in the past 20 years, it may have been a fad that would eventually have faded and been replaced by the latest teachings of a new master. But now that its survival has become an international issue, it will have the notoriety and support to extend its life.

The Reaction in America

Reaction to the Falun Gong affair among the human rights community in the United States has been somewhat ambivalent. The United States State Department's latest annual report on human rights sharply criticizes China for its suppression of Falun Gong. Some members of Congress have also pointed to the crackdown as an important example of the Chinese government's violation of the right to free religious expression. But Falun Gong does not have robust backing from the American constituencies that usually support defense of religious freedom. Currently this constituency consists of an unstable mix of liberals, who support religious freedom as a matter of principle, and Christian conservatives who are especially concerned about the persecution of underground Christians in China. The tolerance of some secular liberals is tested not only by what they perceive as the bizarre nature of Falun Gong teachings about the cosmos but also by the conservative nature of its teachings about morality. In particular, Falun Gong teaches a conservative sexual ethic that prohibits homosexuality and criticizes female equality. And while Christian conservatives in the United States may approve of the Falun Gong sexual ethic, they see Falun Gong as a false religion. Meanwhile, the American political center does not want to push the human rights issue so hard that it would disrupt commercial and political engagement with China.

Thus, although Falun Gong may receive some basic support from the United States and the international human rights community, its capacity to survive will largely depend on its own resources. But it does seem to be extraordinarily resourceful and resilient. Perhaps the Falun Gong affair is an example of the wider role that religious practice will have around the world in the twenty-first century. Secular ideologies have lost their capacity to inspire the great sacrifices needed to ignite social movements. But religions, including Falun Gong, retain their ability to inspire martyrdom. At the same time, the intellectuals who once were the main creators and carriers of secular ideologies have largely been co-opted. In China, for example, many intellectuals who were dissidents in the 1980s are now entrepreneurs or professional consultants to multinational corporations, too busy and too content to lead social movements. However, many in the middle and lower reaches of societies such as China have been left out of the benefits promised by globalization. Religious teachings and practices provide ways to talk about and to deal with their pain and also act as channels of communication with coreligionists around the world. Whatever consequences Falun Gong may have for the short-term stability of China, movements like it will play a large role in the long term of twenty-first-century history.

17. China's New Leadership: The Challenges to the Politics of Muddling Through

September 2002

TONY SAICH

The sixteenth party congress that is to be held this fall should be remarkable in a number of ways. Most important, if Vice President Hu Jintao becomes the new general secretary of the Chinese Communist Party, it will mark the first time that the leadership of the party has changed hands relatively peacefully. Leadership transition, always extremely contested, usually has followed some major policy failure and has been accompanied by factional infighting. Even Deng Xiaoping lost his first two choices as general secretary (Hu Yaobang and Zhao Ziyang) to party intrigue before he settled on the third, Jiang Zemin. Given this track record, the ascendance of Hu would mark a considerable achievement in terms of institutionalizing succession. Not to appoint him would risk throwing the party once again into turmoil and factional fighting.

Hu has been groomed for senior leadership in the decade since Deng promoted him. This does not mean that the current general secretary, Jiang Zemin, will withdraw entirely; even with no official position he will seek to influence the political process from behind the scenes, as did his mentor, Deng. In contrast with past congresses, leadership unity seems remarkably stable but this is premised on continued economic strength. A sharp economic downturn that jeopardized the capacity to dispense economic largesse or an unforeseen crisis could easily undermine the façade of unity and reveal deeper factional cleavages. In addition, the continued presence of Jiang, Prime Minister Zhu Rongji, and National People's Congress Chair Li Peng, all anxious to preserve their various and sometimes conflicting legacies, means that the new leadership will have limited capacity to launch radical initiatives.

These factors could set serious constraints for the new leadership since it will face many challenges, some of which will require new thinking and clear action. The economic challenges will be difficult enough to meet, but the leadership will also have to come to grips with the problem of social inequity that has arisen during the transition. And it must provide better governance and some kind of effective moral vision to give purpose to and bind together an increasingly diverse society.

Reform: Now for the Hard Part

The fundamental problem for the new leadership is that all the easy parts of reform have been completed. Deng Xiaoping's strategy was to move first in those areas of reform where there was least resistance and that would bring maximum benefit to the most people. Politically, this was extremely important in building credibility to shift China away from state planning to an increasingly marketized and open economy. Deng's successors must complete the reform process by dealing with intractable problems in the enterprise, financial, and rural sectors. Inevitably, reforms also create losers, at least temporarily, as well as those who will not benefit as much as others have. Membership in the World Trade Organization (WTO) will provide external discipline that will hasten the need for further reform.

Problems in the economy can no longer be isolated and dealt with discretely and individually. The problems are nested one within another, thus requiring comprehensive solutions. The core challenge is how to allocate resources more effectively within the economy to ensure that markets function better. The nonperforming loans in the financial sector cannot be addressed adequately without improved performance by the state-owned enterprises (SOEs). Until these problems are resolved, it will not be possible to redirect sufficient credit to those sectors of the economy that can use it more effectively and that are currently starved of funds. In turn, this will make it difficult to create enough jobs to meet the needs of those laid-off, the newcomers to the job market, or those who will have to leave their farms.

Entry into the WTO will further expose the structural problems in the Chinese economy. In particular, it will cause more unemployment in the state sector, reduce fiscal revenues, and dramatically shift the party's traditional preference for self-sufficiency in basic food supply. At the same time, it offers the potential for growth in new sectors of the economy, particularly in the high-tech and service industries, and over the long term should be generally beneficial. The question remains as to whether China can weather the initial storm.

For almost a decade some policymakers have realized that the boom-bust economy China was experiencing was not a result of cyclical fluctuations but instead derived from structural problems within the Chinese economy. In 1993 and 1994, a group rallied around Deputy Prime Minister Zhu Rongji to outline a blueprint for future economic reform. Almost for the first time, the leadership seemed to be setting out a program that would place it at the forefront of the reform process rather than appearing to react to short-term contingencies. The program called for a renewed role for the center in managing key macroeconomic levers and an extensive role for the market; it also called for modernization of the enterprise system and, for the first time, highlighted the need to restructure the financial system. To back up the reforms, substantial policy innovation would be necessary in the provision of social welfare, especially in the urban areas. This agenda began to address the tough parts of reform, all of which could have been dealt with much easier earlier had it not been for the lack of political consensus. These included state enterprise reform, removing the institutional impediments to rural-urban labor flows, improving the banking system, and integrating domestic markets with foreign competition.

Progress has been made in all these areas but, given the ramifications of this blueprint, it has been deeply contested; subsequent political debate has revolved around the depth and speed of its implementation. Vested interests in central ministries and in local administrations have deflected policy in many key areas, and fears of social unrest have been used to slow the pace of structural transformation. The new leadership has the onerous task of completing this reform agenda, but time is running out.

A good example of the future challenge is state-owned enterprise restructuring and nonperforming loans. The number of SOEs has dropped from 100,000 in the mid-1990s to under 60,000, and the share of the nonstate sector in industrial output rose from 22 percent in 1978 to 74 percent in 2000, with the private sector growing from 2 percent in 1986 to 16 percent in 1998. The problems are still significant, however, and distort the state's capacity not only to lend to more productive sectors of the economy but to invest more in education, health, and research and development. State policy and its organizational structure still do not reflect the basic fact that the economy is a mixed economy, with the continuation of preferential policies for the state-owned sector, bias against the nonstate sector, and an administrative structure that cleaves too closely to that of the prereform era. For example, credit policy still directs 70 percent of bank lending to state enterprises.

From the mid-1990s two important reforms were introduced in an attempt to improve this sector. The first was the establishment of a social welfare system independent of the individual enterprises and regulated through the government. The second was to harden the budget constraints by gaining control over bank loans, trying to introduce better discipline over lending, and commercializing loans. By the end of 1999 and throughout 2000, officials began to highlight statistics that showed the situation for loss-making state-owned enterprises was beginning to turn around. This turnaround is not surprising. First, many of the hopeless cases were taken off the state books through mergers and acquisitions with more profitable companies. Second, asset management companies (AMCs) have bought the debt for many of the larger enterprises, moving it off the books of the SOEs. Most important, these SOEs are no longer paying a large amount of interest on their bad loans. In this way many bankrupt state enterprises have turned from basket cases to seemingly profitable businesses overnight. Whether the problem of SOE inefficiency is resolved is an entirely different matter; many have avoided the necessary structural reforms to enable them to compete in the future WTO market.

China's new leaders will need to move more quickly on governance in this area to avoid provoking a financial crisis that will be exacerbated by WTO entry. The consequences for what China has signed on to are enormous. By 2005 no restrictions will be placed on foreign banking activity in China, and prudential, not national, criteria should apply. Unless the AMCs and China's banks are able to clear the debts within five years, the challenges could create a banking crisis in China. Even with the AMCs assuming most of the current bad loans (but only the pre-1996 nonperforming policy loans), the banks will have to improve dramatically future lending habits. To prepare its banks for international competition, China must accelerate the liberalization of domestic interest rates, seek fuller integration between domestic and international capital markets, and speed toward full convertibility of the currency. The new government will need not only to withdraw from the SOE sector but to end preferential policies and lending practices that redirect valuable resources to that declining sector, which is unlikely to turn around.

The Challenge of Inequality

The costs of WTO entry—unemployment and increasing inequality between geographic regions and sectors already favored by reforms—are
concentrated and visible, while the benefits, such as a more efficient economy, cheaper consumer goods, and better governance, are diffuse and not
visible.[1] China's development strategy has eschewed social equity and followed Deng Xiaoping's principle that it is natural that some should get rich
first. There is nothing wrong with this, but the question is whether those
left behind initially will be afforded the opportunity to catch up or at least
not continually fall farther behind.

Regional disparities are growing, as are disparities between and within
urban and rural areas. Foreign direct investment (FDI) has increased regional inequalities, with greater wealth concentration in the eastern
coastal areas. In 1998 Guangdong alone received 27 percent of FDI; the
three major municipalities of Shanghai, Beijing, and Tianjin received a
total of 18 percent; and Jiangsu province 15 percent. By contrast, the nine
provinces and one municipality in northwestern and southwestern China
received only 3 percent of all FDI. This results in differential per capita
rural and urban income.

In urban areas real income is consistently higher, and the gap is increasing. By the end of the decade, the urban dwellers of Shanghai enjoyed a real
income twice that of the northwest and 60 percent more than the southwest. The rural income for the coastal areas was about twice that of the
southwest; Shanghai was three times higher. The better incomes for rural
dwellers in the coastal areas come from greater opportunities for off-farm
employment. These imbalances and the poverty associated with an exclusive reliance on agricultural employment are the drivers for the massive
migration we are witnessing in China. Anywhere from between 80 million
and 120 million people are estimated to be on the move, and over the next
decade another 100 million could leave the land.

Rising income inequality, combined with the unequal distribution of
resources and the incentives for spending priorities, accounts for the
huge variation in the provision of public goods and services during the
transition. Access to health and education services was still widely available in the 1980s but became more dependent on incomes in the 1990s.

1. On these issues see Joseph Fewsmith, "The Political and Social Implications of China's Accession to the WTO," *The China Quarterly,* no. 167 (September 2001), pp. 573–591, and Tony
Saich, "China's WTO Gamble," *Harvard Asia Pacific Review,* vol. 4, no. 1 (2002), pp. 10–14.

For example, in 1998 22 percent of those in high-income areas were covered by cooperative medical facilities but only 1 to 3 percent in poorer areas were covered.

The urban bias of central policy has clearly heightened the unequal access to public goods and social welfare, with individuals increasingly left to find the best support available with their own resources. This has been particularly noticeable with health care provision. Government health spending is inadequate and is heavily biased toward urban areas. In fact, the state's financial commitment to rural health services has been declining as a percentage of the total medical and health expenditure from 22 percent in 1978 to around 10 percent in the 1990s. With health costs rising it is not surprising that illness is one of the most cited reasons for poverty among the poor, a condition exacerbated by the collapse of the prepaid collective medical system during the disbanding of the communes in the early 1980s. As a result, some 90 percent of rural households have to pay directly for almost all the health services used.

The inequality of service provision between the urban and the rural, which has always been a feature of Communist Party policy, has become more complicated with the rapid increase in migration over the last decade. Migrant labor has been crucial to the urban economic boom, whether in supplying workers to the foreign-invested factories in coastal China, providing construction crews for the massive building expansion, or feeding the burgeoning service sector (ranging from the hotel and restaurant industry to the more unseemly services of the sex trade). It has also been crucial for rural development, both in terms of remittances and also as migrants have returned to the villages and brought with them capital, new skills, and social networks that extend beyond the narrow village confines.

Should the new leadership be worried about this inequality—and does it matter? Yes, for political and economic reasons. First, it is important if the ruling party wishes to represent and speak for the entire nation. A policy that channels resources to the urban elite and leaves many of the rural dwellers to fend for themselves and that treats migrants to the urban areas as second-class citizens can be politically destabilizing over the long term. Second, unless good education and health care facilities can be assured for the vast majority of the rural population, growth may slow and China may not be able to climb the ladder to follow the model of its East Asian neighbors.

The leadership apparently has understood the seriousness of these problems, but it will fall to the new leaders to address inequality and its consequences. They will need to continue the development of a set of social guarantees to ensure that those left behind are provided with minimum benefits, articulate a more inclusive vision for China's development, and alter the urban and coastal bias of current policy. While great progress has been made in the first area, the last two, which will require a more substantial rethink, are less likely to occur.

Recasting the Party

The party leadership has recognized that it requires a stronger basis of legitimacy beyond its capacity to deliver economic growth. Experimentation has ranged from a clearer focus on the national interest in foreign policy, the promotion of nationalism, a curiosity with neo-Confucianism, and a fascination with social democracy as practiced in northern Europe. However, it is a significant problem for the new leadership to articulate a vision of China's future that resonates with the Chinese people.

In early 2000, Jiang Zemin launched a campaign to study the "Three Represents," a program enthusiastically endorsed by Hu Jintao. The campaign is intended to enshrine Jiang as a great theoretician and to indicate that the Chinese Communist Party is still relevant to China's future. In a shift from the past, it is claimed that the party represents the "advanced social production forces," the most advanced culture, and the fundamental interests of all the people. While many have ridiculed the campaign as irrelevant to contemporary challenges or as a throwback to Maoist days, it does highlight that the party needs to think about its future role. It may not be enough, but it is an attempt to claim contemporary relevance.

The campaign seeks to portray the party as leading not only the new and dynamic areas of the economy, but also the newly emerged technical and economic elites. It furthers the process of distancing the party from sole reliance on the proletariat it created 50 years ago. The proletariat is consigned to the past, and the party now claims a broader constituency of representation. The continued need to cover policy direction with the fig leaf of socialism, however, makes it difficult to outline what future society would look like and how the relationship between state and society will change.

If the party cannot provide a moral framework for society, it will increase the centripetal tendencies within society. People are more likely to seek spiritual guidance in alternatives or simply adopt a "me first" or "family first" approach to life. The breakdown of a civic morality during the

Cultural Revolution in the 1960s has produced a highly instrumental view of personal relations today. The resultant moral vacuum presents a problem for any future leaders since no civil society exists to provide a bond should the Communist Party collapse.

Policy initiatives, rhetoric notwithstanding, have not been inclusive, as can be seen from the social exclusion of migrant communities. Recently there has been recognition that rural incomes must be raised and that the poorer parts of China, especially in the west, need to be given the chance to develop. But policy has not been coherent and still favors the urban and the coastal areas. Many analysts feel that the initiative to "develop the West" serves more political purposes than genuine development needs. A recent report by the Organization for Economic Cooperation and Development, *China in the World Economy,* states that better integration of China's regions is important for equity reasons and because poor integration is becoming an impediment to meeting other development goals. The report points out that key features of the initiative, such as using "growth poles," launching major infrastructure projects without considering regional demand, and supporting declining sectors of the local economy, have not worked elsewhere and most likely will not work in China.

At the highest levels of party leadership, no representative currently serves in the poorest provinces, confirming their marginalization in the Chinese body politic. Sichuan, the most important province in the west, has not had a Politburo representative since 1992. Given this, it is not surprising that policy has reflected the political bias of the most powerful, vociferous, and visible groups. As a result, policy has focused on the needs of the state officials despite retrenchment, has been receptive to the policy prescription of its (urban) professional classes, and has sought to soften the blows of the market transition for the urban proletariat. By contrast, it has left the rural poor, the migrants, and the nonstate-sector employees to their own collective or individual devices, and they have remained politically marginalized. If the Communist Party wishes to maintain social stability over the long term, this may not be the best road to follow.

Rethinking the State

Many inside and outside of China have high expectations that Hu Jintao and the new leadership will undertake significant political reforms. Apart from wishful thinking, no evidence indicates this will happen. Yet clearly the question of governance, whether corporate, administrative, or political, deserves serious policy innovation. The new leadership will need to complete the transition of governing structures from those that oversaw a communist state and planned economy to those that can run a modern market economy.

The Chinese state has undergone significant transformation during the reform period. New agencies have been created to oversee marketization and internationalization, a reduction in the state's control over the economy and intrusion in people's daily lives, and a redistribution of power between different agencies and levels of the state apparatus. Thus, while political rule may still be authoritarian, China is no longer a traditional communist state. At the same time, China does not possess an effective modern state that has a clear vision of what it should or should not be engaged in. In some areas (financial and industrial policy) it clearly does too much, while in others it does too little (rural health care).

The new leadership will have to develop a better capacity to rule through indirect mechanisms and to rely less on direct intervention to secure macroeconomic stability. This will require state administrators to develop new skills. Far from becoming easier, the entire process of governing will grow more complex. Most important, an effective—as distinct from strong—state structure is a precondition for any hope for successful reform. Certainly, the role of the state in the economy will change with a narrower set of interventions and less direct administrative interference. An increase in state capacity is a prerequisite for an effective market to function. The state must adjudicate the increasingly contentious nature of economic market transactions. This means that it is the obligation of the state to establish a sound legal system. In addition, the state must manage the key macroeconomic variables and ensure that economic and investment policy is not distorted by price fixing or subsidy supports that have outlived their rational lifetime. It must deal with revenue collection and distribution, which will help the state provide minimum social services and welfare guarantees to protect those who are vulnerable in the shift to a market economy.

How much political reform the Communist Party is willing to countenance is debatable and will also depend considerably on external circumstances. However, further reform will be necessary to deal with enhanced accountability, transparency, and the quality of governance. The major challenge lies in providing the good governance that will help the Chinese leadership deal with the political and social consequences of its own phenomenal economic success.

Beginning a process of serious political reform would have many benefits and would aid in coming to grips with numerous problems.[2] First, it could help strengthen the legitimacy of party rule. A more democratic system would provide a residual legitimacy as the regime negotiates the difficult transition ahead.

Second, political reform would derive the pragmatic benefits of ensuring a better environment for the economy and helping mediate potential social unrest. A system that would make local officials more accountable to the populations they are supposed to serve would immensely benefit virtually all concerned. Currently Chinese reform attempts have concentrated on making the system, particularly at the local level, more transparent. This has included new tax regulations that provide a clearer idea of tax revenue streams and what should be divided between the different administrative levels (including the ratio of the division), and public posting of village and township government accounts and financial information about officials. Less attention has been paid, however, to making the system more accountable. Incomplete transparency without accountability will not provide a basis for the reduction of the systemic corruption that plagues China. One fruitful area in which to expand accountability would be to raise the level of direct elections from the villages to the township and county administrative levels.

A more open political system that increased citizen participation would provide channels to address some inequities during the transition. This would be a preferable alternative to rioting and other nonsanctioned forms of political action. The lack of accountability can also lead to the redirection of government policy or to perverse outcomes that undermine the intent of the original policy.

The conditions for long-term social stability are not likely to improve unless the party trusts its people to organize themselves to provide more and better social services and if the party itself does not reform and change significantly its relationship to state and society. With the decreasing financial capacity of the state, the decline in the party's moral authority, the downsizing of the workforce, and with more individuals increasingly responsible for their own welfare provision, the party will have to allow greater autonomy to society to organize and prioritize its

2. This last section is based on Tony Saich, *Governance and Politics of China* (Basingstoke: Palgrave, 2001).

own affairs. Not to do this will mean that many needs will go unmet as the state cannot provide adequate services. This, in turn, will lead to an increase in the kind of unrest that the party seeks to avoid.

The political challenges are increased by the nature of China's involvement with the world outside and the pressures of globalization. It will take enormous skill on the part of the current leadership and its successors to prevent the challenges from further undermining the power and legitimacy of the party. While the leadership has shown itself to be skillful at adapting to economic change, it has been unable to confront the social and political consequences that arise from this change. Each time the need for far-reaching political reform is floated, the senior leadership has backed away, hoping that its authoritarian power structures will enable it to crush any overt opposition and ride out any unrest.

Those who take power at the sixteenth party congress will not be able to rely on traditional Communist Party methods of controlling the country and will be under considerable pressure to find new ways to manage the Chinese polity. Clearly, the forces of globalization will require a considerable shift in the way the party governs the system and will require political reform that tries to make the system not only more transparent, but also more accountable. The new leaders will have to deal with a much more fluid domestic and international political order where many key decisions affecting China will be taken by international organizations that will not respect the Communist Party's outdated notion of sovereignty. Given its record to date, this will be a significant hurdle for the Chinese leadership to overcome.

The capacity to respond will be hampered by the difficulty the new leadership will face in undertaking any dramatic new initiatives that depart from what Jiang Zemin sees as his legacy. Whoever succeeds Jiang will take almost a full term to consolidate his position. This means that, absent an unforeseen catalyst, the politics of muddling through will prevail for much of the next five years. An essentially technocratic approach will continue while the leadership tries to maintain an authoritarian political structure combined with growing economic liberalization. Minimal reform is likely in the political system with a continued focus on strengthening the legal system and building capacity and skills within public administration.

Whether this politics of muddling through will be sufficient for the next period is debatable—the leadership might be pressured to take a more dynamic approach. The requirements for China to maintain continued high growth are greater information, declining coercion, less hierarchy, more accountability by means of representative institutions, and a marketplace in which priorities of goods and services in the economic sphere are balanced by needs and wants in the political sphere. Whether the Chinese leadership can deal with these challenges of governance will attest to whether it can retain its leadership over China's development in the twenty-first century.

18. China's Environmental Challenge

September 2005

ELIZABETH ECONOMY

In late July 2001, the fertile Huai River Valley—China's breadbasket—was the site of an environmental disaster. Heavy rains flooded the river's tributaries, flushing more than 38 billion gallons of highly polluted water into the Huai. Downstream, in Anhui province, the river water was thick with garbage, yellow foam, and dead fish. Although the authorities quickly proclaimed the situation under control, the incident represented a stunning failure for China's leadership. Only seven months earlier, the government had proclaimed its success in cleaning up the Huai. A six-year campaign to rid the region of polluting factories that dumped their wastewater into the river had ostensibly raised the quality of the water in the river and its more than 100 tributaries to the point that people could once again fish, irrigate their crops, and even drink from the river.

Sadly, the saga of the Huai River Valley is typical of today's China. Throughout the country, centuries of rampant, sometimes willful, destruction of the environment have produced environmental disasters:

- *Flooding.* In 1998, the Yangtze River flooded, killing more than 3,000 people, destroying 5 million homes, and inundating 52 million acres of land. The economic losses were estimated at more than $20 billion. The culprit: two decades of massive deforestation and destruction of wetlands.
- *Desertification.* Desert, already covering one-quarter of the country, continues to spread, with the pace of desertification having doubled since the 1970s. Efforts to stem the advance of the desert through afforestation and development of grassland have had limited success. Since 1998, northern China, including the capital of Beijing, has been

shrouded in dust for days at a time. Year by year, this dust has traveled increasingly far afield, darkening the skies of Japan and Korea and even a wide swath of the United States.

- *Water scarcity.* Water scarcity born of changing ecosystems, skyrocketing demand, increasing pollution, and inadequate conservation efforts has limited access to water for more than 60 million people, and almost 10 times that number drink contaminated water daily. As a result, factories are closing, tens of millions of people are leaving their land, public health is endangered, and the government faces a future of expensive river diversion and pollution remediation projects, even in areas once rich in water resources.

- *Dwindling forest resources.* China's forest resources rank among the lowest in the world. Demand for furniture, chopsticks, and paper has driven an increasingly profitable, environmentally devastating illegal logging trade. By the mid-1990s, half of China's forest bureaus reported that trees were being felled at an unsustainable rate, and 20 percent had already exhausted their reserves. China's Sichuan province—home to the famed pandas—now possesses less than one-tenth of its original forests. Loss of biodiversity, climatic change, desertification, and soil erosion are all on the rise as a result.

- *Population growth.* Underpinning much of China's resource degradation has been the continued pressure of a burgeoning population. China's top leader until March 2003, President Jiang Zemin, called the country's population size his biggest problem, particularly in the countryside, where many routinely defy the coercive one-child policy. Prime Minister Wen Jiabao, in his December 2003 address at Harvard University, commented that "any small individual problem multiplied by 1.3 billion becomes a big, big problem." Even if the 2000 official census is accurate, China's 1.3 billion people exceed by almost 300 million the goal set by China's leaders a decade earlier.

A Legacy of Devastation

The roots of China's environmental crisis run deep. Current environmental practices are shaped by the dramatic economic and political reforms that have been transforming the country since the late 1970s. These reforms have significantly diminished the role of the state and encouraged newfound reliance on the market and the private sector to meet the economic and social welfare needs of society. They have also introduced new actors, institutions, and ideas into the political system. Yet, at the same time, the reforms have reinforced some of China's traditional policy attitudes and methods, sometimes in surprising ways. China's current environmental challenges, as well as its approach to environmental protection, reflect this rich, sometimes complicated mix of deeply rooted links to the past and dynamic new pressures and opportunities.

Through the centuries, the relentless drive of China's leaders to amass power, consolidate territory, develop the economy, and support a growing population led to the plundering of forests and mineral resources, poorly conceived river diversion and water management projects, and intensive farming that degraded the land. This exploitation of natural resources, in turn, contributed significantly to the wars, famines, and natural disasters that plagued China. The result was a continuous cycle of economic development, environmental degradation, social dislocation, turmoil, and often violent political change. China's leadership has typically approached the environment through frequent campaigns and mass mobilization efforts for large-scale infrastructure projects, such as dams or river diversions that wreaked havoc with local ecosystems and were undertaken with little consideration for the actual environmental and scientific factors necessary to achieve success.

History therefore offered little environmental wisdom to China's post-Mao reformers. As economic reform took hold, China experienced dramatic average annual growth rates exceeding 8 percent, the elevation of hundreds of millions of Chinese out of poverty, and, eventually, the transformation of China into a global economic powerhouse. No effort, however, was made to account for the costs that reform levied on the environment, and natural resources remained priced far below their replacement costs in order to encourage continued rapid economic development. China's leaders were well aware that they were trading environmental health for economic growth. The maxim "First development, then environment," was a common refrain throughout the 1980s and much of the 1990s.

The reform period has taken an enormous toll on the environment. Air and water pollution rates have skyrocketed. By 2002, China had become home to six of the ten most polluted cities in the world. Acid rain now affects about one-third of China's territory, including approximately one-third of its farmland. More than 75 percent of the water in rivers flowing through China's urban areas is unsuitable for drinking or fishing. Desert now covers 25 percent of China's territory, and deforestation and grassland degradation continue largely unabated.

The leadership has begun to witness the broader social and economic costs of its environmental failures. Over the next decade or two, Beijing anticipates the migration of 30 million to 40 million Chinese—some voluntary, many forced—as a result of depleted or degraded resources. If not managed properly, the combination of migrant laborers and unemployed workers could trigger serious conflict in urban areas, as has already happened in some cities. Managing this process of migration and urbanization successfully will challenge the Communist Party's ingenuity and organization, not to mention its financial resources.

The economic costs of environmental degradation and pollution are dramatic. Already they are the equivalent of 8 to 12 percent of China's annual gross domestic product. In addition, pollution-related illnesses are soaring. There have been serious outbreaks of waterborne disease, as well as long-term health problems in riverside communities reflected in rising rates of spontaneous abortion, birth defects, and premature death. Air pollution alone, primarily from coal burning, is responsible for over 300,000 premature deaths per year.

Perhaps most threatening to the Chinese leadership, protests over polluted water, damaged crops, air pollution, and forced resettlement contribute to the increasingly pervasive social unrest already confronting the regime. Top leaders have commented on the danger that environmental protest poses to the authority of the Communist Party and the stability of the state, noting that it is one of the most important sources of social unrest in the country. In 2005 alone, violent environmental protests that involved tens of thousands of people took place across the country.

At the same time, China's leaders are grappling with the legacy of the past as population and national security concerns continue to shape environmental practices. While an aggressive family planning effort has cut the birthrate in half, there are wide regional discrepancies, with important economic and environmental implications. And, even as national security concerns over issues such as civil war have diminished, others have emerged. In the mid-1990s, declining grain yields and growing reliance on international grain markets prompted concerns over China's food security, resulting in yet another massive land reclamation and grain-growing campaign to ensure grain self-sufficiency. Today, the Chinese leadership has turned its attention to China's west, where it confronts a combination of discontent among minority populations and lack of economic development. In response, officials have initiated a massive economic development campaign to raise the standard of living and to secure China's borders from separatist movements—at further risk to the environment.

A Patchwork of Protection

China's reforms have also changed the political landscape for environmental protection in more positive ways. Spurred on by both environmentally concerned Chinese officials and the country's participation in the 1972 UN Conference on the Human Environment, China's leaders in the 1970s and 1980s began the long, slow process of developing a formal environmental protection apparatus both at the central and local levels. At the same time, they began to build a legal infrastructure for environmental protection, drafting increasingly sophisticated laws, signing onto international environmental agreements, and, beginning in the 1990s, training lawyers and judges on issues of environmental law.

Yet challenges remain. Beijing has still not sufficiently empowered its environmental protection infrastructure to meet the vast array of environmental challenges. The State Environmental Protection Administration and local environmental protection bureaus remain weak and underfunded, often incapable not only of advancing their interests in the face of more powerful development-oriented bureaucracies but also of using the nascent legal infrastructure to protect the environment.

Moreover, devolution of authority to local officials, which contributed to such dramatic economic development in many regions of the country, has produced a patchwork of environmental protection. Some regions have moved aggressively to respond to environmental challenges, while others, such as in the Huai Valley, have been far slower to develop the necessary policies and implementation capacity.

Some of the difficulty rests in the nature of the political economy at the local level. Local government officials often have close ties with local business leaders and indeed may be part-owners in local factories. It is difficult to police polluting factories that are at least partly owned by the local government and directly contribute to the wealth of local officials. Moreover, local environmental bureaus are embedded within the bureaucratic infrastructure of the local governments; enormous pressure may be brought to bear on local environmental protection bureaus by officials concerned with maintaining high levels of economic growth no matter the environmental costs. In some respects, this devolution of authority perpetuates a form of the traditional, personalistic system of governance that characterized Imperial China and produced wide regional variation in environmental protection.

In addition, in the 1990s, as the Chinese leadership gradually withdrew from its responsibility to meet all the social welfare needs of the population, including health, education, and environmental protection, it welcomed greater public participation in environmental protection. China's leaders have thus allowed the establishment of genuine nongovernment organizations, encouraged aggressive media attention to environmental issues, and sanctioned independent legal activities to protect the environment, partly to compensate for the weakness of its formal environmental protection apparatus. Grassroots ngos have sprung up in many regions of the country to address issues as varied as the fate of the Tibetan antelope, the deterioration of China's largest freshwater lakes, and mounting urban refuse. Nonprofit legal centers have emerged to wage class action warfare on behalf of farmers and others whose livelihood and health have suffered from pollution from local factories.

The media have played a crucial role, directing a harsh public spotlight on enterprises that refuse to respect environmental laws, investigating the accuracy of government accounts of environmental cleanup campaigns, and exposing large-scale abuses of the environment such as rampant logging. In this way, the Chinese leadership hopes to fill the growing gap between the people's desire to improve the environment and the government's capacity or will to do so. Meanwhile, there is the potential for society to become more vocal in its demands for a cleaner environment and to bring a new level of accountability to the Chinese government's environmental policies and proclamations, and perhaps even to the entire Chinese political system.

Inviting New Players

China's leaders have also looked abroad for inspiration and assistance. The government has eagerly gobbled up technical and financial help from international institutions, as well as other countries. China is the largest recipient of environmental aid from the World Bank, the Asian Development Bank, the Global Environmental Facility, and Japan. The international community has supported China in virtually every aspect of its environmental protection work, including the development of a legal system, monitoring systems for air pollution, and exploring energy alternatives to coal.

However, deepening integration with international actors carries with it a set of unpredictable challenges. Involvement by the international community brings not only financial assistance and technical expertise but also an array of political and social considerations that often diverge from the interests of many within the Chinese government. Infrastructure projects involving massive forced resettlement or programs involving minority populations, for example, often alarm international donors and focus unwanted international attention on China's human rights record. China's weak incentive system and enforcement apparatus for environmental protection also often thwart effective cooperation. Corruption siphons off money and goodwill from both donors and intended recipients.

Inviting participation from both domestic and international actors outside the government is an enormous gamble in other respects; once unleashed, independent social forces may be very difficult to contain. In the former Soviet Union and Eastern bloc countries, intelligentsia, including writers, scholars, scientists, and other professionals, as well as college students, used environmental protection as a cover for the sharing of broader grievances, and environmental ngos helped develop the germ of civil society. Many environmental ngos in these countries allied with other social interest groups to focus more directly on revolutionizing the political system.

Similarly, in the less dramatic cases of China's Asia Pacific neighbors, environmental ngos have been consistently at the forefront of political change. In advancing the cause of environmental protection, they have exposed the institutionalized corruption and lack of accountability of the entire system of governance. In countries such as South Korea, the Philippines, and Thailand during the 1970s and 1980s, environmental activists became closely linked with the democracy activists who agitated for broader political reform. In these instances, environmental issues did not serve directly as a catalyst for regime change but did permanently enlarge the political space for social action. Already, several of China's leading environmental activists leave no doubt as to their desired outcome: not only the greening of China but also the democratization of the country.

Thus, China's path to its current environmental crisis and its environmental future depend significantly on how not only the central government but also local officials, citizens, and the international community manage the environmental legacy of the past and respond to the challenges and opportunities that reform presents for environmental protection today.

Assessing the Trends

Looking back over the period since China began its reform process, trends in environmental pollution and degradation alone would suggest that economic reform has contributed to a significant deterioration in China's environmental situation. Yet, scratch beneath the surface and an additional, more useful set of observations concerning China's current and future environmental challenges emerge.

First, while the reform period marks a break in both the nature of the environmental challenges that China confronts and the opportunities it has to respond to them, important continuities remain from centuries-old practices and ideas concerning environmental protection. In some respects, the reforms reinforce these traditional approaches to environmental protection: maintaining a campaign mentality, relying on local officials for core aspects of environmental protection, and viewing the environment in terms of national security.

Second, the Chinese government has made dramatic strides in developing institutions and a legal system to protect the environment, but the nature of Chinese politics, including endemic corruption and a lack of transparency, often renders the system dysfunctional.

Third, within China there is extraordinary variability in environmental pollution and degradation statistics. As others have discovered looking at issues such as agriculture, automobiles, and technology, the decentralized nature of the state and decades of devolution of power to local officials virtually ensure that policy choices will be made and implemented differently from one region to the next.

In a few select regions of the country, the reform process has already produced dramatic new benefits for China's environment and society. Still, in many others, it has contributed to a slide deeper into environmental crisis. Those regions in which reform has produced a positive environmental outcome, where pollution and environmental degradation are being aggressively and effectively addressed, share some common features: the top local official supports or is perceived by other local officials to support environmental protection goals; there is a strong level of environmental support provided by the international community; and the domestic resources available to local leaders to address environmental challenges are significant. The losers, in turn, are those regions with much weaker links to the international environment and development community; whose leaders are still overwhelmingly concerned with economic development and perceive the environment as a costly luxury; and, often, whose local resources to invest in environmental protection are far less than those in other parts of the country.

Finally, as the interplay of political and economic reform exerts an impact on China's environment, it becomes clear that the environment comes back to influence the reform process in critical ways. Most clearly, environmental degradation and pollution constrain economic growth, contribute to large-scale migration, harm public health, and engender social unrest. Moreover, there is the potential, already evident in nascent form, for the environment to serve as a locus for broader political discontent and further political reforms, as it did in some of the former republics of the Soviet Union and in some countries in Asia and Eastern Europe.

A Rising Star Tarnished?

In the early years of the twenty-first century, China's leadership can claim much to celebrate. The communist regime has brought unparalleled economic growth and well-being for the Chinese people, the expansion of Chinese influence throughout the Asia Pacific and beyond, and the return to Chinese control of Hong Kong and Macao. Only Taiwan remains to fulfill Beijing's dream of a Greater China. China's rise to major player status on the world stage was confirmed in 2001 as the country completed negotiations to join the World Trade Organization, hosted the Asia Pacific Economic Cooperation summit, and won the right to hold the 2008 Olympics in Beijing.

But these successes come at a heavy price. Ignored for decades, even centuries, China's environmental problems now have the potential to bring the country to its knees economically, with the costs of environmental pollution and degradation taking a large toll on the country's gross domestic product. Moreover, pollution and resource scarcity have become major sources of social unrest, massive migration, and public health problems throughout the country.

How China's leadership balances its desire for continued economic growth with growing social and political pressures to improve environmental protection has profound implications for the world beyond China. Resolution of the world's most pressing global environmental challenges, such as climate change, ozone depletion, and biodiversity loss, requires the full commitment and cooperation of China, one of the world's largest contributors to these environmental problems. Regionally, China's economic development contributes to problems of transboundary air pollution, fisheries depletion, and management of international water resources such as the Mekong River. The continued stability of China—a major global trading power and pillar of East Asian security—also is drawn into question by the relentless press of sociopolitical problems, some of which have roots in the government's failure to address environmental concerns.

Beyond this lies the fundamental question of the future of China's political and economic system and its orientation toward the rest of the world. The authority and legitimacy of the Communist Party depend on how well China's leaders provide for the basic needs of their people and improve their standard of living. Fundamental to the state's capacity to meet this challenge is the environment. Access to resources for household and industrial consumption, improvements in public health, and continued economic growth are all predicated on Beijing's ability to slow or reverse the forces of environmental pollution and degradation. Thus, the environment will be the arena in which many of the crucial battles for China's future will be waged.

The Environment and the Future

Millions of people concerned with the environment, both in China and elsewhere, are hoping that a scenario combining growing prosperity and democracy with environmental protection becomes reality. But this is by no means assured. Both China's domestic reforms and its deeper integration into the international system require a fundamental change in values. The nationalistic and occasionally violent demonstrations that have taken place in the country in recent years demonstrate that, within at least some sectors of Chinese society and the Chinese leadership, the commitment to this kind of change is a tenuous one.

The world community has an opportunity to assist in the process of developing China's approach to environmental protection. The impact of the international community on China's environmental practices has already been substantial. In every regard—technology transfer, governance, and policy development—the international community has helped to shape the evolution of China's environmental protection effort. Fortunately, this involvement shows no evidence of abating and, indeed, seems likely to grow in the future.

Yet much more remains to be done. Technology transfer and adoption of new policy approaches await the development of a stronger legal and enforcement apparatus. Here, the international community, in particular the United States with its strong environmental enforcement apparatus and history of public participation in environmental protection, could be far more active in contributing to the development of China's environmental future.

The environment provides a natural and nonthreatening vehicle to advance US interests not only in China's environmental protection efforts but also in its basic human rights practices and trade opportunities. Several simple steps could be taken to help shape China's future environmental, political, and economic development. Chief among these is removing restrictions on the involvement of the Overseas Private Investment Corporation and the US–Asia Environmental Partnership in China. Lifting these restrictions would permit US environmental industries greater access to China's market by offering them some level of US government assistance.

The United States Agency for International Development (USAID), with its broad emphasis on governance, public health, rule of law, and poverty alleviation, could be especially valuable in helping to address China's most pressing needs and the United States' most direct interests. For USAID to become actively and directly involved in such activities, however, would require the United States to remove either the prohibition on USAID funding of communist states or the label of communist state from China. The United States has the chance not only to benefit more significantly from China's current reform process but also to aid in the future evolution of that process in ways that serve broader US political, economic, and environmental interests.

And yet, no matter how extensive China's interaction with the United States and the rest of the world, China itself bears the brunt of the challenge. As the story of resource degradation and governmental failure in the Huai River Valley makes clear, a future in which China fully embraces environmental protection will require new approaches to integrating economic development with environmental protection. Indeed, China has begun to experiment with calculating a green GDP, using tradable permits to control sulphur dioxide emissions, and promoting cleaner production. Equally important, however, will be a commitment by China's leaders to develop the political institutions necessary to ensure such a future and to bring true transparency and accountability to the system of environmental protection.

Speculation remains as to the boldness of President Hu Jintao and Prime Minister Wen Jiabao, communist China's fourth-generation leaders. Yet change will require nothing short of boldness. China's governance is a system thousands of years in the making, one in which the greatness of leaders has often been achieved at the expense of nature, through grand-scale development campaigns to control and exploit the environment for man's benefit. Today, greatness may well depend on resisting this tradition and instead developing a new relationship between man and nature.

Chronology of Recent Events

People's Republic of China

1993

Jan. 28—A shuffle of the armed forces in which new commanders or political commissars have been named for six of the country's seven military regions has been completed, the *New York Times* reports. The changes have greatly lessened the influence of half-brothers Yang Shangkun and Yang Baibing; Yang Shangkun, a former general, is finishing a term as China's president, and Yang Baibing was removed as the army's top political commissar.

Feb. 17—The government announces the release from prison of Wang Dan and Guo Haifeng, student leaders in the 1989 democracy movement; it says all students held in connection with the movement have now been released, although several are reportedly still in custody. Dissidents Wang Xizhe and Gao Shan were released earlier this month.

March 15–31—The First Session of the Eighth National People's Congress takes place. Jiang Zemin, the general secretary of the Communist Party, is elected on March 27 as the country's president, and reelected as chairman of the Central Military Commission. This is the first time since 1980 that the top posts in the party, government, and military have been concentrated in one leader's hands. Revisions to the state constitution, approved on March 29, make explicit commitment to economic reform and opening up as well as modernizing the country according to the theory of "building socialism with Chinese characteristics." The Basic Law of the Macao Special Administrative Region of the People's Republic of China is promulgated on March 31.

April 6—The number of registered companies in China rose 88% last year, to 486,000, reports the *New York Times*; the capital of private businesses also grew 79% over the year, to $3.9 billion.

April 27–29—The chairmen of Chinese mainland's Association for Relations Across the Taiwan Straits, Wang Daohan, and Taiwan's Straits Exchange Foundation, Koo Chen-Fu, meet in Singapore. The two sides issued a joint communiqué and signed three specific agreements.

May 24–25—In the largest demonstration in several years, some 600 people in Lhasa, the Tibetan capital, protest economic hardships and Chinese control of Tibet. Police disperse the crowd with tear gas.

June 6—In Renshou, Sichuan province, paramilitary police fire tear gas at thousands of peasants who surrounded them and threw stones. The police were attempting to arrest leaders of a recent rebellion against county officials who imposed a tax for the construction of a road.

June 20—The State Council, in response to widespread discontent among peasants, rescinds 37 central government taxes and fees. All locally issued burdens are abolished.

June 30—It is announced that Li Guixian, one of the state councilors, will no longer be the governor of the central bank after some 100,000 Chinese investors lost more than $175 million in the Great Wall bond scandal earlier this month. He will be replaced temporarily by Deputy Prime Minister Zhu Rongji.

July 2—The American brewer Anheuser-Busch, in the first such foreign acquisition allowed by China, acquires about 6% stock share in Tsingtao Brewery Company by converting convertible bonds to stock shares after Tsingtao becomes the first mainland corporation to be listed on the Hong Kong stock exchange.

July 17—The Hong Kong newspaper *Ta Kung Pao* reports that 44 people were convicted two days ago in Fuzhou, the capital of Fujian province, of smuggling people out of the country and sentenced to terms in labor camps. Another 32 have received prison terms of from 1 to 5 years for the same offence.

Aug. 12—The government announces it has closed 1,000 of the 1,200 economic development zones set up by local officials to attract domestic and foreign investment, often by offering unauthorized tax breaks

and incentives. In July the state began an effort to cool down the economy, which grew 14% last year. Earlier this month the government made public plans to turn one-third of state-owned enterprises into limited-liability corporations responsible for their own losses.

The official newspaper, *China Daily*, announces that a social insurance system providing all urban workers with guaranteed unemployment benefits will be established within two years.

Aug. 20–25—The second plenum of the Central Discipline Inspection Commission takes place. President Jiang Zemin calls for a crackdown on corruption in government. The official New China News Agency reported recently that between 1990 and 1992, the Communist party disciplined 605,689 of its members for corruption.

In Hong Kong, the government informs Han Dongfang—whom police expelled from mainland China a week ago—that his passport has been revoked because of subversive activities abroad; Human Rights Watch says Han, who organized China's first free labor union during the 1989 pro-democracy protests in Tiananmen Square, is at least the fourth dissident to be expelled in the last year.

Sept. 4—At the Saudi Arabian port of Damman, U.S., Chinese, and Saudi representatives certify that a detained Chinese freighter has no illicit cargo aboard after U.S. intelligence reports said the vessel was carrying materials for the production of poison gas to Iran; the Chinese Foreign Ministry condemns "self-styled world cop behavior" by the United States.

Sept. 20—In Beijing, Wei Jingsheng, China's best-known dissident, appears publicly for the first time since his release from prison last week, 6 months before the end of his 14 1/2-year sentence for antigovernment activities during the 1978–1979 Democracy Wall movement.

Oct. 5—China conducts an underground nuclear test.

Oct. 31—Five of nine draft laws are adopted at the fourth Standing Committee Session of the Eighth National People's Congress. Among them, the "Amendments to the Law on Individual Income Tax" stipulate that all Chinese residents and nonresidents who have income from China should pay income tax.

Nov. 11–14—The Third Plenum of the Fourteenth Central Committee takes place. An important document is approved—"Decision of the CCP Central Committee on Certain Questions Regarding the Establishment of a Socialist Market Economy"—and the official communiqué emphasizes the establishment of a modern enterprise system, including separating government administration from enterprise management.

Nov. 14—Lu Yonghua, deputy director of the State Commission for Economic Restructuring, announces that beginning next year, 100 large state-owned factories will be run as private corporations whose managers will have sole responsibility for financial decisions and results. If the program is successful, all 11,000 medium-size and large state-owned firms in China will be similarly restructured in 3 to 5 years.

Dec. 15—The State Council promulgates its decision to introduce a tax-sharing system (*fenshuizhi*) in 1994 to replace the fiscal contract system (*caizheng baoganzhi*), which was implemented in 1980.

Dec. 28—In the third such incident this month and the tenth this year, a couple accompanied by their young son hijacks a Chinese jetliner and forces the pilots to fly to Taiwan. The couple is held by Taiwanese authorities rather than being extradited.

The Central Bank announces that, beginning January 1, it will unify its two-tier system of official exchange rates and much lower semiofficial swap-center rates for a single controlled floating exchange rate based on market supply and demand.

1994

Jan. 12—In a joint statement, France and China announce that relations have been completely normalized after a pledge by French Prime Minister Edouard Balladur's conservative government not to authorize any new arms sales to Taiwan. French companies have effectively been excluded from competing for contracts in China since the previous socialist government approved the sale of 60 Mirage jets to Taiwan in 1993.

Feb. 20—Four rival clerics from Zheherenye, an officially tolerated Islamic sect, have received sentences of from 15 years to life in prison in connection with a clash between their followers last May over succession, the *New York Times* reports. Troops were called in to quell the fighting in Xiji, Ningxia province, and 20 of the clerics' followers were killed.

Feb. 28-March 3—The State Council holds a working conference on national poverty reduction. The government says it will lift most of the remaining 80 million poor above the poverty line during the seven-year period from 1994 to 2000. The plan is known as the "8–7 Plan."

March 4—A Beijing court convicts Shen Taifu, the former chief of the Great Wall Machinery and Electronics Group, on bribery and corruption charges and sentences him to death for his role in a $115 million corporate bond scandal exposed last year. Li Xiaoshi, a former deputy minister at the State Science and Technology Commission, receives a 20-year prison sentence for accepting bribes from Shen.

March 31—Twenty-four tourists from Taiwan and 8 tourists from mainland China die on a pleasure boat on Qiandao Lake in Zhejiang province. In April, Taipei refuses to accept the explanation that the deaths were caused by fire on board and suspends trade and cultural exchanges. Three suspects are sentenced to death on June 12 and are executed on June 19.

April 1—In Beijing, police arrest Wei Jingsheng, the leader of the 1978–1979 Democracy Wall movement.

April 23—The government releases Wang Juntao, a leader of the 1989 democracy movement serving a 13-year prison sentence, and sends him to the United States for medical treatment.

May 10—A ceremony is held at the People's Congress Hall for the publication of the 13-volume *Chinese Language Dictionary* (Han Yu Da Ci Dian), which is the product of 18 years of effort by over 1,000 scholars.

June 3–8—The inauguration and the first general assembly of the Chinese Academy of Engineering takes place. Like the Chinese Academy of Science established in 1949, it is under the direct administration of the State Council.

June 10—China conducts underground testing of a hydrogen bomb, one of a new generation of miniaturized warheads, in the region of Xinjiang.

July 5—The State Council promulgates a decision to further protect intellectual property rights.

July 30—The Securities Regulatory Commission orders a halt to new stock listings for the rest of the year to stem declines on the country's two exchanges associated with the government's tight-money policy; the three-year-old Shanghai exchange has lost 80% of its value since February 1993, most of it in the last three months.

Aug. 8—After the government's announcement July 30 that new stock issues would not be permitted for the rest of the year, trading on the Shanghai exchange reaches a one-day record of $1.34 billion, four times higher than the total in Hong Kong.

Aug. 24—The cabinet orders government at all levels to fight inflation, which in 35 major cities in July reached an annual rate of 24.2%. The directive mandates increased supplies of goods, especially food, and punishment for price gouging and other economic crimes.

Sept. 2—In an apparent show of support for its ally North Korea, China withdraws its representative from the Korean Military Armistice Commission, which became inactive after North Korea's withdrawal in 1991.

Sept. 12—The Standing Committee of Beijing Municipality's People's Congress promulgates a regulation under which the city government will levy a charge on the average annual wage for people from outside the capital who become permanent residents. The regulation is to be abolished in 1999.

Nov. 14—The identification of a fetus's sex by technical means for purposes of sex selection will be prohibited under a law to take effect in January, health officials announce.

Nov. 21—The People's Bank of China proclaims that foreign exchange certificates will cease circulation on January 1, 2005, but can be converted until June 30.

Dec. 14—The Three Gorges dam project officially begins.

Dec. 20—The government announces that the construction of luxury projects and office buildings will be banned during 1995 in an effort to channel investment into public works.

1995

Jan. 30—President Jiang Zemin issues eight points on the reunification of Taiwan and the mainland. Under the idea of "one country, two systems," Taiwan would be allowed to have high degree of autonomy, including keeping its party, government, military systems, and armed forces.

Feb. 9—The Central Committee of the Chinese Communist Party issues the Temporary Working Provisions on the Selection and Appointment of Party and State Leading Cadres. The formal document is to be issued on July 9, 2002.

Feb. 25—Twelve leading intellectuals present the National People's Congress with a petition calling for the establishment of a constitutional democracy with independent legislative and judicial branches. The petition also calls for freedom of speech and freedom of the press.

Feb. 26—The United States and China sign a trade agreement that averts $1 billion in punitive tariffs that the United States would have levied against China for the illegal copying and sale of U.S. music and movies. Under the agreement China will enforce intellectual property rights and patent, trademark, and copyright laws.

March 5—In his opening address to the National People's Congress, Prime Minister Li Peng reports that the annual inflation rate in 1994 was 21.7%, the highest since the Communist Party took power in 1949.

March 13—In Beijing, U.S. and Chinese officials sign an accord under which the United States will back China's entry into the World Trade Organization. China agrees to dismantle some trade barriers for American goods.

April 4—Wang Baosan, the deputy mayor of Beijing, is reported to have committed suicide. Wang was under investigation for "economic crimes," according to Xinhua, the official news agency.

April 10—Chen Yun, the architect of China's centrally planned economy and second most powerful leader in the reform age, dies.

April 27—Government officials report that Chen Xitong, a member of Politburo and the party secretary of Beijing municipality, has been implicated in a corruption scandal and has resigned. Chen is sentenced to 16 years in jail on July 31, 1998.

May 29—Japan reports that China launched its first solid-fueled long-range intercontinental ballistic missile in a test today.

June 16—The government recalls its ambassador to the United States, Li Daoyu, after the president of Taiwan, Lee Teng-hui, was allowed to enter the United States on a private visit on June 9.

July 8—The government announces that is has arrested Harry Wu, an American-naturalized citizen, for espionage. He is sentenced to 15 years in prison on August 25 and is immediately expelled to the United States.

July 11—The World Trade Organization admits China as an observer.

Aug. 11—China's first joint venture investment bank licensed by the People's Bank of China, China International Capital Corporation Limited, opens.

Sept. 25—Prime Minister Li Peng notes two fundamental shifts of China's development when addressing the Fifth Plenum of the Fourteenth Chinese Communist Party Central Committee: from a traditional planned economic system to a socialist market economic system; and from an extensive to an intensive mode of economic growth.

Oct. 24—President Jiang and U.S. President Bill Clinton meet unofficially in New York.

Nov. 22—The government charges dissident Wei Jingsheng with trying to overthrow the government. Wei had been seized by officials in 1994 while on parole after serving 14 1/2 years of a 15-year prison sentence for "counterrevolutionary activities."

Nov. 29—Following the traditional ceremony of drawing lots, six-year-old Gyaincain Norbu is confirmed by the State Council as the eleventh Panchen Lama, the second-holiest Tibetan Buddhist leader. The exiled Tibetan Dalai Lama's previous choice for the reincarnated Panchen Lama was rejected.

Dec. 19—The U.S. aircraft carrier *Nimitz* passes through the strait dividing Taiwan and mainland China on December 19, 1995. This is the first time a U.S. navy ship has entered the strait since 1979.

1996

Jan. 16—American military attaché Colonel Bradley Gerdes and Japanese military attaché Colonel Kenji Maetani are expelled on charges of espionage.

Jan. 26—The Preparatory Committee of the Hong Kong Special Administrative Region is established. On March 25, the committee approves the decision to establish a provisional Legislative Council composed of permanent Hong Kong residents.

Feb. 8—A seminar on legislative and legal affairs is held for party leaders in Zhong Nan Hai. In a speech, President Jiang Zemin's speech calls for the rule by law, the first time a leader of the party has made such a declaration.

March 8—The military begins a series of missile tests off the northern and southern coasts of Taiwan. The island's first free presidential elections are scheduled for March 23. The United States sends the aircraft carriers *Independence* and *Nimitz* to provide a stabilizing presence.

April 26—The presidents of China, Russia, Kazakhstan, Kyrgyzstan, and Tajikistan signed in Shanghai an agreement on military confidence building in border areas. The alliance is known as "Shanghai Five."

June 17—U.S. and Chinese negotiators announce that a settlement on intellectual property rights. The United States and China will cancel proposed sanctions and countersanctions respectively.

July 6—The State Council issues a decision for tighter control of off-budget funds.

Sept. 1—The Beijing-Kowloon Railway, which connects Beijing and Hong Kong, goes into service.

Oct. 28—The National School of Administration, which will train high-rank civil servants, opens.

Nov. 27—Dai Xianglong, governor of the People's Bank of China, announces that China will introduce current account convertibility of the renminbi, China's currency, on December 1.

Dec. 11—Hong Kong legislators elect Tung Chee-Hwa chief executive of the Hong Kong Special Administration Region. On December 16, the State Council ratifies the selection.

Dec. 25—A bomb wounds five people outside government offices in the Tibetan capital of Lhasa.

1997

Feb. 5—The government says that at least 10 people were killed when 1,000 Uyghur Muslims rioted in Yining, a town in northwestern Xinjiang.

Feb. 19—Paramount leader Deng Xiaoping, the architect of China's economic modernization program, dies. Because of Deng's long illness, power has for some time been in the hands of President Jiang and Prime Minister Li.

Feb. 25—Nine people are killed and 68 wounded by bomb explosions on three buses in Urumuqi, the capital of Xinjiang. Uyghur separatists in Kazakhstan later claim responsibility.

March 7—A bomb explodes on a Beijing bus, seriously wounding at least 10 people. The bomb reportedly was similar to those used in the February 25 attacks by Muslim separatists in Urumuqi.

March 18—The government sends high-level North Korean defector Hwang Jang Yop to the Philippines, where he is expected to stay before going to South Korea. The move ends a diplomatic standoff that began February 12 when Hwang sought political asylum at the South Korean consulate-general in Beijing.

May 21—The State Council forwards regulations that prohibit state-owned enterprises and companies listed on stock markets from speculation in stocks.

June 30—The United Kingdom formally hands over control of Hong Kong to China. Besides taking the tiny Hong Kong Island in 1842, the United Kingdom rented the New Territories (over 90% of Hong Kong) for 99 years from China on July 1, 1898.

July 1—The Hong Kong Special Administrative Region is formally established with Tung Chee-Hwa as chief executive and the Basic Law as the constitutional document.

July 17—The New York–based group Human Rights in China reports that earlier this month police in the southwestern city of Mianyang broke up a protest by 100,000 workers, injuring as many as 100 and arresting more than 80. The workers were demanding jobs and welfare payments after several large state-owned factories declared bankruptcy. On March 3, 1998, the official *People's Daily* admits a petition by several hundred people but denies that any arrests were made.

Sept. 12–18—The Fifteenth National Congress of the Chinese Communist Party takes place. New members to the Central Committee and the Central Discipline Inspection Commission are elected. Qiao Shi, the number three man in the party, retires from his party posts and will fully retire at the end of his tenure as chairman of the National People's Congress in March 1998.

Sept. 19—The First Plenum of the Fifteenth National Congress of Chinese Communist Party takes place. The new Politburo and its standing committee are elected. Jiang Zemin continues as the general secretary and the party's chairman of the Central Military Commission.

Oct. 16—After approval by the State Council, the People's Bank of China determines that Chinese enterprises are allowed to reserve a certain ratio of foreign currency income.

Oct. 21—A UN spokesman says that two UN human rights officials, for the first time, earlier this month privately interviewed about 30 inmates, including political prisoners, in Chinese prisons. The interviews were at China's invitation.

Nov. 10—Russian President Boris Yeltsin and Chinese President Jiang sign a joint declaration that the demarcation work on the eastern border between Russia and China has been completed.

1998

Jan. 19—U.S. Defense Secretary William Cohen tours a military command center for air defenses in the Beijing region. The tour is the first of the facility by any foreigner.

Feb. 14—An explosion on a bus kills at least 16 people and wounds at least 30 in Wuhan in Hubei province; no group takes responsibility.

Feb. 20—The party Central Committee and the State Council approve the suggestions made by the State Planning Commission to react to the Asian financial crisis. China successfully maintains the stability of the renminbi's exchange rate with the U.S. dollar and provides $4 billion for the IMF to help the suffering countries.

Feb. 24—In a letter received by Taiwan's government, Beijing offers to resume talks with Taiwan on the future of the island. Talks begun in 1993 were broken off by the mainland in 1995 after President Lee in Taiwan was granted a U.S. visa.

March 5–19—The First Session of the Ninth National People's Congress takes place. Jiang Zemin is reelected as China's president and Li Peng is elected chairman of the congress. Zhu Rongji is appointed prime minister.

April 16—About 500 retired workers block trains linking Dalian and Harbin to protest a state metal factory's failure to pay wages for six months.

April 18—The State Council issues a circular to prohibit multilevel marketing.

May 5—The Preparatory Committee of the Macau Special Administrative Region is established.

May 25—The first Legislative Council of the Hong Kong Special Administrative Region is elected. Among the 60 members, 20 are elected through geographic constituencies, 30 are elected through functional constituencies, and the remaining 10 are elected by an 800-member Election Committee. About 53.29% of 2.8 million registered voters cast their ballots.

June 15–17—A working conference is held for the reform of housing institutions in cities and towns. From the second half of 1998 on, direct distribution of housing in cities and towns will be stopped.

June 22—The Finance Work Commission of the Central Committee of the Chinese Communist Party is established to strengthen the party's leadership of financial institutes.

June 25-July 3—U.S. President Clinton visits China. Washington and Beijing confirm that progress has been made toward the establishment of a "constructive strategic partnership."

July 9—The Central Work Commission of Large Enterprises of the Central Committee of the Chinese Communist Party is established to strengthen party leadership in large enterprises.

July 21–22—A meeting is held by the four general departments of the People's Liberation Army to deal with the issue of smuggling. Jiang Zemin points out that from now on, the armed forces are no longer allowed to do business.

July 22—The State Council approves the Ministry of Public Security's four-point proposal on the reform of the household registration (*hukou*) system to remove some restrictions on domestic migration.

Aug. 7—The south dike of Chang River breaks at Jiujiang, Jiangxi province. It is reinforced in five days. The flooding that China suffers in most major water systems in July and August is the worst since 1954.

Oct. 1—In New Delhi, India, the Tibetan government-in-exile acknowledges that it received $1.7 million a year from the U.S. Central Intelligence Agency in the 1960s to train volunteers and support guerrilla operations against China.

Oct. 5—At UN headquarters in New York, China signs the International Covenant on Civil and Political Rights.

Oct. 14–19—Koo Chen-Fu, chairman of Taiwan's Straits Exchange Foundation, visits the mainland with a delegation of the foundation. Four common understandings are reached with Wang Daohan, chairman of the mainland's Association for Relations Across the Taiwan Straits.

Oct. 17—The State Council approves the reform of People's Bank of China. Its provincial-level banks will be replaced with nine regional branches.

Nov. 25–30—President Jiang Zemin visits Japan. It is the first visit by a Chinese head of state to Japan. A joint statement is issued with the absence of an explicit and overt apology for Japan's wartime activities as a significant omission.

Nov. 28—The State Council decides to relax control over cotton and to make the market the major mechanism for the resource distribution of cotton.

1999

Jan. 8—Police use clubs and tear gas against thousands of peasants gathering in Daolin, near Changsha, the capital of Hunan province, to protest excessive local taxes. One peasant is killed and dozens are injured.

Jan. 25—A nail bomb kills at least eight people and wounds 65 in Yizhang, in Hunan province. On January 17 a homemade bomb exploded on a bus in Changsha, the provincial capital, seriously injuring four people. No group has claimed responsibility.

Feb. 25—China votes in the UN Security Council against a draft resolution to extend the mandate of the UN Preventive Deployment Force in Macedonia, which established diplomatic relations on February 9 with Republic of China in Taiwan.

March 5–15—The second session of the Ninth People's Congress takes place. Constitutional amendments are adopted that include the addition of Deng Xiaoping's theory and rule by law to the constitution.

April 25—More than 10,000 followers of the religious sect Buddhist Law (Falun Gong) stage a silent protest outside Zhongnanhai in Beijing, the largest protest in the capital since the 1989 Tiananmen Square demonstrations. The sect claims to have more than 100 million adherents in China. Its leader, Li Hongzhi, moved to the United States two years ago.

May 1—Purchased housing with an ownership certificate is allowed for resale on the market, starting today.

May 8—U.S.-led NATO jets launch five missiles at the Chinese embassy in Belgrade. Three Chinese are killed and over 20 are wounded. Thousands of students and residents protest at the U.S. embassy in Beijing and consulates elsewhere in China. In a phone call with President Jiang on May 14, U.S. President Clinton pledges to investigate the attack.

May 15—Edmund Ho, He Houhua, is named chief executive of the Macau Special Administration Region. On May 20, the State Council ratifies the selection effective as of December 20, 1999.

June 17—In a colloquium in Xi'an on the reform and development of state-owned enterprises in five northwestern provinces/autonomous regions, President Jiang emphasizes that the development of the western region is now a strategic task for the party and the state.

July 22—The Ministry of Civil Affairs bans Falun Gong and the Ministry of Public Security outlaws pro–Falun Gong activities. On July 19, members of the Chinese Communist Party are forbidden to practice Falun Gong.

August 30—The Eleventh Session of the Ninth People's Congress Standing Committee amends the personal income tax law and approves personal income tax on interest payable on deposits and savings.

Oct. 30—The Standing Committee of the National People's Congress, by a 114–0 vote with two abstentions, passes a strict law aimed at cracking down on Falun Gong. The law calls for jail terms of three to seven years for active cultists and more than seven years for recruiters. The passage follows six consecutive days of Falun Gong protests in Tiananmen

Square in Beijing in which hundreds of followers were detained by police.

Nov. 15—Minister of Foreign Trade and Economic Cooperation Shi Guang-sheng and U.S. trade representative Charlene Barshefsky sign an agreement in Beijing under which the Chinese government will reduce some import tariffs and lift trade barriers that prevent American companies from expanding in China. In exchange, the United States will support China's bid for entrance into the WTO.

Nov. 20–21—China first spaceship successfully accomplishes its first flight.

Dec. 3—China and Vietnam reach agreement on their land borders.

Dec. 20—China officially takes control over Macau from Portugal.

2000

March 15—The State Council promulgates provisional regulations to supervise state-owned enterprises and financial institutes.

March 18—Chen Shui-bian, candidate of the Democratic Progressive Party, wins the presidential election in Taiwan with a narrow margin over independent candidate James Soong. The official Nationalist Party (Kuomintang) candidate, Lien Chan, comes in third.

April 1—The State Council promulgates regulations under which an individual is required to show his or her identification certificate and use his or her real name to open a banking account.

April 20—The Central Discipline Inspection Commission announces

that Cheng Kejie, vice chairman of the Standing Committee of the National Congress, has been expelled from the Chinese Communist Party. Cheng is sentenced to death in a court in Beijing on July 31.

June 5—The Central Committee issues a decision to strengthen and improve party schools.

Sept. 4—The Information Center for Human Rights and Democracy, a Hong Kong–based human rights group, says that the government has indicted 85 members of the China Fangcheng Church, which Beijing has declared an "evil cult." Last month in Henan province, 130 members of the evangelical Christian church were detained, and three American missionary members were expelled. The Cardinal Kung Foundation, a U.S.-based advocate of the underground Chinese Catholic Church, says that 24 Catholics were arrested last month in Fujian province.

Sept. 25—Approved by the party Central Committee, the State Council establishes the National Social Security Fund and sets up the National Council for Social Security Fund.

Oct. 1—The Ministry of Foreign Affairs issues a protest against the Vatican's decision to canonize 120 Chinese saints and foreign missionaries; the ministry announces some of them "committed wicked crimes in China."

Dec. 25—President Jiang and Vietnamese President Tran Duc Luong sign an accord in Beijing that ends the 21-year Gulf of Tonkin border dispute. The settlement includes a demarcation of territorial waters, exclusive economic zones for the two countries, and a fishing agreement.

2001

Jan. 23—Five 4people set themselves on fire, and one dies, in Beijing's Tiananmen Square, apparently to protest the government's 18-month crackdown on Falun Gong. Falun Gong leaders in Hong Kong deny that the sect is involved, saying their beliefs forbid suicide.

Feb. 19—The China Securities Regulatory Commission says Chinese can now trade B shares with legally held foreign currencies.

Feb. 27—The Boao Forum for Asia is established in Hainan; it is the first international organization with headquarters in China.

April 1—After colliding with a Chinese Jian-8 fighter plane above the South China Sea, a U.S. Navy EP-3 reconnaissance aircraft lands at Lingshui Airport on Hainan. The Chinese fighter plane crashes and the pilot, Wang Wei, is missing. None of the 24 U.S. crew members are injured.

April 12—The 24 U.S. crew members are released after U.S. President George W. Bush agreed to say that the United States was "very sorry" for the presumed death of the Chinese pilot and for the U.S. plane's landing without permission.

June 14—The Shanghai Five admits Uzbekistan and changes its name to the Shanghai Cooperation Organization.

June 29—The construction of the Qinghai-Tibet railway begins.

July 13—Beijing is chosen as the venue for the 2008 Olympic Games by the International Olympics Committee. Four hundred thousand people celebrate in Tiananmen Square in Beijing at night.

Aug. 13—Deputy Foreign Minister Wang Yi urgently meets the Japanese ambassador to protest Japanese Prime Minister Koizumi Junichiro's visit to the Yasukuni Shrine, where WWII war criminals are also enshrined. The Japanese prime minister has visited the shrine every year during his tenure.

Sept. 11—President Jiang sends a message to U.S. President Bush expressing sympathy to the U.S. government and people for today's terrorist attacks, and reaffirms the Chinese government's stand against all terrorist acts of violence.

Oct. 8—In answering questions concerning U.S. military actions in Afghanistan, a Chinese Foreign Ministry spokesman assures the United States of Chinese support for antiterrorist actions.

Nov. 21—The government expels 35 foreigners, including 6 Americans, who demonstrated yesterday in Beijing against the government's repression of Falun Gong. The police say the protesters broke laws on protest, assembly, and cults.

Dec. 11—China becomes the 143d member of the World Trade Organization.

2002

Jan. 24—A Chinese Foreign Ministry spokesman does not deny that listening devices in a U.S.-made Boeing 767 jet bought for the personal use of President Jiang have been discovered. A U.S. State Department spokeswoman has no comment on the reports that blames U.S. intelligence agencies for the devices.

Feb. 21–22—U.S. President George W. Bush visits China. The two sides agree to extend and strengthen cooperation.

June 3—The General Offices of the party Central Committee and State Council issue a circular calling for transparency in state-owned enterprises and collectively owned enterprises.

Aug. 3—Taiwanese President Chen Shui-bian declares in Japan that Taiwan and mainland China are "two countries on either side of Taiwan Strait," and calls for a referendum to decide the future of Taiwan.

Sept. 5—Chinese and German officials say they have reached a deal on 15 North Korean asylum seekers who took refuge in a German diplomatic compound in Beijing two days ago. In the past year about 80 other North Koreans have been granted permission to leave China for South Korea by way of a third country after seeking shelter inside foreign diplomatic missions.

Oct. 6—Business tycoon Yang Bin, who was recently appointed by North Korean leader Kim Jong Il as chief executive of that country's newly created Sinuiju Special Administrative Region, is placed under house arrest by police in the northeastern city of Shenyang on suspicion of tax evasion and other economic crimes.

Nov. 8–14—The Sixteenth National Congress of the Chinese Communist Party is held. Amendments are made to the party's constitution to add the theory of "Three Represents," which in effect accommodates businessmen and entrepreneurs. All members, except Hu Jintao, of the Politburo's Stand-ing Committee of the Fifteenth Central Committee, step down from the Central Committee.

Nov. 15—The First Plenum of the Sixteenth Central Committee takes place. A new Politburo and its nine-member standing committee are elected. Vice President Hu is selected general secretary of the Communist Party. Jiang remains chairman of the party's Central Military Commission.

2003

Jan. 26—A passenger plane belonging to Taiwan's China Airlines lands safely at the Shanghai Pudong International Airport after a brief stopover in Hong Kong. It is the first Taiwan passenger plane to land in the mainland in over half a century.

March 5–18—The First Session of the Tenth National People's Congress takes place. Hu Jintao and Zeng Qinghong are elected president and vice president, respectively. Wen Jiabao is named prime minister. Jiang Zemin is elected chairman of the state's Central Military Commission.

April 13—The State Council holds a working conference in Beijing regarding the prevention and cure of severe acute respiratory syndrome (SARS). Executive meetings of the State Council and the Politburo Standing Committee are held later in April to deal with SARS. The minister of health and the mayor of Beijing municipality are dismissed later in the month for concealing the truth of the epidemic.

June 22–27—Indian Prime Minister Atal Bihari Vajpayee visits China.

The Indian prime minister signs a joint declaration with Chinese Prime Minister Wen Jiabao on June 23. The two leaders agree to develop a long-term constructive partnership. India acknowledges that Tibet is part of China.

June 24—The World Health Organization announces that Beijing has effectively conquered SARS.

June 30—Mainland China and Hong Kong officials sign a trade pact eliminating Chinese tariffs on many goods and removing restrictions on trade in a number of services.

July 1—In a lengthy speech marking the 82d anniversary of the Chinese Communist Party's founding, President Hu says that the "foremost political duty" of China's leaders is to carry out the theory of the "Three Stresses" promulgated by his predecessor, Jiang Zemin.

July 17—Deputy Foreign Minister Dai Bingguo, upon returning from a four-day visit to Pyongyang, North Korea, leaves for Washington as part of stepped-up efforts to broker negotiations between the United States and North Korea.

Aug. 1—President Hu cancels the Communist Party leadership's annual summer retreat at Beidaihe, a resort on the Bohai Sea.

Aug. 27–29—Beijing hosts six-nation talks on nuclear issues on the Korean peninsula. Beijing was instrumental in organizing the talks, which include Russia, the United States, South Korea, and Japan. It conducted shuttle diplomacy while pressuring North Korea to participate.

Sept. 1—Police officials announce that measures to ease overseas-travel restrictions will be expanded to 100 cities. Citizens will be allowed to apply for passports on their own instead of first obtaining their employers' approval. Amid a general easing of controls on individual freedoms and movement in China, authorities also lift requirements for employer approval of marriage plans and reduce restrictions on migrants seeking jobs.

The government announces plans to cut 200,000 soldiers from the People's Liberation Army as part of its efforts to modernize its military, the world's largest. The move will leave the army with 2.3 million troops and will coincide with the introduction of more high-tech battle systems.

Sept. 3—U.S. Treasury Secretary John Snow, meeting in Beijing with Chinese leaders, fails to persuade them to allow China's currency to float freely anytime soon. China for nearly a decade has fixed the remninbi's exchange rate at about 8.3 to the U.S. dollar.

Sept. 5—Police arrest Zhou Zhengyi, one of the richest men in China, after months of investigation into loans worth $240 million that he received from a state-run bank.

Sept. 20—The State Council makes a decision to enhance education in rural areas with a series of specific measures.

Oct. 8—China is formally included in the Association for Southeast Asian Nations (ASEAN) Treaty of Amity and Cooperation, during the seventh meeting of leaders of the ten members of ASEAN and China, Japan, and South Korea ("ten plus three"). A joint announcement with ASEAN leaders calls for the creation of a strategic partnership between China and the ASEAN.

Oct. 15–16—China's first manned spaceship, the *Shenzhou-5*, circled the earth 14 times in 21 hours of flight.

Nov. 6—The government reports that it has begun providing free treatment, including anti-retroviral drugs, to poor people infected with HIV.

Nov. 11—Government officials report plans to accelerate the privatization of tens of thousands of state-owned businesses that once served as pillars of Communist Party rule. Officials say China will allow foreign and private investors to buy majority stakes in large enterprises that the government had previously refused to sell.

Nov. 12—The Supreme People's Court, the Supreme People's Procuratorate, and the Ministry of Public Security issue a circular to prevent prolonged detainment of suspects or defendants. Those who are responsible for prolonged detainment of suspects or defendants will now be punished.

Dec. 1—Prime Minister Wen appears on state television comforting AIDS patients and appealing for his nation to treat them with "care and love." Wen is the first senior Chinese leader to publicly address the country's fast-spreading AIDS epidemic, which has been officially ignored, played down, and covered up for years.

Dec. 7—China is playing an increasingly central role in efforts to forge a peace pact between India and Pakistan, diplomats from the three countries tell the *Wall Street Journal*.

Dec. 12—Among 14 suggestions to the Standing Committee of the National People's Congress, the Central Committee of the Chinese Communist Party proposes a constitutional amendment that, for the first time since the 1949 revolution, guarantees protection of property rights.

Dec. 30—To start reforms to diversity ownership of the former state-owned commercial banks, the Chinese central government contributes $22.5 billion each to the Bank of China and the China Construction Bank.

2004

Jan. 7—Police raid the offices of a Chinese newspaper, the *Southern Metropolis Daily*, detaining and later releasing the editor and six other journalists. The newspaper was the first media outlet to report on a SARS case in Guangzhou, the paper's hometown.

Jan. 13—A week after bailing out two of China's biggest banks with an investment of $45 billion in foreign exchange reserves, the government says it will write off its $41 billion stake in the banks in a bid to help cleanse their balance sheets of non-performing loans. The move is the latest in a series of steps aimed at fortifying a weak banking system ahead of what could be a difficult year for the Chinese economy.

Jan. 28—Amnesty International says China is holding at least 54 people in prison for allegedly using the Internet to disseminate political opinions or other information that the government considers dangerous.

March 5–14—The Second Session of the Tenth National People's Congress takes place. Among the constitutional amendments are the inclusions of the theory of "Three Represents" and protection of private property. Prime Minister Wen calls for balanced development.

April 21—The *People's Daily* reports that except for Tibet, where the price for electricity is lower in rural areas than in cities, the price is now the same for rural and urban residents.

June 1—Leaders of nine provinces and two administrative regions in southeastern China, struggling to keep up economically with Shanghai and the rest of the Yangtze River basin, announce plans to create a forum to coordinate regional economic policy and increase commerce. With Beijing's approval, provincial leaders portray the move as the start of a regional economic bloc that would have roughly the same population as the European Union.

July 16—The State Council issues a decision on the reform of the investment system. Enterprise projects not using government investment will no longer need to secure prior approval. Among such projects, government authorization is only needed for the "major projects and projects of the restricted categories."

Aug. 7—The *Washington Post* reports that, a week earlier, hundreds of police stormed the rural village of Shijiahe, in Henan province, firing rubber bullets into crowds of unarmed peasants who were protesting seizures of farmland. Dozens were injured in one of the most violent clashes known to have taken place in the Chinese countryside in recent years.

Aug. 15—The ministries of Public Security and Foreign Affairs issue regulations on the approval of permanent residence of foreigners in China.

Sept. 19—Jiang Zemin, paramount leader of the third-generation leadership of the Chinese Communist Party, resigns as the chairman of the Central Military Commission and is replaced with President Hu Jintao, in the Fourth Plenum of the Sixteenth Chinese Communist Party Central Committee. The move gives 61-year-old Hu undisputed command of the state, party, and armed forces.

Sept. 28—A contingent of Chinese riot police prepares to deploy to Haiti, the first unit of Chinese officers to serve as UN peacekeepers.

Oct. 1—Chinese officials participate for the first time in a meeting of the Group of Seven major industrial nations. The talks occur as China comes under growing pressure to change a currency peg that, according to critics, keeps the yuan undervalued, thereby giving China's products an unfair competitive edge. The yuan has been fixed at about 8.3 per dollar since 1995.

Oct. 28—The nation's central bank raises interest rates for the first time in nearly a decade, signaling increased unease with China's breakneck pace of development, especially in real estate. Economists say they expect more efforts to cool an economy now expanding at an annual rate of more than 9%.

Oct. 31—Two days of clashes in Henan province between majority Han Chinese and Hui Muslims leave almost 150 dead and force authorities to declare martial law in parts of the province.

Nov. 19—Chinese President Hu arrives in Chile to attend the Asian-Pacific

Cooperation Forum. In a two-week visit to several Latin American countries, Hu has announced more than $30 billion in new investments and signed several long-term contracts for raw materials that China needs for its factories.

Dec. 7—IBM announces the sale of its personal computer business to Lenovo, China's largest personal computer maker.

Dec. 30—To start the reforms to diversify ownership of the former state-owned commercial banks, the Chinese government provides $22.5 billion each to the Bank of China and the China Construction Bank.

2005

Jan. 13—An executive meeting of the State Council decides to open more industries and sectors to nonpublic capital, and more financing channels to nonpublic enterprises.

Jan. 31—The People's Bank of China issues a report that it intends to deregulate interest rates.

Feb. 1—About 16 million elementary and high school students from poor rural families acquire free textbooks and exemption from fees.

March 5–14—Wen Jiabao announces an exemption to the agricultural tax throughout the country in 2006. An Anti-Secession Law is promulgated on March 14; the law's major purpose is to prevent Taiwan from independence.

April 10—Thousands of Chinese riot in Huaxi, a village in Zhejiang province, overturning police cars and driving away officers after they tried to prevent elderly residents from protesting against chemical pollution from nearby factories.

April 12—Prime Minister Wen says Japan will not be ready for a permanent seat on the UN Security Council until it faces up to its history of aggression and wins its neighbors' trust. Angry protests happen in several cities this month against newly revised Japanese history textbooks that downplay wartime abuses.

May 26—The Ministry of Commerce indicates that it will set up a nationwide alarm system against threats and damages for industries.

June 6—New, more severe restrictions on the Internet take effect, requiring authors of web logs (or "blogs") and owners of personal Web sites to register with the government.

June 21—Beijing appoints Donald Tsang, a career civil servant, as Hong Kong's chief executive for a two-year term. He replaces Tung Chee-hwa, who resigned three months ago. Tsang expresses confidence that the former British colony, returned to China in 1997, will become more democratic.

July 1—Jilin province reforms the public finance management system. The provincial government directly leads county governments on financial affairs instead of through prefectural governments.

July 21—The People's Bank of China announces that China's currency's peg to the U.S. dollar will be changed. It will now be pegged to a basket of foreign currencies.

Oct. 27—The China Construction Bank is registered on the Hong Kong Stock Exchange. It is the first time one of the country's big four state-owned banks has registered on an international stock exchange.

Nov. 8—Chinese and U.S. officials announce an agreement limiting China's clothing exports for the next three years, marking the return of official trade quotas that ended in January.

Nov. 23—Reports indicate that the government has cut off potentially contaminated water supplies to the 4 million people of the city of Harbin because of a nearby chemical plant explosion, stirring new unrest about industrial pollution in the country.

Dec. 16—The State Council issues a resolution to improve the pension insurance system for employees in firms. Measures including personal accounts are emphasized.

Dec. 29—The Standing Committee of the National People's Congress issues a resolution to abolish agricultural taxes, which were adopted in 1958, beginning on January 1, 2006.

Hong Kong

1994

Feb. 24—The colony's Legislative Council approves by voice vote the first stage of an electoral reform plan presented in December by Governor Christopher Patten. The measure would lower the voting age from 21 to 18 and introduce single-member voting districts for council elections this year and next year. In retaliation, China's Foreign Ministry announces that China will abolish the Legislative Council and the remainder of the British administrative system when it assumes control of Hong Kong in 1997.

June 30—The Legislative Council, the lawmaking body in the crown colony, approves Governor Patten's October 1992 proposal for widening the franchise for council elections. Beijing has strongly opposed the changes.

Nov. 4—After years of talks, China and the United Kingdom sign an agreement on financing Hong Kong's new $20 billion airport that sets a cap on borrowing and calls for a portion of the cost to come from Hong Kong's budget. Work on the project has continued and contractors have been paid from the Hong Kong treasury, under protest from China. Major details remain to be resolved before bank loans can be sought.

1995

May 20—Police fire tear gas to quell a demonstration at a refugee camp that erupted after they tried to remove 1,500 Vietnamese "boat people" for deportation. At least 20,000 Vietnamese are being held in Hong Kong.

1996

Dec. 11—Businessman Tung Chee-hwa is endorsed by an electoral college handpicked by Beijing to become Hong Kong's first chief executive when the territory reverts to Chinese rule on July 1, 1997.

Dec. 17—In his first address since being chosen chief executive, Tung Chee-hwa pledges to preserve Hong Kong's British-style legal system and to resist Chinese efforts to gain special economic privileges in the territory.

Dec. 21—In Shenzhen, China, a 400-member committee handpicked by Beijing from Hong Kong's business and political elite selects 60 members for the new legislature to replace the current Legislative Council on July 1, 1997. Hong Kong's Democratic Party boycotts the process and holds street protests, while Governor Chris Patten denounces the procedure as "a bizarre farce."

1997

Jan. 19—Legislation is introduced in China's parliament that would overturn 16 Hong Kong laws, including several major provisions of the 1992 Bill of Rights, when the territory reverts to Chinese rule on July 1.

Jan. 23—Tung Chee-hwa proclaims his support for Beijing's plans to repeal laws protecting civil rights in Hong Kong.

July 1—Some 2,500 pro-democracy protesters march in Hong Kong. The march was organized by the Hong Kong Alliance, a group that Beijing has called subversive.

July 8—Hong Kong's government announces a new electoral system in which 20 legislative seats will be elected by proportional representation and the other 40 selected mainly by business and professional elites. The system's proponents have admitted that it was designed to handicap the Democratic Party, which won the most seats in the last election in 1995.

1998

Jan. 12—Peregrine Investments Holdings, the largest investment bank in Asia outside Japan, closes due to bankruptcy, triggering a fall by mid-morning of almost 10% in Hong Kong's stock market.

May 27—The *New York Times* reports that the Democratic Party and other pro-democracy parties won 55% of the vote and 18 of the 20 directly elected seats in legislative elections held three days ago in Hong Kong. The remaining 40 seats in the Legislative Council are chosen by indirect means favoring business interests and Beijing. The elections were the first since China regained control of the territory last July.

1999

Dec. 3—The territory's highest court rejects the appeal of 17 mainlanders who claimed residency rights because they had at least one parent legally residing on the island. In February the court had decided that such claims were valid, but the ruling was reversed when Beijing reinterpreted parts of Hong Kong's constitution in June. The decision allows Beijing to nullify the legal residency of 1.6 million mainlanders living in the territory.

Dec. 24—Judge Frank Stock rules that a two-year-old boy born in the territory to mainland parents has the constitutional right to live in the territory. The decision, which grants residency to all Hong Kong–born Chinese, negates a government immigration rule that was aimed primarily against mainland women crossing into the island to give birth. The government says it will appeal the ruling.

2000

Although Hong Kong's Gross Domestic Product grows in 2000, it still does not get back to the levels of

1997. Housing prices continue to decline and there are signs of the double-dip recession that hit Hong Kong hard in the 2001–2004 period.

2001

Jan. 12—Chief Secretary Anson Chan resigns, 18 months before the end of her term, citing a desire to spend more time with her family. Many provincial officials believe that Chan, who had been appointed head of the province's civil service in 1993 by the last British governor, was pressured by Beijing to step down because of her stance that the region should retain some autonomy from the mainland.

2002

Jan. 10—The Court of Final Appeal, the territory's highest court, rules that all but 200 of the 5,114 mainland Chinese suing for the right to stay in the territory must return to China. The court says the right to stay applied only to migrants who arrived in Hong Kong before January 29, 1999.

Feb. 28—Beijing-backed political leader Tung Chee-hwa wins a second five-year term as the island's chief executive in today's election. Tung ran unopposed after his nomination last week by 714 out of 800 members of the electoral committee. Any candidate for the post needs 100 nomination signatures to get on the ballot.

April 1—More than 4,000 mainland Chinese immigrants defy today's deadline to leave the territory. Beijing says it will start repatriation proceedings immediately. Eleven weeks ago

the territory's highest court, the Final Court of Appeal, announced that all but 200 of the more than 5,000 mainland migrants claiming the right to stay in the territory must leave. The former British colony reverted to Chinese rule five years ago.

2003

May 23—The World Health Organization removes a recommendation against travel to Hong Kong following a sustained decline in new SARS cases since a peak in late March.

July 1—As many as 500,000 demonstrators take to the streets to protest government proposals for strict internal-security laws widely viewed as restricting freedoms enjoyed in Hong Kong before it was reincorporated into China.

July 7—Hong Kong chief executive Tung postpones action on the internal-security measure in the wake of massive street protests, but insists he will revive it later. Tung had agreed two days before to delete provisions that would have allowed the government to carry out searches and seizures without warrants and to outlaw groups linked to organizations banned in mainland China. Protest leaders vow to continue demonstrations.

July 16—Two top officials on Hong Kong's government, the secretary of security and the financial secretary, resign amid public protests against pending security legislation. Tung insists he will not resign.

July 19—Tung, in Beijing for consultations, says China's top leaders have given their "firm support" for his continuation in office, but he declines to say if they rebuked him for his handling of security legislation and recent mass demonstrations. China's state news media report that President Hu told Tung the central government was "extremely concerned about recent events in Hong Kong."

Aug. 21—Leaders of Hong Kong's main pro-Beijing political party call on the government to delay internal-security legislation for at least a year. Plans to enact the legislation had set off massive street demonstrations earlier in the year.

Sept. 5—Tung bows to public pressure and announces he is withdrawing internal-security legislation that provoked massive protests in July.

Oct. 22—Hong Kong officials postpone a self-imposed deadline to balance the budget in two years, citing economic harm from the outbreak of SARS last spring and public desire for faster growth after six years of a mostly stagnant economy.

Nov. 23—Voters turn out in record numbers for district council elections, rejecting numerous pro-government candidates. Analysts point to a dilemma facing Hong Kong's leaders and their backers in Beijing: if they yield to public demands for more democracy, they risk unfavorable election outcomes; if they resist demands for democracy, they risk provoking more street protests and public anger.

2004

Jan. 1—Tens of thousands of protesters call on the government to allow direct elections of the next chief executive and the entire legislature of the former British colony.

April 6—The government in Beijing declares that it will determine if and when the people of Hong Kong can elect their local leaders. Opposition parties attack the ruling as a blow to democracy and an infringement on the 50-year period of autonomy China promised when it replaced Britain as Hong Kong's sovereign power in 1997.

April 26—Beijing bars the introduction of popular elections for Hong Kong's chief executive in 2007 and rules out any expanded use of democratic voting for the legislature in 2008.

June 4—Tens of thousands of people, including some mainland Chinese, attend a rally in Hong Kong marking the 15th anniversary of the killings of pro-democracy demonstrators at Tiananmen Square.

July 1—Hundreds of thousands march in Hong Kong to demand democracy and protest Beijing's decision to ban general elections.

Aug. 1—China stages its first military parade in Hong Kong since regaining sovereignty over the territory in 1997.

Sept. 12—Democracy advocates score few gains in Hong Kong legislative elections and fall short of winning a majority in the legislature.

Taiwan

1993

Jan. 30—Prime Minister Hau Pei-Tsun announces he will resign; the cabinet will also hand in their resignations; the liberal wing of Hau's Nationalist Party and the Democratic Progressive Party, the main opposition, have criticized Hau for attempting to block democratization that began in 1987.

Nov. 8—In Taipei, the Chinese hijacker of a Chinese airliner requests political asylum and surrenders to Taiwanese authorities, who hold him for trial rather than extradite him; this is the sixth such hijacking in seven months.

1994

Dec. 3—In elections, the ruling Nationalist Party wins the governorship of Taiwan and the mayoralty of Kaohsiung, the second-largest city. The opposition Democratic Progressive Party candidate for mayor wins in Taipei, the capital. This is the first election for governor of the island, and the first for mayor of Taipei since 1967.

1995

April 8—In a speech, President Lee Teng-hui calls on China to publicly renounce "the use of force" and threatening military moves in order to allow formal negotiations to begin "to put an end to the state of hostility" between Taiwan and China.

July 23—Military authorities report that China fired four test missiles near its coast, two of which were launched during the past two days.

Aug. 23—President Lee announces that he will run in the island's first democratic elections, which are scheduled for next year. Lee heads the Nationalist Party, which currently holds 58 seats in parliament.

1996

March 23—President Lee of the ruling Nationalist Party wins the presidential election with 54% of the vote.

Dec. 5—Foreign Minister John Chang announces that Taiwan will cancel all foreign aid to South Africa, suspend most treaties, and recall its ambassador. On November 27 South African President Nelson Mandela announced that his country would transfer diplomatic recognition from Taiwan to China beginning in 1997.

1997

March 22—The Dalai Lama, the exiled spiritual leader of Tibet, arrives. It is the first time he has visited Chinese territory since he fled the establishment of Chinese rule in Tibet in 1959.

May 9—The government of Prime Minister Lien Chan survives a no-confidence vote brought by opposition lawmakers angry over what they see as a deterioration in law and order, highlighted by three recent unsolved high-profile murders. On May 4, tens of thousands of people marched in Taipei to demand the government's resignation.

July 18—The National Assembly approves constitutional changes that increase the president's power and virtually abolish the provincial government.

Aug. 21—Prime Minister Lien resigns. The resignation had long been expected, partly because of popular discontent over rising crime.

1998

Dec. 5—Ma Ying-jeou of the Nationalist Party unseats Taipei Mayor Chen Shui-bian of the pro-independence Democratic Progressive Party in elections, taking 51% of the vote to Chen's 46%. The long-governing nationalists, who favor eventual reunification with China, also won control of the national legislature, taking 123 of 225 seats.

1999

July 12—Following President Lee's declaration three days ago that the government's contact with China is now "state to state," a government spokesman says the "one China" policy, which states that the Chinese mainland and Taiwan are two parts of the same country, has been dropped.

July 30—Koo Chen-fu, an envoy to China, endorses President Lee's statement earlier this month, but says it does not rule out reunification. Beijing has denounced Taiwan's position as a violation of their 1992 agreement recognizing a single Chinese nation.

August 1—The *New York Times* reports that the Chinese coast guard seized a Taiwan freighter and its 10 crew members yesterday near Matsu, a Taiwan-controlled island. The government says the crew was trying to smuggle goods into the mainland; Taiwan maintains that the ship was carrying provisions for Taiwanese soldiers on Matsu.

Sept. 24—The *New York Times* reports that the casualty toll in the earthquake that struck the island on September 21 has reached 2,160 dead and 8,432 injured, with 8,000 still missing. An additional 80,000 people have been left homeless.

Dec. 22—Deputy Prime Minister John Chang, President Lee's chief of staff, resigns after admitting an affair with a former actress. Chang, the grandson of former president Chiang Kai-shek, was the only active Chiang descendent in government.

2000

March 18—Chen Shui-bian of the opposition Democratic Progressive Party is elected president with 39% of the vote. James Soong, running as an independent after breaking with the governing Nationalist Party, wins 37%, and Nationalist candidate Lien Chan earns 23%. Chen has called for independence from mainland China but has said a formal declaration is unnecessary.

March 19—Thousands of people demanding the resignation of President Lee clash with police outside Nationalist Party headquarters in the capital city of Taipei, trapping Lee inside.

March 21—Parliament lifts the 50-year ban on direct trade, transport, and postal links between the offshore islands of Quemoy, Matsu, and Penghu and mainland China.

March 23—Responding to the public's and lawmakers' demands, President Lee resigns as chairman of the Nationalist Party 15 months earlier than scheduled. He will remain in office until Chen is inaugurated May 20.

March 29—President-elect Chen names as prime minister Foreign Minister Tang Fei, of the Nationalist Party.

Oct. 4—Prime Minister Tang resigns after less than five months in office, citing poor health. President Chen names Deputy Prime Minister Chang Chunhsiung to the post. Government analysts say that Tang's resignation is the result of clashes between Tang and the ruling Democratic Progressive Party.

2001

Nov. 7—The government lifts a 52-year-old restriction on direct investment in China, including eliminating a $50 million limit on individual investments, issuing automatic approval of projects less than $20 million, and allowing direct transfers between Taiwanese and Chinese banks.

Dec. 1—Results from legislative elections show that President Chen's Democratic Progressive Party won 87 of the legislature's 225 seats, a gain of 21 seats. The Nationalist Party won 68 seats, down from 110, the People's First Party earned 46 seats, and the Taiwan Solidarity Union 13. Small parties and independents won the rest, and since an absolute majority was not achieved, the DPP must form a coalition to govern.

2002

Jan. 1—Taiwan formally enters the World Trade Organization and becomes the 144th member.

March 29—The Executive Yuan decides to liberalize the policy relating to investment in silicon wafer plants in China.

July 21—After becoming Chairman of the Democratic Progressive Party, Chen Shui-bian made various statements implying China and Taiwan were two separate states. In August 2002, Chen said Taiwan "may go its own Taiwanese road" and "it is clear that the two sides of the straits are separate countries." These statements were strongly opposed by the opposition parties in Taiwan.

2003

Jan. 26—A China Airlines passenger plane, carrying Taiwan's flag, was permitted to land at Shanghai's International Airport to pick up Taiwanese businessmen returning home for Chinese New Year. This reflected an agreement between authorities in Beijing and Taipei that they would allow selected direct flights between the mainland and Taiwan.

Nov. 28—The Legislative Yuan passed the "Taiwan Referendum Act," although the Pan-Blue opposition, the KMT and People's First Party, vetoed most of Chen Shui-bian's proposals. Chen was not able to get authorization for the Cabinet to initiate advisory referendums and the issue of territorial sovereignty was excluded from referendum topics. The basic right to referendums comes from the Constitution of the Republic of China, which states that the people have the right to election, recall, and initiative and referendum. The November 2003 Law opens one route for the executive branch to initiate a referendum: when the nation's sovereignty is being threatened. Authorities in Beijing strongly protested the new law, saying they were "gravely concerned" about the legislation and noted that China would not tolerate a direct vote in Taiwan on independence.

Dec. 3—Chinese military officers say that Beijing would consider a popular vote on Taiwan's political status—recently urged by a faction of Taiwan's governing party—as a cause for war.

Dec. 8—During a visit to the United States by China's prime minister,

Wen Jiabao, the Bush administration warns Taiwan not to provoke China by holding a referendum that could fuel the island's independence movement.

2004

Jan. 16—Under heavy U.S. pressure, President Chen outlines plans for a toned-down referendum scheduled for March 20. It will ask voters two questions: whether Taiwan should acquire more advanced antimissile weapons if China refuses to withdraw missiles pointed at the island, and whether Taiwan should negotiate with China to establish a peaceful and stable framework for interaction. Members of Chen's pro-independence Democratic Progressive Party had earlier suggested a ballot issue opposing Beijing's formula for reunification or calling for Taiwan's entry into the United Nations.

March 19—One day before elections, a would-be assassin's gunshots graze the campaigning President Chen in the stomach and slightly injure the vice president.

March 20—President Chen wins a razor-thin reelection victory with 50.1 % of the vote. His opponent, Lien Chan, questions the result. Voters fail to approve two referendum questions that would have empowered Chen to boost Taiwan's antimissile defenses and engage in peace talks with Beijing on an equal footing.

March 27—After hundreds of thousands of Nationalist Party supporters flood Taipei's streets, Chen agrees to a judicial recount of his disputed reelection.

March 31—China denounces Chen's push to write a new constitution by 2006 as "virtually a timetable for Taiwan independence." China claims sovereignty over Taiwan and has threatened to use force if it formally declares independence.

May 20—President Chen begins his second term, vowing in his inaugural address not to promote independence from the mainland. His apparent retreat from earlier, provocative pro-independence oratory is attributed to the success of threats from Beijing and hands-on mediation by the United States.

Oct. 27—U.S. Secretary of State Colin Powell, while visiting Beijing, tells reporters that Taiwan is not an independent nation and should not seek to become one. His statement draws praise from Chinese leaders and criticism from Taiwan.

Dec. 11—Parliamentary elections leave the opposition Nationalist Party and its allies with the most seats, denying President Chen the legislative majority he had sought as a reinforcement of his leadership and endorsement of his plans to edge the self-ruled island closer to independence. The unexpected results mark the first pause in what has been a decade of steady growth in support for independence among Taiwan's 23 million people. Political analysts predict the election outcome will mean more prudence from Chen's government and perhaps less tension with mainland China.

2005

Jan. 28—On the eve of the first direct flights between Taiwan and mainland China since communists took power in 1949, Beijing offers to restart diplomatic talks with the island. Negotiations between Taiwan and China collapsed in 1999, and Beijing continues to demand that Taiwan abandon any moves toward independence and recognize itself as part of "one China."

April 29—Lien Chan, head of Taiwan's opposition Nationalist Party, makes a historic visit to Beijing and shakes hands with Chinese President Hu Jintzo, formally ending six decades of hostility between the two sides in China's civil war. In a pointed effort to isolate Taiwan President Chen Shui-bian, the leaders pledge to work together to undermine any movement toward Taiwan's independence.

About the Contributors

LIU BINYAN (d. 2005) was one of China's most prominent journalists. He was a Neiman Fellow at Harvard University and the author of *A Higher Kind of Loyalty* and *Two Kinds of Truth: Stories and Reportage from China*.

DAVID B. H. DENOON is Professor of Politics and Economics at New York University. He is the author of many books, including *Real Reciprocity: Balancing U.S. Economic and Security Policies in the Pacific Basin*, *Ballistic Missile Defense in the Post-Cold War Era*, and of the forthcoming *The Economic and Strategic Rise of China and India: Realignments After the 1997 Financial Crisis* (Palgrave). He is a contributing editor to *Current History*.

BRUCE J. DICKSON is Professor of Political Science and International Affairs at the Elliott School of International Affairs at George Washington University. He is the author of *Red Capitalists in China: The Party, Private Entrepreneurs, and Prospects for Political Change* and *Democratization in China and Taiwan: The Adaptability of Leninist Parties*, and is coeditor of four other books.

JUNE TEUFEL DREYER is Professor of Political Science and is the director of East Asian programs at the University of Miami, Florida. She is the author of *Asian-Pacific Regional Security* and the coeditor of *Chinese Defense and Foreign Policy*.

MICHAEL DUTTON is Professor of Political Science at the University of Melbourne. He is the author of *Streetlife China*.

ELIZABETH ECONOMY is C. V. Starr Senior Fellow and Director for Asia Studies at the Council on Foreign Relations. She is the author of *The River Runs Black: The Environmental Challenge to China's Future*.

BARRY EICHENGREEN is the George C. Pardee and Helen N. Pardee Professor of Economics at the University of Califoria, Berkley. He is the author of *Golden Fetters: The Gold Standard and the Great Depression, 1919–1939.*

EDWARD FRIEDMAN is the Hawkins Chair Professor of Political Science at University of Wisconsin, Madison. He is the author of *National Identity and Democratic Prospects in Socialist China,* and with Barrett L. McCormick, *What If China Doesn't Democratize? Implications for War and Peace.*

DRU C. GLADNEY is Professor of Asian Studies and Anthropology at the University of Hawai'i at Manoa. He is author of over 50 academic articles, as well as *Muslim Chinese: Ethnic Nationalism in the People's Republic; Ethnic Identity in China: The Making of a Muslim Minority Nationality; Making Majorities: Constituting the Nation in Japan, China, Korea, Malaysia, Fiji, Turkey, and the U.S.;* and *Dislocating China: Muslims, Minorities, and Other Sub-Altern Subjects.*

PAUL H. B. GODWIN is Professor Emeritus of International Affairs at the National War College, Washington, D.C. He is currently a consultant and serves as a nonresident scholar in the Atlantic Council's Asia-Pacific Program. He is coauthor of *Asian Security to the Year 2000.*

MERLE GOLDMAN is Professor of History, Emerita, at Boston University and Associate of the John K. Fairbank Center for East Asian Research, Harvard University, and is the author of *From Comrade to Citizen: The Struggle for Political Rights in China.*

RICHARD MADSEN is Professor of Sociology and Director of the Council on East Asian Studies at the University of California, San Diego. He is the author of *China and the American Dream* and *China's Catholics: Tragedy and Hope in an Emerging Civil Society.*

BARRY NAUGHTON is Professor of Chinese Economy and Sokwanlok Chair of Chinese International Affairs at the University of California, San Diego. He is author of *Growing Out of the Plan: Chinese Economic Reform, 1978–1993* and *Reforming Asian Socialism: The Growth of Market Institutions, Urban Spaces in Contemporary China,* and *The China Circle: Economics and Technology in the PRC, Taiwan and Hong Kong.*

LUCIAN W. PYE is Ford Professor of Political Science Emeritus at the Massachusetts Institute of Technology and past President of the American Political Science Association. He is the coauthor of *Asian Power and Politic: The Cultural Dimensions of Authority.*

TONY SAICH is the Daewoo Professor of International Affairs at the Kennedy School of Government, Harvard University. From 1994 to July 1999, he was the Chief Representative of the China Office at the Ford Foundation in Beijing. He has written several books on development in China, including *China: Politics and Government; China's Science Policy in the 80s; Revolutionary Discourse in Mao's China;* and *The Rise to Power of the Chinese Communist Party.*

DAVID SHAMBAUGH is Professor of Political Science and International Affairs and is the Director of the China Policy Program at the Elliott School of International Affairs at George Washington University. He has authored four and edited twelve books, including *Power Shift: China and Asia's New Dynamics,* editor; *The Odyssey of China's Imperial Art Treasures,* coauthored with Jeannette Shambaugh Elliott, and *Modernizing China's Military.*

ROBERT SUTTER is a Visiting Professor in the School of Foreign Service at Georgetown University. He is the author of *China's Rise in Asia: Promises and Perils.*

MICHAEL D. SWAINE is Senior Associate and Co-Director of the China Program at the Carnegie Endowment for International Peace. He is the coauthor of *Interpreting China's Grand Strategy: Past, Present, and Future.*

TYRENE WHITE is Professor of Political Science at Swarthmore College. He is the author of *China's Longest Campaign: Birth Planning in the People's Republic, 1949–2005.*